255548

AMERICAN

NATURE

WRITING

1998

Books by John A. Murray

The Indian Peaks Wilderness

Wildlife in Peril:
The Endangered Mammals of Colorado

The Gila Wilderness

The Last Grizzly, and Other Southwestern Bear Stories

The South San Juan Wilderness

A Republic of Rivers:
Three Centuries of Nature Writing from Alaska and the Yukon

The Islands and the Sea:
Five Centuries of Nature Writing from the Caribbean

The Great Bear:
Contemporary Writings on the Grizzly

Nature's New Voices

Wild Hunters: Predators in Peril

Wild Africa:
Three Centuries of Nature Writing from Africa

Out Among the Wolves:
Contemporary Writings on the Wolf

A Thousand Leagues of Blue:
The Sierra Club Book of the Pacific

American Nature Writing 1994

The Sierra Club Nature Writing Handbook

Grizzly Bears

American Nature Writing 1995

The Walker's Companion
(with Dave Wallace, and others)

American Nature Writing 1996

Cactus Country

Alaska

American Nature Writing 1997

Desert Places

American Nature Writing 1998

The Colorado Plateau

The River Reader

AMERICAN NATURE WRITING 1998

Selected by *John A. Murray*

SIERRA CLUB BOOKS
San Francisco

The Sierra Club, founded in 1892 by John Muir, has devoted itself to the study and protection of the Earth's scenic and ecological resources—mountains, wetlands, woodlands, wild shores and rivers, deserts and plains. The publishing program of the Sierra Club offers books to the public as a nonprofit educational service in the hope that they may enlarge the public's understanding of the Club's basic concerns. The point of view expressed in each book, however, does not necessarily represent that of the Club. The Sierra Club has some sixty chapters coast to coast, in Canada, Hawaii, and Alaska. For information about how you may participate in its programs to preserve wilderness and the quality of life, please address inquiries to Sierra Club, 85 Second Street, San Francisco, CA 94105. www.sierraclub.org/books

ISBN: 0-87156-948-5
ISSN: 1072-4723

Cover and book design by Amy Evans
Production and composition by David Peattie

Printed in the United States of America on acid-free paper containing a minimum of 50% recovered waste paper, of which at least 10% of the fiber content is post-consumer waste.

10 9 8 7 6 5 4 3 2 1

In memory of

Michio Hoshino
(1952–1996)
naturalist, photographer, friend

———

Red, red is the sun
heartlessly indifferent to time,
The wind knows, however,
the promise of early chill.
Basho, *The Narrow Road to the Deep North* (1684)

Every so often a person changes your life. Michio Hoshino changed
mine. For those who do not know, Michio was the premier nature
photographer of Japan and published two award-winning books of
photography in the United States (*Grizzly* and *Moose*, both with
Chronicle Press of San Francisco). We first met in 1988 in Denali
National Park. Over the next six years we often photographed
together in Denali. Michio's approach to wildlife was very different
from American photographers, who use powerful lenses and strive
to fill the frame. Michio preferred smaller lenses that show the animal in relation to the landscape. I soon realized his approach was
better—close-up shots can be taken at any zoo—and began to use
similar lenses to achieve a fuller composition.

On August 8, 1996, Michio was sleeping in his tent along the Khakeetsin River in Kamchatka. On two previous nights an adult male brown bear had visited his campsite, which was midway between the river and the cabin where his friends were staying. Apparently, the Khakeetsin bears were restless because the salmon run was late. On the third night, at around four in the morning, the bear pulled Michio from his tent and killed him. The bear was hunted by helicopter and shot the next day.

It is ironic that such a quiet and gentle soul died so violently, and at the hands of the animal he most loved. I can honestly say I never met a person who was more kind, warm, or generous, or a naturalist who was so passionately devoted to environmental education. After the cremation, his widow and young son distributed a portion of Michio's ashes along the road to Wonder Lake in Denali—one of his favorite places. Now he will be a part of the mountains he loved forever.

Out of the clutter find simplicity,
from discord make harmony,
in the middle of difficulty lies opportunity.

ALBERT EINSTEIN

Contents

Preface

It is in changing that things find repose.
Heraclitus

The past five years have seen much change for the good in this country, including passage of the historic California Desert Protection Act, a new million-acre national monument in Utah (Grand Staircase-Canyons of the Escalante), creation of a tall grass prairie national preserve in the Flint Hills of Kansas, gray wolves reestablished in Wyoming and Idaho, red wolves restored to North Carolina and Tennessee, and Mexican wolves reintroduced to Arizona and New Mexico. If the next five years bring as much change, we may see grizzlies restored to Idaho, Colorado, and California (where presently the only grizzlies are on the state flag), gray wolves returned to Utah and Colorado, gray wolves reintroduced to New England, and new national parks designated in such ecosystems as the short grass prairie, the timber country of northern Maine, and the southern Rockies (south San Juans).

Over that same period from 1994 through 1998, the *American Nature Writing* series has taken root and flourished—I thank you all (reviewers, booksellers, readers, nature aficionados) for helping us to make it so. As always, in looking toward next year's volume, I request contributions from readers—I carefully read everything that is sent me with the genuine hope that it will amaze and delight. Please send your work to me at P.O. 102345, Denver, CO 80250. I am particularly interested in writing from those only known locally or regionally but with national potential, from those living in the Midwest, Northeast, and Deep South, and from writers with experiences in nature abroad. The collections are divided equally by gender, and so I am especially interested in receiving works by women writing about nature. Working together—readers and editor—we can continue to build anthologies that, like the first five, hold both literary excellence and thematic and stylistic diversity as the standard.

This year's annual is distinct in several ways. First, several of the selections are of more substantial length than those featured in the past. These include extensive excerpts from Chip Rawlins's memoir of life in the Wind River Mountains of Wyoming ("Head of Murphy Creek"), Dan O'Brien's book on falconry in South Dakota (*Dog Days*), and David Rain Wallace's long-awaited study of the Central American land bridge ("The Bumpy Bridge"). The greater length provides readers with the opportunity to become more fully acquainted with a writer's style and thematic interests. Second, the collection is geographically diverse, ranging from Barry Lopez's essay on the coral reefs of Bonaire in the Caribbean to Mary Beth Holleman's essay on St. Lawrence Island in the northern Bering Sea. Third, the 1998 annual features three nature poets, including a substantial portion of Homer Kizer's celebrated and strikingly innovative sonnet sequence.

I once again thank the writers, agents, and publishers for their wonderfully cooperative spirit—no collection is possible without such enthusiastic assistance. My editor, Jim Cohee, continues to bring good cheer and warm support for the series—without him these books would be impossible. The Murray clan continues to be a source of great happiness, especially my son Naoki, who at seven went for his first extended camping trip with Dad this past summer. His century—the next century—will bring changes to this world that we cannot imagine. It is my hope that books like this are paving the way for that next generation, passing on values, reaffirming choices, and shining the lights of reason into the darkness of this world.

Introduction

From the Faraway Nearby

I

The dangers of life are infinite, and safety is among them.
Goethe

i. In late August, 1992, Duane Crawford and I flew in a twin-engine Beechcraft from Fairbanks, Alaska, where we lived and worked, 150 miles north to Fort Yukon. From there we were flown, one at a time, in a Piper Supercub 75 miles into the Brooks Range, where we established a camp and hunted caribou for a week.

What follows is an account of that trip.

Those who have heard the chronicle have often urged me to make a written version, and so here it is, such as it is, a narrative that has heretofore been available only as a campfire tale, a fugitive artifact of the backwoods, as, they say, the story of the Laestrygonians was once, or any of those anecdotes regarding Odin and Ymir the frost giant, or, for that matter, the Wife of Bath's tale.

ii. The story begins with a phone call. Summer term was over and I was grading English papers in my windowless office—a converted music practice room—in the basement of the fine-arts complex at the University of Alaska. On the phone was Duane Crawford, a former student, saying that his brother-in-law was too sick to accompany him on a caribou hunt and that he needed a replacement. He had to find this replacement by the end of the day, and I was the only person he knew outside of work. In retrospect, I should have realized that Duane's brother-in-law was too sick of

Duane to come on the hunt. In any event, I was, at least then, always willing to render assistance to anyone in need, and so I told Duane, sure, man, I just happen to have a spare week before fall semester, I'll help bail you out of this little situation, yes, yes, of course I understand. Don't worry about a thing. I'll be at the south end of the airport tomorrow morning. Right, 6:00 sharp. Alright, then, 5:30.

The garage turned upside down, all manner of outdoor gear spread across the living room floor, driving around town for supplies, grades handed into the Dean's office, little if any sleep.

Disarray and uncertainty, the parents of every disaster.

On the flight over to Fort Yukon I spent most of my time admiring the White Mountains, a wild glaciated range Alfred Bierstadt would have loved. Duane sat across the aisle reading the morning paper, telling me, among other things, that the latest polls showed his man Bush handily defeating the Arkansas governor. To which I decided the best response was silence. Once past the White Mountains the country flattened into a basin that stretched to the horizons —brown muskeg and green patches of spruce, shallow lakes and ponds, peat bogs and horsetail fens, occasionally the odd hill, aspen or birch covered. We flew across the Yukon Flats on a line as straight as the mark a jeweler cuts on a diamond, and after awhile I saw the big brown river ahead, low and muscular and slow, winding its way across that province of the world as it had been doing since the beginning of time.

The airport was located in a birch forest south of town, which in turn was downstream from the confluence with the Porcupine River. As we made our approach Fort Yukon sprawled below: a community building, the Alaska Commercial Company general store, a busy waterfront, a school with a baseball field, several churches, a couple of log-hewn lodges, and the scattered homes of the 600 souls who called this place home. The pilot circled once, losing altitude, and then lined up with the runway—cabins and outbuildings below, people in flannel shirts cutting wood and working in vegetable gardens, woodsmoke puffing from stovepipes.

Mornings are cold in the valley, even in late August.

After we landed and pulled the gear from the belly of the beast, Duane led the way across the runway to Elden Morris's maroon and white Supercub, tied down beside a 500-gallon aviation fuel tank. The depot served as the international headquarters for Elden's one plane operation, Sheenjek Air. It was an old plane—six years older than me—but Duane said it was a sound machine and that its pilot was not as bad as some. The passenger seat was positioned behind the pilot's seat, and both sat beneath the oversized wing. Behind the passenger seat was enough room for one seabag, a backpack, and a rifle. The plane looked as though it would fly, through no fault of its own.

As we stood there waiting, two Kutchin men drove up on a four-wheeler to say that Elden was on his way. They were his neighbors, Sam and Charlie, and appeared to be brothers. Duane showed them his rifle, a .375 H and H magnum. A man lies in direct proportion to the size of the rifle in his hands—consider that an axiom.

A little while later Elden roared up on a motorcycle with his terrier, Hayduke, and I was introduced to both man and dog. Hayduke would be accompanying us on the trip, Elden announced, because he had proven himself to be a "good-luck charm." Elden was a gentle giant, half Kutchin and half Canadian, and was thick-necked and big-shouldered as all firewood cutters are. He wore a faded "Midnight Sun Fun Run" T-shirt and a Sourdough Roadhouse baseball hat. His jeans were stained with the recent blood of moose and salmon. On his feet were well-worn surplus army boots, the sort girlfriends are always trying to throw away but wives do not mind so much. In the village he was famous among schoolchildren for owning the only Harley-Davidson north of the Arctic Circle.

Elden told us that he had been having minor engine problems all week but that he believed everything would be alright today, or at least he sincerely hoped that would be the case.

Duane, who had previously insisted that he go first, now generously suggested that I have the privilege, and so we loaded the plane with my gear and some of his. After waving goodbye to Duane and the men still admiring his howitzer, I squeezed into the seat behind Elden with Hayduke on my lap, careful not to disturb the cables on the floor that controlled the rudder and flaps in the tail.

Elden started the engine, which smoked at first from a "bad gasket—nothing to worry about," and we idled to the main runway, stopped on the numbers, received clearance from the tower, and proceeded to takeoff. Or tried to. A couple of hundred yards down the runway, at an altitude of ten or twelve feet, the engine sputtered, stalled, started up again, and then completely conked out. After losing power we dropped back heavily and unevenly onto the runway, first on the right wheel and then on the left, and then back again, careened toward the edge of the pavement, and then braked so abruptly that Hayduke cut his lip on the back of Elden's seat.

Both pilot and passenger climbed out and pushed the plane into the grass so that Elden could install new spark plugs. I was assigned the task of hammering the right wheel support, now partially bent, into a straight position. The support had been previously repaired with a section of hollow plumbing pipe and so I had to be careful with the framing hammer.

While we were working on the plane a military transport touched down—a C-130 Hercules—and it was exhilarating to stand a few yards from a landing aircraft. Crew members stared incredulously from cockpit windows. The dog was transported into a state of religious ecstasy by the experience, barking so energetically his feet left the ground.

Forty-five minutes after the aborted liftoff we attempted to become airborne again—and this time actually made it.

Shortly we were flying over the Yukon Flats, the quiet village and the broad muddy river behind us.

From the air we saw the north country as the white-fronted goose or the black plover sees it. And it was a beautiful country, far more so from five hundred than from five thousand feet. The wild grasses were dry and hay-colored with winter approaching and the birch groves and aspen parks held the last of their gold to the sun. In every low place there was water. Around every lake, and there were thousands of old sloughs and stranded oxbows and dead muskeg ponds, you could see the trails of moose. They led through the smoky yellow willows into the forests where the moose slept, heavy and dark and still as the centuries. A rock was a rarity. Anything stationary soon disappeared into the mouldering green moss. From the sphagnum grew many things, but the tallest and most striking were the spruce. They were as numberless as the quills on a porcupine and they came in two varieties: thin and very thin. Across the whole landscape there was not one sign of the human race. Not one cabin. Not one boat dock. Not one smoke plume from one campfire. Here was the New World before the cross-bearing conquistadors, before the slave plantations, before Wounded Knee and the Dust Bowl and the Trinity Site. Here was the beginning and the end.

"You know," Elden said through the headsets, "I was the first person to land on this mountain."

"When was that?"

"About two weeks ago."

Elden spoke in a soft, restrained voice, as if superstitious that raising his voice or speaking disrespectfully about anything would bring him bad luck. I adjusted the earphones and tried to move my knees into a more comfortable position. The dog was staring out the window as intently as a person.

"How do you know you were the first?"

"No wind sock. First thing a pilot does is put down his flag. Country's big enough we don't bother each other. At least most of us don't. Nobody in Yuk knows about this mountain, and I plan to keep it that way. Do you see that lake coming up on the right?"

I told him I did.

"That's Kwittevunkud. My middle son Ronnie killed his first bull moose on the lake a year ago."

"How old is he?"

"Thirteen next month."

I spotted a lanky black bear eating blueberries on the shore of the lake, and Elden said if the bear didn't put on more weight it wouldn't survive the winter.

"You see them sometimes," he continued, "in the middle of the winter. They come out on the ridges, covered with frost. They don't last long at fifty below. A week later you see where the wolves have found them."

I asked him how he found the mountain, and he said that he was taking a shortcut home from a Dall sheep camp on the Wind River, dropped through a hole in the clouds, and "there it was." He spotted a pair of shed moose antlers and landed on the tundra to pick them up.

"What do you do with them?"

"I just like to have them around the yard."

I knew that wasn't true, but didn't say anything.

I asked him if we could see the mountain yet and he said no, we were still too far away, but that after awhile it would appear dead ahead. I peered over his shoulder and past the vibrating gauges and through the blur of the propeller at the foothills of the Brooks Range, about seventy miles away. Behind the foothills were the clear sharp peaks of the Arctic Divide. Above the Arctic Divide were clouds, high and brilliant white with summits trailing plumes and plunging misty canyons—the cumulus clouds of summer still.

Elden told me about the country as we flew north, about how the Brooks Range was the northernmost mountain range on the planet and was home to everything from polar bears to flying squirrels; and how each November he counted moose for the state in aerial surveys; and how the perpetually burning summer fires caused the broad sweeping patterns of dead and living forests we were seeing. He pointed to Burnt Mountain, a vast unfinished pyramid of a mountain to the northeast, and said the government built a remote seismic detector there to listen for Soviet nuclear tests at Novaya Zemlya. Burnt Mountain was, Elden claimed, the quietest seismic location on earth. In bad weather he often landed just below the summit to wait for blue skies, and sometimes poked around the "top-secret" strontium-90 generators that every ten-year-old child in Fort Yukon knew about. I asked him about his family, and he told me about his Kutchin wife Monica, a nurse in the village, and his three children, and how this bushpiloting was sure better than anything he had done before, fighting fires for the BLM, or trapping lynx with his brother from homemade dogsleds (snowmobiles being unreliable in the deep cold of January) on the Coleen River, or working as a deckhand on a Yukon freighter barge.

Suddenly the plane lurched into a steep left-hand bank and I felt a stab of adrenaline. Even without looking I knew the cause. Before departing Fort Yukon, Duane—worried he had too much gear for the second trip—had insisted that we take along his empty backpack. The only place for it had been tied loosely to the left wing strut, which angles from the bottom of the plane to the center of the wing and holds the wing in place. Because Duane had tied the pack the wrong way, the main bag had blown open in the airflow and was dragging us down. Elden worked the plane back to our cruising altitude of 500 feet and was now constantly fighting the plane's tendency to bank in the direction of the resistance.

It took awhile, but our hearts finally slowed from a gallop to a canter.

"Boy," Elden said, his neck muscles bulging as he grasped the yoke, his voice now strained, "I just wish there was some way I could climb out there and cut it loose. That thing could make landing tricky. And if it blows off and hits the tail…"

His voice trailed into silence.

I pictured a sudden wind gust on final approach, the left wing dropping sharply, the plane cartwheeling across the steppes.

After a few minutes of battling the yoke, Elden said, "Do you think—"

I finished the sentence. "Yeah, I can do it."

"How?"

I explained my proposal and asked if he could safely reduce air-speed a little to make it easier, and he said yes.

"Elden, do you by any chance have any rope under your seat? I've got some in the pack but it's hard to reach."

"I've got plenty of rope."

"Good. Give me as much as you can."

Elden reached under his seat, one hand on the yoke, and handed me a coil of blood-stained half-inch rope over his shoulder.

"Don't forget to take your glasses off," he said.

"Right."

I placed my glasses in my baseball hat and laid it under the seat. I could feel Elden throttle back. I didn't like the sluggish feel of the plane at lower speed, and we were already losing what little altitude we had, but it would hopefully only take a minute.

"Everything okay up there?"

"No problem."

"Alright, here goes."

I unfolded my skinning knife and laid it beside me on the seat, unsnapped the safety belt, put Hayduke on the floor, took off my headsets, and lowered the window. Loose items began flying around the cabin immediately—an aerial map, a paper cup, the page from a mail-order catalog—and were promptly sucked out the window into the maelstrom. I squeezed my head, arms, and torso through the window, leaned into the airflow—which was like leaning into the side of a tornado—and tied one end of the rope to the top of the pack frame, with three half-hitches behind the knot to hold it secure. When that was done I slid back in and tied the other end of the rope to the crossbar under the bottom of the seat, tightly. I then reentered the wind tunnel with knife in hand and began cutting away the quarter-inch nylon rope that held the pack to the wing strut.

When every inch of Duane's rope was five miles behind us I wrestled the pack through the window—it just fit, at the widest angle and with considerable wrenching and pulling. Once the pack was inside—temporarily pinning Hayduke to the floor, but he seemed to understand the importance of being still just then—I raised the window and locked it tight.

"Everything secure?" Elden asked, looking over his shoulder. I didn't have my headsets on yet, and so it was hard to hear him over the engine.

"Yeah," I said.

I snapped my seatbelt and put the headsets on. My whole body was numb, my right ear felt strange, and my eyes hurt. The headsets had become unplugged, and so I had to search for the plug until I finally found it above me. Once I was settled in, Hayduke crawled into my lap and began smelling the pack. It was a nuisance there between me and the left side of the plane, and so I worked the pack between the back of Elden's seat and my knees—a tight squeeze but better than having it on the strut.

The knife was on the seat beside me. I snapped it shut and put it back in my pocket. After that I put my glasses and baseball hat back on.

The plane was gaining speed—and altitude.

"I can feel the difference already," said Elden.

"Me, too."

"I'll never do that again," said Elden. "I tie antlers to the struts all the time. But I had no idea how dangerous a pack could be."

The plane was flying straight and normally now.

Elden studied the wing for awhile and then, as if guilty for something he was thinking, said, "Still, Duane's a good guy. Don't tell him this, but I'd fly him up here for free I like him so much."

I knew the only reason Elden said that was because Duane's agency—the Bureau of Reclamation—was a major source of his income.

"Yeah, he's an interesting person," I said.

"How'd you two meet?"

"He was a student of mine."

Duane had dropped out after a month. The reason for his enrolling in the night class, a writing seminar, was never clear, perhaps related to work.

As we talked I scanned the terrain. The level earth stretched out evenly toward every horizon, with mountains rising at a distance in all directions. The mountains to the north were considerably closer than the others. Soon we would be over the foothills. Everywhere I looked there were places I had never seen, places I would never go. I was so happy I wanted to shout for joy, or cut loose with a rebel yell, but restrained myself with the microphone.

"Are we in the Arctic Refuge yet?"

"Just crossed the southern boundary."

"Man, this is beautiful."

"Oh yeah."

We were in the mountains now, a tumbled hill and valley country with the gentle contours and rounded knolls of the oldest grounds. The fall colors, the reds and oranges and yellows, were like an oriental tapestry, and there were caribou moving across the tundra domes. Down below, in the wide timbered valleys, beaver ponds backed the clear cold water up into grassy swales and cattail marshes and moose thickets, and from the sheer number of ponds I would have guessed that no one had trapped this country in about 10,000 years. We were flying low enough to see the Arctic grayling in schools just beneath the surface of the ponds, and once I spotted a pair of trumpeter swans and pointed them out to Elden, who nodded and said they would be turning south to Oregon soon. Far to the east a flock of white cranes the size of a jumbo jet fluttered south, and I watched them until they vanished. It was the finest country I'd ever seen. In my life I had never been so many hundreds of miles from a road, and I probably never would be farther, and so I scanned the whole country in every direction several times to get a complete sense of its scope. Wherever I looked there were mountains in every size and shape, as if this was the warehouse where God came when he was building a new range and needed a mountain.

To the east twenty miles was the wide cut of the Sheenjek River, and I marked its drainage carefully, for the Sheenjek is where, Elden was saying, we would have to hike if anything happened to him and the plane. "Just follow any drainage east and you'll wind up on a gravel bar beside the Sheenjek. Build three smoky fires and wait."

Ahead of us and beyond the foothills was the cordillera of the Brooks Range, which looked like the Rocky Mountains west of Denver, and I asked if we would be flying much closer to the high peaks.

"Not today. And I'm glad. You can't tell from here, but the wind is blowing through those passes like a hurricane right now."

A minute later Elden motioned to a prominent mountain underneath the left wing and told me not to talk anymore, that he needed to concentrate on the landing. From the air the mountain resembled an enormous island rising from a sea of forest. The greater length of the mountain measured about five miles, and two side ridges extended a mile or so from the central mass. Elden pointed with his finger to the compass on the instrument panel, and I saw that the needle was spinning wildly, as if we were flying over a magnet. As we neared the mountain I could feel its power. The midday thermals buffeted the wings like the first punches of a boxer early in the round. The plane banked abruptly and then made a sharper turn and began losing altitude rapidly as Elden lined up with some point I could not see.

All the time we were bucking regularly and things were falling down—Elden's spiral-bound logbook lodged between the instrument panel and the windshield, the small pair of binoculars stored in the net bag over his seat. My head was banging against the top of the plane, and I held on to the bottom of the seat and kept an arm around Hayduke. I studied the main ridge closely, rising ahead of us like the back of a moose, and wondered where a plane could possibly land. Every instinct in my body told me there was no place to land a fixed-wing aircraft, and I wanted to suggest that we pull up while there was still time and fly elsewhere, but Elden had asked me

not to speak and he was sitting in the pilot's seat. Before I knew it
we were over the trees. I could not believe we were that low, with
nothing resembling a safe landing place ahead, and that we hadn't
hit a tree yet. If I had been sitting on the wheel brace my feet would
have been dragging on the tops of the spruce trees. I put my head
down so that I would not see what was about to happen, and then,
not able to resist, I looked up. As we came in a bit too fast, with the
wing's pivoting back and forth on the ground winds and the rubber
tires a few feet over the last trees and the engine throttled just
above stall and nothing ahead but reindeer moss and rocks and a
scattering flock of ptarmigan, I was fairly certain it would be a fatal
crash.

But we didn't crash and the forty-five-year-old plane bounced
and braked to a fairly quick stop on the gravelly slope near Elden's
wind sock, which was a blaze orange scarf tied to a dead white
spruce.

Elden said it was okay to get out, and so I removed the earphones,
opened the door, and jumped down after Hayduke. It was good to be
on the ground again—real good. Elden followed, relieved himself on
the dead spruce with Hayduke, helped unload the gear, looked over
the plane, then stood with his hands on his hips, surveying the landscape as if he were the owner, which in a way he was.

"This is the country, eh?" he said.

That it was—in every direction, a place so stunning it would be
a national park anywhere else in the world.

"You know, people live their entire lives and never see anything
like this. Just think of all the people right now in the Lower 48 who
would kill to be where we are."

I agreed.

"I never forget how special the Arctic is," he said. "Even a bad day
here is better than the best day any place else. Still—." He paused, a
flock of chickadees chirping by on a gust of wind without a care in
the world. "I don't want to be doing this forever. Not with kids to
raise."

Elden then mentioned there was no water on top of the mountain and that we would have to hike to the bottom of yonder valley for water. No big deal, we both agreed, although it looked to be a four-mile round trip.

"Just out of curiosity," I asked, "how close is the nearest person?"

"That would be Arctic Village—60 miles in that direction."

He pointed to the northwest.

I remembered all the crowded places I'd been, the tedious lost years in cities and suburbs and even small forgotten towns that were bustling centers of humanity compared to the absolute solitude of the bush, and I felt fortunate.

As Elden and Hayduke got back into the Supercub, a sort of time machine if you thought about it, he turned and said, "Remember everything I said and have a good hunt."

He gave me a little salute and I returned it. And then the door closed and he was gone, the little red-and-white plane bouncing down the slope and off into the big blue, and I was more alone than I had ever been in my life, with the pale sky curving away deep and far and empty. The air was more clean than anything I'd ever breathed. It was an extraordinary air born on the northern ice and washed by the swells of the Arctic Ocean and scrubbed by the glacial peaks and freshened by a million square miles of open tundra. It reminded me of ocean air, only it was better, for it carried with it the scent of snow and winter and, somewhere nearby, caribou. It smelled of distance, of space that had never known a surveyor's transit or a township line, and never would.

I stood there for quite some time just taking it in, feeling a great sense of relief, as an ailing patient does when finally placed in the hands of a competent physician.

After awhile I carried my gear down the hill to timberline and made camp. I found a perfect place, a dry terrace surrounded by blueberry bushes, facing east and out of the wind. There were even a few spruce trees to give the place a little more life and comfort.

I then returned to the top of the mountain.

The views were immense—in every direction. To the north and west were tundra highlands—low massive hills, grassy swales, isolated granite tors. South of the mountain the country sloped off through wooded foothills toward the Yukon Flats, and to the east was the Sheenjek Valley—heavily forested, cut north to south by the river, with treeless uplands on the far side.

In all the sky there was not one cloud.

It was a clear warm day. There was a soft autumnal light over the hills, as in those Winslow Homer paintings of Newfoundland, and the sky was flawless in its clarity. It was the sort of day when a sound, however small, carries a long way—the cry of a raven, the chatter of a pine squirrel, a spruce half fallen and creaking against another. The landscape was filled with color, though in the subtle tones of the spent earth: the rusted stalks of fireweed, the salmon-hued clumps of blueberry, the dull orange streaks of dwarf birch, and, under it all, the grayish cream of reindeer moss.

I looked at my feet and saw many old friends—cotton grass, cranberry, crowberry, cloudberry, moss campion. Because of the rainy summer, the blueberries were thick. Some were dangling from twigs and others were lost in the leaves. Most were sweet, but a few, touched by frost, were tart. All showed variations on the color blue —from Prussian blue to pinkish blue and everything in between. Among the blueberries were a few late bloomers: yellow dryas, white bistort, and bright red shooting stars, each deeply bedded in the mat of reindeer moss and heather.

I walked a mile west across the ridge, to where it joined the main ridge, and stopped where the trees ended. I had forgotten—always do—how hard it is to walk on tundra, which more or less levitates over the permafrost. There was grizzly scat on the ground in several places, filled with berries, and I took note of the fact that the bears had passed through earlier that day, an adult and her nearly full-grown cubs. At the edge of the trees, half buried in the moss, was the lichen-covered skull of a bull caribou. The lichens were orange and ochre and olive and resembled the encrustations of coral on a reef, colonizing dead matter with the bright colors of the sea. One painted antler protruded upward, the other was covered with moss and fallen willow leaves. The antler that stuck up had been gnawed on by a porcupine on its furthest tines. Down lower the size of the teeth marks indicated something smaller—a boreal mouse or red-backed vole. Tilting the skull upward from its resting place, I saw that the bone was stained green and black where it touched the ground—the earth had begun to reclaim its loan.

What else?

A spider had occupied one eye socket for the short summer—bits of web and a few ant carapaces remained in the cavern.

The single protruding antler resembled a hunting bow in the grace of its curve, and I saw how easy it would be to fashion a bow from the antler, with the proper tools. Even sharp stones would do, and for a bow string perhaps fibers twisted from the thin supple roots of spruce.

And what of those cliffs over there—couldn't caribou be driven over them? What a treasure trove could be obtained, and so easily. And there would be furbearers drawn by the scent—wolf, wolverine, lynx, fox—and they could be snared, their fur the difference between life and death when the cold of outer space came to earth.

The mind considers such things, alone and in a wild place.

Old memories, strange but familiar, return from the past.

Suddenly a keen chill flowed across the land—a bitter western wind—and I heard the persistent annoying buzz of an airplane.

III. It was evening now and Duane sat across the fire against a stump, a steel cup of tea in his hands. We'd already burned one timberline tree, and had started another. I hated to burn those beautiful dead trees—it was like destroying works of art—but the fire felt good against the Arctic cold. Behind Duane was what looked like the Ur-backpacking tent from the sixties. The zipper had long ago been torn off, and the front flaps were held together with a dozen safety pins. It was the first time I had ever really looked at Duane.

He was a big man, with a rising tide of gray in his mustache and thick eyebrows and shaggy hair, and the widening paunch of a man approaching fifty who has spent too much time behind a desk. His eyes were set back under a prominent bony arch, and so he looked out at the world as from a cavern. The right eye squinted frequently, as if he knew that one bad thing you did once. The only other notable feature on his face was a red spot on his cheek where the frost had paid a visit—a not uncommon feature to those who have wintered in the Arctic.

The western sky held its violet-cobalt blue light until past seven, and then slowly darkened through a Phoenician purple to an ivory black, revealing stars and northern lights. The moon was low in the east and so the sky was fine for northern lights. The auroras were like self-contained theatrical events, beginning in the north with a minor rustling of green or red, then building to a whirling crescendo at the zenith and finally playing out toward the south. I never tired of watching them—wave after wave they came on, some as delicate as the light reflected on the ceiling of a grotto, others the visual equivalent of a Jimi Hendrix guitar solo.

As I sat there carving on a piece of wood, and occasionally looking up to admire the northern lights, Duane was pretty much holding court, and I was letting him run with himself, curious to see where it led. Unfortunately, as the evening progressed and he revealed more about himself ("Pardon my profanity but this is the way I talk"), I began to realize the grotesque nature of my plight. The man across the fire, whom I'd known only casually in town and consequently made many false assumptions about, was my polar opposite. In fact it was worse than that. Duane was of the nature of an evil twin or anti-self, an antipodal character such as populate the works of Joseph "The Secret Sharer" Conrad. In story after story, one disturbing revelation after another surfaced from his murky depths. First was the incident from Vietnam, which involved the killing of a civilian in retaliation for a series of casualties suffered by his unit, and with no remorse on his part. Next was the elaborate fiction concerning a self-inflicted wound in his foot that brought him, a troubled draftee, back home six months early. Then came a rambling piece of vitriol concerning the various races, Duane unaware that my first wife was Jewish, my second wife was Japanese, my sister-in-law was black, and so on. The whole thing reminded me of the Star Trek episode in which Captain Kirk and his nemesis the reptile captain were marooned on a desert planet by invisible superbeings as part of some sort of interstellar behavioral experiment.

Indeed.

What happened?

After an hour, tired and disgusted, I got up, and, despite the inconvenience, moved my tent and gear under the stars to the far side of the mountain, the bright side of the planet, and a quarter of a mile from Duane. I told him that I could not tolerate one thing in this world and that was racism. I also told him I had seen my share of the human condition in the service, but that nothing in that experience quite compared with what I had just heard. I told him that we were stuck together in this place for the week and I would be polite and make the best of it, but that I preferred some distance between us.

I had lived long enough to know there was little point in trying to reform a person over the age of forty, particularly one whose vulgarity ran in such a deep fissure from circumference to center.

As I left, Duane, surprised someone had finally stood up to him, mumbled something about it being better to camp together because of the bears.

That was the first night, before things got really bad.

In the morning the clouds had moved in from the west and lowered over the top of the mountain and fog was running everywhere, thick and cool and translucent, through the green forest and across the red and orange meadows, creating an optical effect such as you see in a coral reef when a storm has roiled the sand and reduced visibility. Everything was covered with a fine mist, as if the world had just been born and was covered with afterbirth. As I was putting on my rain pants and my rain jacket, which would be worn continuously for the next week, Duane walked over, ready to hunt. He seemed to have forgotten about the previous night entirely, or at least was trying to make it appear so.

Even as I stood there trying to decide what to do with him, the fog was dissipating, the drizzle gathering strength.

I walked west on the whale-backed ridge toward the last stand of spruce, Duane following. Beyond that was a country of rolling tundra. Along the way I noted fresh caribou tracks pressed into the wet ground. Duane straggled behind, explaining how the storm was the remnant of Typhoon Iniki, which had leveled the Hawaiian Islands earlier in the week. He said there would be snow soon, as the first blizzard of the season rolled in from Siberia.

The man was a perpetual font of good news and cheer.

At the juncture of the ridges Duane spotted two, then three, bull caribou on a hill to the south. He told me to stand aside and watch the master as he killed them in succession from right to left (the legal limit being four per day). Duane emptied his cannon—five rounds, and each one painfully loud in the gallery-like silence—and never came close.

He then blamed me for not spotting the shots.

Repelled by the entire spectacle, I parted company with him, saying I would spend the rest of the day exploring to the north, away from the trees, and out on the open tundra.

"Good luck," he exclaimed sarcastically.

Fifty yards later he called out and said that all kidding aside he would really appreciate it if I killed one for him, because there might be something wrong with his scope and his wife would make his life miserable if he spent all that money and returned with no meat.

Something wrong with his rifle scope? I wanted to say there might be something wrong with his head.

It was good to be away from that maniac, and after awhile I

slowed my pace and enjoyed my surroundings. It was, after all, a new and good country.

I hiked for several hours at a very slow pace, not so much hunting as exploring. The going was slow on the muskeg, with the grassy mounds and tangles of heather, and with each step I became increasingly wet. Water was everywhere—at one point I sank to my thighs in a hidden baptismal pool. Near noon I came to a hill topped with granite tors, each twelve or fifteen feet tall, grouped by nature in such a way as to evoke Stonehenge. Beyond the tors was a hummocky region of *baydzheraki*, or Siberian cemetery mounds—soft green remnants left behind when ice wedges melt. It would be a quagmire in that region, and so I decided to rest awhile and have lunch among the druid stones. After eating I laid down, spread the poncho over me like a tent, and fell asleep.

Hours later I awakened. The rain was drizzling steadily on the poncho, and the light told me it was much later in the day.

Ptarmigan were clucking all around.

I sat up. The flock of ptarmigan fluttered off, their wing and chest feathers already winter white, the rest of the plumage still summer brown. Nothing had changed. In all directions, fog and rain and lovely bleak tundra.

I was happy to be far from civilization and its discontents, and far from my companion, the reincarnation of Captain Ahab, and, not wanting to turn back to camp just yet, I decided to hike another mile and see what happened.

I crossed the Siberian cemetery, climbed another Labrador tea hill, crossed another peat bog, and then something far ahead made me stop. I had no binoculars or telescopic sight, and so all I could do was squint. There, at the edge of vision, was movement. I tilted my glasses to make the lenses stronger and saw there were a couple of caribou perhaps 300 yards ahead, feeding away from me, heads down. When they raised their heads I could see they were mature bulls with heavy necks and racks. I dropped my survival pack,

marked the location—a lone spruce with a split main branch due
east—and ran to an exposed grassy point 200 yards ahead, hidden
from view by an intervening ridge.

Once there, on top of the knoll, the length of a football field from
the animals, I sat down, placed my elbows on my knees, and centered the iron post on the shoulder of the nearest one. At that exact
moment the caribou stopped feeding and looked around, sensing
some disturbance, but the wind was in my face. I held my breath,
squeezed the trigger, felt the recoil, and watched the near caribou
drop. There was a second shot as he struggled, as all life does, with
the strange new freedom of death.

The other caribou, including three I had not seen, ran for the
horizon, every horizon, including mine—one passed at a distance of
twenty feet, unaware in his panic of my presence.

When I reached the bull he was dead, sprawled out in the grass,
the light gone from his amber eyes, and, as always, I was appalled at
what I had done. I felt particularly bad when I noted the condition
of his hooves—torn, cracked, frostbitten—and couldn't escape the
sense that I had committed a crime for which I would one day be
held accountable. Regret attends every death inflicted by a hunter,
but on that occasion, in those surroundings, the act of sport hunting
seemed particularly absurd. Even though I had hunted since I was
nineteen, and had worked my way through college partly as a hunting guide, I resolved that I would never kill another animal again,
unless personal survival was involved. He was—or rather had been
—a beautiful animal, the size of a bull elk, with antlers still in velvet.
He had a long-muzzled, square-nosed face, a glistening white neck,
and a dense white mane. The whiteness spread over the shoulder
and down the back, which was as gray as the Arctic twilight. His
hooves were flat and rounded, perfect for the tundra. I touched a
long blade of grass to the eye several times to make certain he was
dead, and then I put my rifle down, unfolded my knife, and opened
the body from the pelvis to the sternum. After that I rolled up my

sleeves, pulled loose the viscera, and reached past the diaphragm for the lungs and finally the heart.

All this was done in twilight, largely by feel, and in the rain, and with fresh grizzly sign on the nearest hill. I worked quickly and carefully and finished in twenty minutes, and then I set back for camp through the fog and darkness, retrieving my pack along the way, hoping the rough compass heading I had followed on the way out was correct in reverse.

Sometime after nine o'clock, moving in the darkness at the speed of a ninety-year-old on the way to the day room, I spotted Duane's distant fire and veered toward his campsite.

I told him about the caribou, and that he could have some of the meat, and then retired to my campsite over the hill, crawled into the tent, and slept among the dead.

In the morning, quite early and in the continual presence of our faithful companion the freezing rain, we hiked the three miles to the carcass and deboned the meat, Duane to have whatever he could carry. During this process Duane nearly cut his left thumb off, exposing the flesh to the bone from the first joint to the knuckle. It was a deep ugly wound, but he bandaged it and kept working on his end of the caribou. With perhaps 200 pounds of meat divided between us on our pack frames, we trudged back, me in front and him behind, with our rifles at port arms and stopping periodically to scan behind us. During the last mile we had to stop every fifty yards, Duane's bad foot having been wrenched in the tussocks.

That night we established a truce—Duane's self-inflicted injuries were forming a pattern—and I joined him at his fire and listened to the extended version of his life story. It was a century-long saga involving a German immigrant turned pioneering Oklahoma sodbuster, a prosperous ranching clan that lost everything in the Great Depression, a forced exodus to the city and the purgatory of urban wage-labor, and then a concluding chapter about his now-stalled-before-retirement career with the agency. The story of his loveless marriage, senile live-in mother-in-law, and ungrateful children could have been written by Dickens.

Before I departed for my camp that night, Duane began shifting around uncomfortably, and then awkwardly announced he had something to say. He cleared his throat and, staring at the fire, said he was sorry for "carrying on like I did the other night." The apology was accepted, but with the knowledge that the statement was not made from any fundamental change in character.

The next morning we hiked over for the rest of the meat, but three grizzlies were feeding on the remains, accompanied by a gathering of ravens. The bears had heavy square heads and contoured shoulder humps and each time they moved the silver fur rippled over their bodies. Occasionally the younger ones stared at us, but the mother fed without distraction, apparently confident we would not approach any closer. She may have never seen a human before—certainly she had never been shot at, or she would have run at first sight. Duane wanted to kill the sow, which was legal because the cubs were almost as large as the mother, but I prevailed upon him to spare the animal. As we sat there and watched the grizzlies crack the bones in their teeth and use their claws to retrieve the marrow, I told Duane about the past five summers I'd spent in Denali observing grizzlies and the book I was writing about them. For all its reputation, "the American Serengeti"—with its sightseeing buses, helicopter tours, and citation-writing rangers—now seemed about as wild as Central Park, compared to the far north.

We then returned to camp, both feeling as though the hunting part of the trip was over. For one thing, Duane's thumb was a mess, and his foot was too stiff to walk for more than a few miles. For another, a storm was on its way, and packing meat through snow would give new meaning to the word travail.

And so we organized our gear and began to disengage ourselves from the trip and prepare to return to civilization. The trip was already receding into the past, to an extent, and to become part of that dust cloud that forever drifts behind us on the road.

Or so we mistakenly thought, unaware that the real adventure, the life and death struggle that is always just a moment away in the wilderness, was about to begin.

That afternoon I hauled my gear to the top of the mountain and walked over to Duane's camp. Elden was scheduled to stop by and fly out any meat, and so around one o'clock Duane placed his radio among the branches of the tallest spruce, uncoiled the 50-foot wire antenna, draped it around the neighboring trees, and found the frequency used by local pilots from Fort Yukon and Arctic Village.

After several minutes of white noise we heard the following transmission: "Sheenjek Air. Mayday, mayday. Engine fire. Going down south of KV."

Five or six seconds later we heard an ominous crackle of static, followed by repeated unanswered calls to Sheenjek Air from the tower at Fort Yukon.

At which point Duane turned off the radio to save the batteries. We sat down by the fire and considered the situation. It was not as bad as it could be, nor was it as good as it had been. This much was certain: The only person who knew where we were had just crashed near Kwittevunkud Lake 40 miles to the south and was possibly dead, the season's first major snowstorm would soon arrive and we had no snow gear, we were 20 miles from the nearest regular route of travel for local pilots, current food supplies would not last indefinitely, and Duane had a hand injury and could not hike any distance on his foot.

For quite some time we didn't say much, mostly stared at the fire, somewhat in a state of disbelief, almost expecting Elden to arrive as planned. The crash, in those circumstances, seemed to belong to that category of events one reads about now and then in the Fairbanks newspaper, that occur to the friend of a passing acquaintance, or to the cousin of someone at the other end of the street, or to a high school classmate of the office secretary, but never to anyone close to you. For years, life goes on like that, the comfortable illusion that nothing bad happens inside the circle of family and friends, and then one day, in an instant, everything changes, and suddenly you are confronted once again with one of the many unpleasant facts of this small world—that, for example, worn oil gaskets fail and hot engines catch fire and smoking planes fall from the sky.

Nothing had changed in the landscape around us—the Bohemian waxwings still fed among the blueberries up the hill and the ravens still talked back and forth in their ancient corvid dialect—and so the event we had just overheard seemed unreal, part of another universe, both related and not related to us.

I tried to inject a sense of humor, as usual, even a bit of gallows humor (such as the fact that, on the bright side, if no one came for us at least we wouldn't have go to work anymore; or that we could now live out every man's dream and spend the rest of our days hunting, fishing, and trapping in the wilderness). Duane, however, good old migraine-headache Duane, thought the situation was too serious for humor. My philosophy is the reverse—the more serious the situation, the more essential the need for humor—but of course he could not be persuaded to join the revolution.

His answer to the situation was to tell the story about the wildlife photographer. Apparently a few years earlier a *cheechako*, or inexperienced newcomer from the Lower 48, had been dropped off in the Brooks Range by an unreliable pilot with a drinking problem. The pilot returned to his cabin near Fort Yukon, settled into his usual routine, and proceeded to forget about his client, completely. The body was found about a week too late—the photographer had already shot himself, thinking he would never be rescued and not wanting to die from starvation and exposure.

As I say, Duane was a missionary in rags for the creed of optimism, a student by candlelight of the works of Aristophanes, high priest for the Cult of Perpetual Happiness, perennial poster boy for the Royal Good Fellow Society, and the actual person on whom producers based the cartoon character "Chuckles, the Happy Clown."

And so on.

At around three o'clock a 747 passed overhead—several made the high-altitude transit every afternoon, en route from Heathrow to Narita—and Duane went into his tent and pulled out a small two-way radio he had not told me about that enabled him to communicate with the pilot on an emergency frequency. His transmission went like this: "Ground party in Arctic Refuge to passing transpolar jetliner. We are in urgent need of assistance. Please respond, over." Unfortunately the pilot, flying for the Hong Kong-based carrier Tiger Air, was Chinese and spoke only enough English to land at airports. He had no idea what Duane was saying. Even if the pilot had been more fluent, Kutchin words such as Kwittevunkud or Sheenjek would not have meant much to someone whose native language was Mandarin. Another complication was that we only had a couple of minutes before the plane passed out of antenna range. The *coup de grace* was that the batteries went dead in the middle of the brief conversation, Duane having forgotten to recharge them after his last trip.

Duane proceeded to throw an "all hope is lost" fit, and I suggested that he try to adapt the batteries from the other radio. He worked on that project, like Dr. Spock in the Edith Keiller episode (Captain Kirk and company stranded on twentieth-century Earth, with Joan Collins as the doomed Edith Keiller fighting the fascists), for the rest of the afternoon without any success.

The diversion, though, enabled me to finalize my plan, and over dinner I told Duane I would hike out the 20 miles to the Sheenjek and build the three signal fires, as Elden had instructed.

Duane asked if I could actually complete a cross-country trek without a map or trails, and I told him it would be no problem, providing it didn't snow. I would simply follow the streams to the river. Twenty miles is, after all, not that far. In the Marines we hiked 20 miles before noon. In Denali I day-hiked that far all the time, and never with the luxury of a trail. It would be no problem.

Duane gave me a look. I knew he thought I couldn't make it, and that was all I needed *to* make it.

So that settled the matter—one of us would go out "there"—*into that howling wilderness beyond their lonely outpost* (as Jack London might have phrased it)—and *that unfortunate man never heard from again* would be me.

Duane was in considerable pain from the thumb, which had begun to change color, and after dinner I convinced him to cauterize the thumb with boiling water, which was a screaming but necessary ordeal. I then tried to suture the wound with a sterilized needle and thread from his medical kit, but after the first shallow stitch Duane started throwing up. After that he took some heavy-duty prescription painkillers and passed out. He had previously declared that if necessary he would consume the entire bottle, which he carried for this sort of contingency.

And so in the pages of my journal I quietly bestowed upon him, as has long been the custom on the American Frontier, the honor of a nickname, a phrase that would capture his essence for posterity, an appellation such as was given to Francis "The Swamp Fox" Marion, or "Honest" Abe Lincoln, or "Grizzly" Adams, or "Buffalo Bill" Cody, or "Cactus Ed" Abbey.

The name I chose for Duane was "Mister Sunshine."

And what of myself? Well, by then I had more than earned the sobriquet of "The Idiot" for having been so foolish as to go on a wilderness excursion with someone I barely knew.

We waited one more day, just to make certain no one was coming, and then decided, from the condition of the sky and the lowering temperatures, there could be no further delays.

iv. The following morning I departed at first light, my frame pack stripped to the essentials. The sky was overcast and the wind was blowing from the west. Once off the tundra and in the woods, I felt more relief than concern. It was good to be moving, especially with the snow coming and the understanding of what that would mean. And it was good to be among trees—a more protected and congenial realm than the alpine. Whatever lay ahead, at least we had a better chance with one of us going for help. It was also nice to finally be away from Duane, and that dismal place he lived in.

For the first mile, the woods were open and parklike and there wasn't much brush or deadfall. I soon began to feel warm from the exertion and unzipped the rain jacket, opened my coat, and pushed my hat back on my head. I didn't want to become overheated so early in the day. The pack was heavy, and so was the ten-pound rifle in the bend of my arm, and I had to pace myself, find a comfortable rhythm, and stay to it.

There was not a sound in the woods, and the air was still. The songbirds of summer had long since departed. It would be a quiet trip, but at least there would be no mosquitoes. At its far end the main ridge diverged into two ridges. The northern ridge dropped steeply over a layer of exposed shale into a side drainage. The eastern ridge extended in the proper direction, but then descended into a forested plateau that appeared to be an excellent place to become lost. I decided, at the risk of alder, to follow the water.

And so I hiked downhill a mile into the basin and stayed parallel to the stream, following the trails of the moose.

Thank god for the moose. In Africa, the trailblazers are the elephants. In Alaska, the pioneers are the moose, boldly leading the way—impassable thickets, tangled stretches of black timber, godforsaken mountain ranges—in their determined quest for food.

The only problem was that moose don't mind wet hooves, and sometimes I had to climb a hill or detour through a woods to avoid a marshy area.

But steady progress was being made, about a mile an hour, and at that rate I would reach the Sheenjek by the next day, hopefully in advance of the snow.

I had just made that calculation when it began to snow. Not a lot, but enough to hurry the general pace.

About an hour later, as I was hiking along absorbed in these thoughts, I entered a clearing and a covey of spruce grouse, feeding on cranberries, exploded in front of me.

Nearly producing a cardiac event.

But mostly it was quiet in the woods, deadly quiet. Old spiderwebs in the grass, shed moose antlers, sun-bleached bone yards, dry fallen leaves rustling crisply underfoot, the patient cheerful trickle of water in the stream.

And all the while a steady dusting of fine snow, as when a teacher knocks the accumulated chalk powder from two erasers.

Left, right, left—your military left you at the end of first squad. Hour after hour.

As I hiked along I saw once again how a forest is composed of different neighborhoods. Here was an old burn rich in firewood, and here a dry slope poor in blueberries. Here was an aspen grove with a bird nest in nearly every tree, and here a sedimentary outcrop where the fossil hunting would be good. This spot would be ideal for a little cabin, and that spring up the hill could provide a reliable source of water.

At the end of a long day—four-thirty and dead-tired—I reached an exposed rocky point that overlooked the country I would traverse the next day. I had come perhaps ten miles. Perhaps a little more, perhaps a little less. But around that, around halfway. The point offered a commanding view—ahead were creeks, ridges, divides, low passes, and timber domes, all sloping toward the river. Across the Sheenjek, which was running dark and unfrozen at the bottom of the valley, was more hilly country, topped with treeless tundra. Upriver the back range had come partially into view— eroded crags with vertical headwalls, hanging glaciers, and soaring pinnacles. All views to the south were blocked by intervening ridges.

A decent place to camp.

For half an hour I dragged dead trees in from the forest and then, using one of the lantern candles, built a bonfire that could be seen from the space shuttle—there is nothing like a fire at such a time.

I pitched the tent beside a shelf of rock, so that the heat of the fire would be reflected back—it would be nice and warm through the night.

Dinner consisted of a freeze-dried chili dinner with chunks of caribou tenderloin. The more I ate the better it tasted. "Hunger is a good sauce," as Captain Bourke wrote toward the end of his dusty career on the Mexican border. Bloody good tucker, mates. And all that. By firelight I wrote in my journal in the manner of the lifelong naturalist—that, for example, I was camped beside a blocky tor of horizontally foliated metamorphic rock and that down the slope was a broken scarp of the same material. The rock was porphyritic granite, I wrote, identical to that I'd found on Primrose Ridge in the Alaska Range and on Wickersham Dome in the White Mountains.

That was the last thing I wrote before sleep.

v. The first vague morning light showed about three inches of fresh snow had fallen during the dark hours and more was falling. The thermometer on the pack registered 24°F. It felt colder, but it naturally tends to in a situation like that—200 miles from the nearest road. I didn't restoke the fire, only nibbled on some cookies for breakfast, and then quickly packed up and set off.

Mount up and move out, Bravo One.

Not 50 yards from my camp, a moose had bedded down for the night. The snow was melted and glassy from his body heat, and nearby was a pile of black pellets, not yet frozen. His antlers had left impressions in the snow and the blades of grass near the front of the bed were still frosted from his breath. Perhaps he felt safer near the fire, sensing wolves wouldn't come near, or perhaps that was one of his customary bedding locations.

As I hiked along I could see where he had fed on twigs, branches, bark, leaves—anything green.

There were a lot of moose in the valley. The rut would begin soon, and they were drifting in from the hills. Tracks were everywhere—herd bulls and upstart bulls, barren old cows and fertile young ones, abandoned yearling calves and those fortunate ones still with their mothers, all about to commence with the moose version of the Mardi Gras.

The valley woods were not as lifeless as the highlands. Down lower, there was considerably more activity, and I frequently had company: A red fox eating rose hips that was startled, perhaps even embarrassed, when I walked by and said hello; a troupe of black-beaked magpies playing in a thicket, the young ones almost as large as their parents, seven in all, clamoring about like busy happy families everywhere; a cow moose plodding along through the snow, head lifted, completely ignoring me, late, it would seem, for an important appointment.

It was a gentle familiar woods, the woods of home.

Late in the morning I came upon the scene of a wolf attack, the evidence no more than a few hours old. I saw in the snow where the wolves had brought a moose to bay and torn a piece of its hindquarters off. The moose ran for a hundred yards through the snow, trailing spots of blood, and the tangle commenced again. It became a prolonged engagement that went on for half a mile along my route of travel. In the end, the moose ran for the safety of an alder thicket, where it could cut its tormentors to pieces with those sharp hooves, and the wolves, two adults and two young of the year, trotted over the side of the hill into another valley—they would return after a day or two, in the hour before dawn, the killing hour.

I followed neither trail, but remained on the high ground.

At midafternoon I stopped for ten minutes and ate the last of my cookies. After that, it would be blueberries pulled from the branch.

Hour after hour, striding along, avoiding deadfalls and thickets, checking my compass, my breath in a ghostly plume behind me, always the soft crunch of the snow beneath the felt-lined paks.

The storm began to taper in the afternoon. As it did, the clouds lifted and the light was beautiful—a rose-gray glow to the southwest casting subtle shadows over the land, and in the east a venous blue edging into violet, which gave the sky in that quarter the appearance of a healing bruise.

At three o'clock, hiking down the last side valley, I was joined by a raven, who chattered incessantly in that peculiarly human voice of ravens, and followed me through the woods as if he was the local real estate agent. I was near the flood plain of the Sheenjek now and the snow was abating and my pace was slowing—the end was near. I enjoyed the antics of my new friend the raven—they are among the most intelligent birds, with over 100 sounds in their language. After awhile the moose trail we were following led off into a basin of beaver ponds—heaven to a moose, hell to a man—and so I climbed a hill to avoid becoming soaked and then cut back through the woods toward the sound of the river.

As I was walking through the woods I saw the raven sitting on an oddly angled object in the trees. I stopped and stared at the raven. Something about the scene was not quite right—an unexpected mass, an unnatural angle—and so I made a detour.

The object that did not fit into its surroundings turned out to be the collapsed remnants of an antique cabin and a tipped-over meat cache of the same vintage. The ruins had been there for quite some time, judging from the lichens. Near the cabin was a large crystalline ridge that ran above ground for hundreds of yards. Resting on the side of this ridge was a rusted pick, the wooden handle long ago devoured by porcupines. I took off my pack, for I was very tired, and slowly walked up and down the ledge, trying to figure out what it was. The wall appeared to be a nearly pure vein of milky quartz, and on closer inspection the rock was marked with the cobalt blue of copper, the corroded gray of silver, and the bright unmistakable flecks of gold. I found a piece that filled my gloved hand and put it in the pack.

The river was calling and so I resumed the march. A quarter of a mile later, there she was—the river Sheenjek, running bank full—and what a welcome sight. I set up my orange tent on a gravel bar beside the river. It would be cold there, but at least the tent would be visible from the air.

VI. And I didn't have to wait long. Early the next morning, tending my three fires in what had become a driving blizzard, I heard human voices. Shortly, two fourteen-foot flatboats, their engines out of the water and drifting with the current, came into view. I waved and shouted and they pulled over. The occupants were Dorothy and Leo Peters, Kutchin residents of Fort Yukon, their teenage son Richard, and a gregarious wolf hybrid that liked to lick your face named Hooch. Dorothy and Leo were physically as different as two people could be—Leo short and small-boned, Dorothy, in a word, massive. Richard appeared more related to his mother than his father but still had his father's strong chin and thick eyebrows. All three wore rubber hip boots and parkas.

They were in a hurry because the river was dropping and they had to get through something called "Peel Canyon" before nightfall, and so after explaining my situation they said I could ride in the boat with their son and his dog but that we must leave now. What about my companion? I asked. "God help him if he's up there in this blizzard," answered Dorothy. "Now hurry up and get in, or stay, it's up to you."

I stuffed my gear in the pack, took one final look at Fort Necessity, Population 1, and stepped into the boat with Richard.

My job was to man one of the 10-foot aspen poles and help steer the craft, something I'd never done before but would now have the opportunity to learn.

It was cold on the river, even with seven layers of clothing, and I shivered a lot. They told me that they had never been that far up before—nobody had—but the record rains had enabled them to explore farther than in past years. I asked if they were hunting moose, and the mother laughed—she was the boss and did all the talking—and said nobody in their right mind would hunt moose this far from Yuk. No, she said, look under the tarp.

Under the canvas tarp was the tusk of a mammoth, six or seven feet long and mottled green and dark tan and light gray. It was as big around as my thigh.

"How much does this thing weigh?"

"About as much as the gasoline it took to get here," said Dorothy, with a smile.

She said they found the tusk in a cutbank a few miles above my camp. They spotted another but couldn't dig it out because of the ice and with the dropping water decided to come back some other year if the water ever got this high again.

We had just drifted by an eagle nest in a cottonwood tree, and I was trying to estimate the diameter of the nest (10 feet? 12 feet?)—when I heard a roaring downstream. I turned toward the other boat to ask what was happening and was immediately instructed to pull up the pole—it would be useless in the rapids—and find a safe place to sit in the middle of the boat.

Rapids?

"Look alive, man," the father sternly warned, the first words he had spoken. "We're gonna run the canyon. Richard knows what he's doing. Keep your weight in the center and don't move around."

By now the rock walls had risen on either side of the river and the current was accelerating and the roar of the rapids was tremendous. A huge volume of water was compressed between the rocks and there were white-crested waves everywhere. The sounds were amazing—midtones and overtones and under it all something like a big bass drum banging away, throbbing, resonant. The acoustics were superb—it was a place to sing "Shenandoah" at the top of your lungs. Or a place to die, in an instant.

Up and down we went, over churning waves and into sucking troughs.

There were stumps and whole trees riding by on the current, and Richard deflected them with his oar. Sometimes he was only partly successful, and they collided with the boat, branches reaching. They were half-submerged from their own sodden weight and turned slowly in the current, like drowning people lifting an arm before going under.

And all the time it snowed—unrelenting, the end of the world, All Souls' Day, the sky falling.

Just when I thought we were free—cliffs lowering, gorge widening—the river grabbed the paddle from Richard's hands—it was gone in the time it takes to read this aside—and he turned to his parents and shouted something. I looked toward the other boat. Leo was yelling, but we couldn't hear him.

I was sitting in the back of the boat and Richard was telling me to turn on the engine, turn on the engine. I looked for a cord, didn't find one, turned to ask Richard where it was and saw a rock in the middle of the river. Rock? It was the size of a Ryder truck and it divided the river in two, one side half as wide as the other. There was a white mist hanging around the rock, and I realized there was a whirlpool beyond it and that we must somehow go through the wider of the two channels.

But it was too late.

We could not stop and in a few moments hit the rock to one side, crunching the side in, and I felt the water lift us up, as if the river was studying us for a moment, and then we plunged through the wrong gap, sideways, and were spinning around and around in circles and I thought for sure the boat was going to turn over and spill us out but then we were suddenly in the next stretch, floating backward in the wide, deep, and quiet water, everything calm.

It happened that quickly.

Richard stepped over Hooch and started the engine as you do a lawnmower, with a pull cord on the outboard side. In a moment Dorothy and Leo came through the gap.

Dorothy was laughing.

Leo smiled, the spaces in his teeth showing, and called over the water: "Rivers are like the government—they can't be trusted."

He started the engine on his boat and we cruised together down the lovely empty river through the snow.

We covered 45 miles that day, according to Dorothy, and the farther we went the more the river began to meander, like a string a cat has been playing with on the carpet. There were side streams and islands, logjams and floating trees, sweepers and unexpected rocks, and on either side, always, the snow-covered spruce forest, fronted with willows and alders.

We saw one beaver that day, and nothing else, and it never stopped snowing.

We camped above the confluence of the Sheenjek and the Porcupine, about 60 miles from Fort Yukon. It was a level spot in the spruce where river travelers have probably camped for 10,000 years. Leo set up a canvas tarp between two trees in such a way as to make a three-sided tent. Dorothy built a fire in front of it and inside the tent it was as warm and dry as inside a cabin—we laid out our sleeping bags and made it quite comfortable.

Dinner consisted of the last of my caribou meat mixed in with macaroni and cheese and eaten from a large suet-covered steel pot, all of us gathered round with forks in one hand and bread in the other.

At some point after dinner I asked what the land status of the area was—whether we were on federal land, or not.

That was a big mistake. Dorothy's face flushed and she started in on a long tirade about the federal government—"How would you feel if someone came in and took over your country and stole your land and then made you pay taxes on top of that?"

Leo made a face that said, "You don't want to get her started."

Richard got up to take a walk, even though it was nearly dark.

"I hate those people," Dorothy continued. "They come into the village and don't try to get to know anybody. They just start ordering us around like we're children."

Leo started telling jokes, trying to mollify his wife. Such as,

"Why is the fed standing with his hand on the lightbulb?"

"He's waiting for his three assistants to spin him around."

And,

"How do you know the feds have been in the village?"

"The dogs are pregnant and the trash cans are empty."

She finally smiled, a little.

Later that night, when I was looking for my toothbrush, I found the piece of milky quartz in my pack and showed it to them.

"You guys ever see anything like this before?"

Leo took the rock, his eyes a few inches from it. He handed it to his wife. She held the crystal toward the campfire and traced her fingers over the planar faces, the light of the flames passing through the quartz and onto her face.

"Where'd you find this?" she asked.

"In the hills behind where I was camped."

"What was it like where you found it?"

I described the wall of milky quartz and the cabin.

They spoke back and forth excitedly in their language.

"What are you saying?" I asked.

Dorothy proceeded to relate the story of Robert Hess, a Canadian who wandered into Fort Yukon in the summer of 1909 or 1910, purchased a river boat and supplies, and then disappeared into the wilderness for two years. When he returned to Fort Yukon he claimed to have discovered gold on the upper Sheenjek and had a bag of gold to prove it. No one knew exactly where the mine was —he kept the location secret, but he did mention an exposed quartz ridge. Over the next four years he brought in $20,000 worth of gold, just working by himself and sometimes with his brother Lancaster. After the war started, the Hess brothers went down to Vancouver and enlisted in the British Army. They promised to return and take a company of men upriver to work the mine, but both were killed when a German submarine sank their transport in the North Atlantic. The location of the mine died with them. After years of futile searching everyone forgot about the Hess Mine, except the old people, who kept the legend alive during the winter nights—it was their north-country version of the Lost Dutchman Mine, for whosoever found the Lost Hess Mine would be forever transported from the realm of earthly cares, the gold both an element on the periodic chart and a metaphor for some sort of paradise the human race hasn't known since Mesopotamia.

There followed a lively discussion, in which I played little part, about whether the site was in fact the Hess Mine and, if it was, what should be done. Leo wanted to file a claim and tell the world. Dorothy insisted the discovery be kept secret and that only a small amount of ore be removed every now and then, very discreetly. That way they wouldn't have to deal with the dreaded "feds."

When asked my preference, I replied that I had no interest in the subject. The information was theirs to do with as they wished. They could even keep the rock. I had no desire to ever return to the place.

You have never seen three more surprised people.

When I turned in that night they were still talking around the fire in their language, which reminded me of Navajo. It is a musical language, beautiful in its phrasing and intonations, and is pleasant and relaxing on the ear.

The next day it snowed much harder, big flakes. Snowing, snowing, the river hissing against the bottom of the boat, Hooch sleeping soundly on top of the trophy bone he had dragged in from the field, which would make him king of all the dogs back in Fort Yukon.

We stopped once—to ask to use a camp radio—but the radio was broken and everyone was drunk. "You don't want to stop at some of these camps," Dorothy warned. She believed there was a difference between people who lived in the villages and those who did not, who maintained small cabins along the back sloughs and lived strange impoverished lives.

The confluence with the Porcupine was amazing—like motoring out on a lake, compared to the narrow Sheenjek. It was a wide slow-moving river, with the greenish color of an aquarium that has not been cleaned in six months, and we roared along, watching always for snags and sandbars, whirlpools and riffles, and seeing only the occasional flight of mergansers or buffleheads waiting out the storm.

Approaching Fort Yukon by flat boat was like paddling a canoe toward St. Louis in the year 1820—a crowded, perpetually busy waterfront, a modest supply post of a village in the woods beyond, the immense river in front serving as the sole highway into a vast unsettled territory. Here was the last stop before the "last great wilderness on earth," the muddy portals to the primeval, the worm-hole entrance to that other, older universe, and on the well-worn banks were all variety of frontier folk, most with the bark still on them. I imagine the end of the world to be such a place, a final cluttered weigh station before eternity, an unadorned aperture into the unknown, a glimpse across the waters to a place that will be both the same and different for each traveler.

After we dragged the flatboats from the water and unloaded the gear and the giant tusk into a caravan of four-wheelers, I presented Dorothy with my rifle in gratitude for the passage (the gun quickly handed to a beaming Richard), wished them well, and asked directions to the troopers' office.

At the top of the hill I found the local office in the same building as the clinic. I kicked the snow from my paks, stepped in, dropped my pack, and identified myself to the officer on duty, who was putting on his down coat and was about to leave. On the wall behind him was a topographic map of Alaska, including the Aleutians, divided by state trooper districts, and a framed painting of Alexander Murray, who founded Fort Yukon in 1847.

"What happened to Duane?" I asked.

"He was picked up the day after you left. He's at Fairbanks Memorial."

"Infected thumb?"

"No, he walked into the airplane wing and cut his head open."

"Weren't you guys going to look for me?"

"Sure, once the storm cleared. But we can't launch an aerial search in a blizzard. Not without a beacon locator or anything. We knew your general route. We would have started tomorrow."

I asked him if I could use the phone to call Fairbanks, but he said the lines were down, a now deceased porcupine having chewed through the cable to the Alascom satellite dish. He then headed for the back door and told me to lock the front door on the way out.

There are two lodges in Fort Yukon, one run by the Kutchin and the other not, and I walked over to the first to rent a cabin for the night—Dorothy and Leo had politely invited me to spend the night at their place, but I didn't want to impose any further. As I was registering at the counter of the Gwitchyaa Zhee Lodge a man closely resembling Elden Morris walked in, a man in fact who appeared to be Elden Morris.

I blinked at the sight, not trusting my senses, and then glanced at the woman across the counter, to see if she, too, saw the visage. She did.

"I thought you were dead," the figure said, stepping closer and punching my shoulder.

"I thought *you* were dead," I said, realizing it was indeed Elden and shaking his hand in both of mine.

"Dorothy briefed me," he said, motioning toward the street.

In a moment, everything was explained. Earlier that month a pilot named Trent Collier had started flying side jobs for Elden and using his call sign, Sheenjek Air. Elden had been en route to our camp when Trent, in an overloaded Cessna, went down. Elden turned back, landed near the crash site, pulled the most critically injured hunter out, and flew him to Fort Yukon. The rest of the day was involved with the crash. The following day Elden had to fly to Beaver to pick up a woman in labor. The day after that he put skis on his plane and flew to our camp, but by the time he arrived I was miles away and the snow had begun to fall.

We shook hands again and said goodbye and I walked to a table, ordered the beef stew dinner, talked with the waitress for awhile, and read a three-day-old newspaper. After awhile a couple of children came in and played with their toys by the fireplace. I ate dinner and watched the evening news—another Republican member of Congress indicted on some minor felony, rumors that the Democratic presidential candidate was given to a loose interpretation of the seventh commandment, my favorite football team already a long shot for the playoffs.

America.

The high point of the day was having hot apple pie and vanilla ice

cream with the waitress and then going for a ride through the woods
on her snowmobile, something, over four Alaskan winters, I'd never
done.

By the time I reached the cabin I was so tired I didn't build a fire.
I dumped my pack on the floor, spread the sleeping bag on top of the
bed, and collapsed. Outside the dogs were barking and howling at
something. Inside a mouse was already scratching around the pack.
Suddenly the light of the moon streamed through the window. The
storm had finally blown off to the east.

And then there was a knock on the door—an armful of kindling
for the fire.

A deep cold settled over the land that night, and stayed for eight
months.

VII. The walk, the weather, the sky, the solitude, the river—they
would become sweeter over time. It is well sometimes to see a
country as it was before we were here. To recall freedoms lost and
gained, and to understand where we may be on the more extended
journey, and to gaze through our longest lens, which is the past, into
the future. To remember the world as it was in the beginning, and to
listen again to a harmony that expresses itself in silence.

Down from the hills I had traveled, and I would never regard
wilderness, civilization, or myself in the same way. I saw that what
we call civilization is more wild than that which is commonly given
the name, and that the gulf between who we are and what we are is
as great as the span between the cry of a newborn baby and a handful of ash in an urn.

In after-years memories return: of vast steppes lying desolate
under clear skies, of a mighty river making its way to a distant Arctic sea, of a snowy forest where the only darkness was the eye of a
raven, of a place so immense and still that I can hold it close whenever I feel myself at turmoil, and instantly be at peace. The generations that follow should always allow for such places to endure,
places where the wild animals roam freely and the storms last for

weeks, places where time is measured in the melting ice and shooting stars blossom in the moss, places that the human race leaves
undisturbed as we leave undisturbed the hearts in our chests that
beat and give us life.

II

> *The fruit of silence is prayer,*
> *The fruit of prayer is faith,*
> *The fruit of faith is love,*
> *The fruit of love is service,*
> *The fruit of service is peace.*
> Mother Teresa

Many of the writings in this year's collection are concerned with
advocacy, with words used consciously in the service of a particular
cause or idea. This tradition in American nature writing began with
George Caitlin's 1841 book *Letters and Notes on the Manners, Customs,
and Conditions of the North American Indians*. In that work the
artist/naturalist, fresh from years of exploration in the Far West,
proposed creating "a nation's Park" at the headwaters of the Missouri River:

> What a beautiful and thrilling specimen for America to preserve and
> hold up to the view of her refined citizens and the world, in future
> ages! a *nation's Park*, containing man and beast, in all the wild and
> freshness of their nature's beauty! I would ask no other monument
> to my memory, nor any other enrollment of my name amongst the
> famous dead, than the reputation of having been the founder of such
> an institution.

Fifty years later, in 1872, President Ulysses S. Grant established
Yellowstone National Park and made Caitlin's youthful dream a reality. Subsequently, the impassioned writings of John Muir led to the
formation of Yosemite National Park in 1890, and the pioneering

essays of Aldo Leopold resulted in the formation of the world's first wilderness area, the Gila, in 1924. More recently, Rachel Carson's 1962 book *Silent Spring*, which documented the effects of DDT, so moved President Kennedy that he formed a presidential commission, which led to a governmental ban on the insecticide in the United States.

Time after time, nature writers have made a difference—building a constituency for Southwestern deserts (Edward Abbey, *Desert Solitaire*); generating support for the Alaska Lands Bill (John McPhee, *Coming into the Country*); challenging centuries of predator prejudice (Barry Lopez, *Of Wolves and Men*); chronicling the plight of higher primates (Diane Fossey, *Gorillas in the Mist*); fighting for equatorial rainforests (Edward O. Wilson, *The Diversity of Life*). In their essays and books, these and other nature writers remind us of the legendary figures of old—Noah, who saved imperiled nature from a rising flood of iniquity; Beowulf, who slew the dragon of fear and ignorance; and Arthur, who formed a powerful unity—the Round Table—from a rabble of petty factions. Collectively, their works attest to the fact that there is no greater power in this world than the written word, and that a slender book can defeat any opponent on the planet, however wealthy or well-armed, by simply stating the truth.

The writers in this volume know this in their bones.

Rick Bass comes to mind first on the subject of advocacy, as he makes a heartfelt plea in *The Book of Yaak* for the preservation of a remote Montana valley threatened by development:

> My valley is on fire—my valley is burning. It has been on fire for over twenty years. These essays—these pleas to act to save it—it's all I know how to do. I don't know if a book can help protect a valley, and the people who live in that valley.... It is a place to save—a place to exercise our strength and compassion—that last little bit that the advertisers have not yet been able to breed, or condition, out of us. This valley still exists in the Lower 48 as a chance to explain to corporate America...that we can only be pushed and herded so far. What do I want? I want the last few roadless areas in this still-wild valley to remain that way.

The essay included in this collection from *The Book of Yaak*—"Metamorphosis"—gives eloquent expression to the author's deep love and loyalty for this home valley. It is probably only a matter of time before the logging restrictions and wilderness area designation that Bass is fighting for are implemented, if only so that officials are no longer deluged with letters, faxes, petitions, e-mail, and phone calls from his growing army of supporters.

Similarly, Pulitzer prize-winning poet W. S. Merwin makes a strong case in "The Winter Palace" for the beleaguered Monarch butterfly. Each autumn these beautiful butterflies—so familiar to everyone in the United States or Canada who has ever maintained a flower garden—migrate south across the border into Mexico, where they wait out the cold winter months. Unfortunately, the mountain forests where the butterflies seek refuge are now threatened by the rapacious Mexican logging industry:

> Up until now the Mexican government's administrative flourishes establishing sanctuaries and preserves and regulations of the over-wintering area have amounted to little more than environmental rhetoric to convey the illusion something has been done, while allowing business to proceed as usual, a phenomenon that has become familiar on both sides of the border.

One can only hope that essays by formidable writers like Merwin exert an influence on U.S. governmental policy *vis-à-vis* its trading partner to the south in this regard (rumor has it that Robert Pyle, author of *Wintergreen*, is devoting an entire book to the plight of the species).

Many other selections in this anthology are concerned, either directly or indirectly, with advocacy. One thinks of Terry Tempest Williams, who speaks on behalf of the humble desert tortoise at a family roundtable; Jan Grover, who mounts a defense of the logged-over backwoods of the Upper Midwest; and Dave Wallace, who has spent years in the lost jungles of Central America exploring the links between the past and the present, the northern and southern hemispheres, the diverse people of the New World and tropical nature. All these writers are acutely aware of the fact that the world is changing at an unprecedented rate, and that if defense is not rendered now, there will be little to save in the future. In every generation there have been those who fought for the defenseless and gave voice to the voiceless. This book gathers together writings from some of these individuals, who, like the medieval knights of old, have become sworn defenders of that which has saved them.

III

We do not understand that life is paradise, for it
suffices only to wish to understand it, and at once
paradise will appear in front of us in all its beauty.
Fyodor Mikhaylovich Dostoyevsky

In his book *The Grand Canyon of the Colorado* (1920), John Van Dyke, an art history professor at Rutgers University, looked at the Grand Canyon—an emblem for nature—and asked, "What does it mean?"

He attempted no answer and provided no further guidance. He simply posed the question, as a teacher should. But in the absence of an explanation, I have—for I am the eternal student—often pondered his words.

It is a good question. Perhaps too good, for it strikes at the heart of the matter, and I do mean matter.

There are two possibilities: Either nature means nothing, or it means something. Edward Abbey embraced the former point of view: "What does it mean? It means nothing. It is as it is and has no need for meaning. [Nature] lies beneath and soars beyond any possible human qualification. Therefore, sublime."

Sublime?

Here's where I've always felt that sort of response failed. Sublime, a term introduced by the Roman philosopher Longinus, means "glorious, resplendent, majestic." Something is sublime if it causes a "lifting up" (*ekstasis*) of the spirit. How does it help our understanding to simply state that nature is beautiful? And if it is beautiful—organized according to regular laws and patterns—how can it mean nothing? Why should there be beauty—systematically arranged matter—if there is no purpose? If matter had no purpose, wouldn't the reverse be true—anarchy instead of order? Doesn't beauty prove by its very form that its existence is not without reason?

To me, and I believe to most of the writers in this volume, nature and, by inference, human life do have meaning. The writings in *American Nature Writing 1998* affirm and celebrate that meaning. We are here for a purpose, each of us, and we are bound together by a shared past and a common destiny. The writers in this book remind us that we must always try to remain natural people in an often unnatural world. Their words, collectively and individually, lead us away from the artifice and alienation of civilization and back to the authentic and amiable world of nature. Here we enter the kingdom of change, the unchanging. Here a person may stand on Earth and catch a glimpse of eternity, which is, as a wandering carpenter once predicted, and with the confidence of someone who has seen it, an immensely calm and beautiful place.

John A. Murray

Alianor True

Firefinder

First publication

It's late August, temperatures are cooling down, and yellow tints the quaking aspen. It's my second to last day on the fire crew, and I've been assigned to tower duty. Nine hours, spent in solitude in a 6 x 6-foot enclosure, 180 feet off the ground. Crowded, with a folding army cot, a wooden chair on chipped glass insulators, and a centered pedestal. Streaked windowpanes comprise the upper half of the four metal walls, giving me views of the park, the forest. It is cool today, and cloudless skies lift away above the forest, just like the past two days. No recent lightning or storms; no sleeping fires are likely to creep up on us today. I scan the canopy through binoculars. To the north, the Kaibab National Forest stretches away, shaded ridgelines concealing chains of connected meadows. To the west, the park: Kanabownits, the Basin, Crystal Ridge, and to the southwest, Swamp Ridge and Fire Point. Though shadows and distance conceal the details, I don't need the topographic map to know where these places are and how to get there.

I know Greg didn't have to send me up here today. I know he's doing me a favor, giving me a chance to reflect on what we both know has been an amazing season. Thinking of the winter flurry of phone calls and job applications that had landed me at the North

Rim of the Grand Canyon. My first time out West, living in near isolation on a high, forested plateau in the middle of the Arizona desert. My first year in wildfire, a green college girl from back East, years younger than the rest of the crew. And this summer has seen the worst drought in over forty years. The biggest wildfire in Kaibab Forest history, the 53,000-acre Bridger Knoll Complex. The thrill of watching the canyon fall away beneath the helicopter, the thud of heavy blades all around. And the less grand memories: my knack for flat tires on distant roads, the pulling tension between crew members, the monotony of fire camp food.

I sit up here, occasionally pacing the cramped space around the centered chest-high pedestal, on which sits a prized firefinder. The Osborne Firefinder, a tool that determines the bearing and angle of a fire from a lookout tower. The brass ring sits atop the pedestal, placed over and coordinated with a topo map, vertical sight and front sight opposite each other. The flat ring rotates over the map. Find and center the smoke in the horsehair of the front sight while looking through the vertical sight, check for bearings and direction, and you've found yourself a fire. A simple tool, outdated by modern technology, where tour planes report the smokes, and dispatch finds the fires with GPS. But when wind and rain keep planes grounded, when GPS is paralyzed, firefinders are indispensable. In a 180-foot tower made of steel, even compasses won't work, their needles confused by the metal's own magnetic field.

This has been an extreme season. With less than 12 percent of the annual snowfall, and a bone-dry spring, the plateaus of northern Arizona began the season in a dry deficit. Situated between 8,000 and 9,000 feet, this area is not usually a center of wildland fire activity. Modest fires, maybe up to ten acres, but mostly less than one, are the norm. Nothing a small fire crew can't handle. But this year has been spent almost entirely in Level IV, at a "very high" fire danger. And crews from all over the West have been rotated through the Southwest. Every year there is a hot spot, and extra crews from areas of low fire danger are sent there to supplement the regular fire crews. It was Yellowstone in '88, Idaho in '94. In 1996, it's the Southwest, and I've worked with hotshot crews from California, from Idaho, engine crews from Montana and Wyoming. The highest level, V, "extreme," is where our parched conditions really place us, but the overhead at fire management won't acknowledge this reality. They don't want to have to work the 12-hour days, 21-day shifts. I can't say I do either, even if I do get paid by the hour.

This summer has been a collection of atypical occurrences: "Now, we wouldn't usually do this." "In a normal year...." "When we get some rain, when we go down to Level III, it'll all be different." Chris and Steve, returning for their second season, tell me that the North Rim is usually a mecca for wildflower enthusiasts, but all I see this year are a few wilted Indian paintbrush lining the sides of the roads. And Kristy and Ann of the prescribed crew work weeks upon weeks doing prep work, thinning the drop zones of prescribed burns, too dry to actually burn the plots. We have had more fires than usual this year, though smaller than the models predicted. They serve to punctuate the growing list of maintenance and upkeep jobs on the office clipboard. "Make two new benches for the lodge walkway," "Replace steps at Kanabownits tower," "Brush the E-4 road." Amid the daily toil of brushing trails, felling hazard trees, and refilling distant water tanks, I have seen some good fire. And it is due to these routine tasks, in addition to actually fighting wildfire, that I have become acquainted and familiar with the North Rim.

It is today, on fire watch, checking and rechecking the landscape, that I realize the familiarity I have gained over these three months. The recognition of ridges and ravines, the different trees and their forms, the weather, constant and assertive. I have begun to feel this strange land. This place was so foreign just yesterday, and while I will not pretend to have mastered this landscape, I can admit to a thorough introduction. Now the evergreens have become white fir with flat, flexible needles, Engelmann spruce with sharp, four-sided ones. Subalpine fir with smooth, pale gray trunks, blue spruce with hanging cones and rough-textured branches. I am reassured by the inland winds that prevail from the southwest and the constant canyon winds at the rim, upslope during the day and downslope, rushing into the deep shadows, at night. I can approximate my elevation from recognizing that ponderosa pine dominate the upper 7,000s, while fir, spruce, and quaking aspen prefer the 8,000- to 9,000-foot range. Driving down the winding road that leads to the surrounding desert, I see pinyon and juniper, known to us as "p-j," crowd the roadsides from 5,000 to 6,000 feet. I have even met the elusive Kaibab squirrel, the endangered species evolutionarily isolated from its South Rim cousin by the foreboding canyon. The Kaibab squirrel, with its white tail and tufted ears: Over 60 percent of them die every year because they don't store food for the long snowpacked winter.

I remember exploring the North Rim under the guise of work. An endless task of brushing the W-1 road, clearing the dirt track of debris up to the berm, but really exploring the whole west side of the park. And the rutted W-1 opens the door; it leads to the Ridge road, and up to Lindbergh Hill. The W-1 road runs through the Basin, an enormous collection of meadows dotted with wooded hillocks and crisscrossed with gopher burrows. It is the way to Crystal Ridge, and to Point Sublime, made famous by Edward Abbey. Eventually it gives way to the W-4, a route to Kanabownits, to the Big Springs dip site, to Swamp Ridge and Fire Point. It is this last area, far to the west, that has seen the most fire activity this season. It is as if a lightning rod has been centered there, directing the storms to release their fury on this distant area, concentrating the smoke reports and fires, leaving the whole eastern region of the park virtually flame free. King Arthur's Court has seen the most action. A wide stone-framed amphitheater whose isolated monuments grace fanciful names. Elaine's Castle, Lancelot Point, even the Holy Grail, a narrow stack of rocks piled impossibly high, no way to reach the top.

I cannot see King Arthur's Court from here. In fact, no one can see that collection of monuments except from a rare helicopter flight or a long hike from a little used dirt road. And it is now, in reviewing the landscape and the season, that it occurs to me that our knowledge is so limited by access. A simple fact, that we can only know what we experience. I think of the tourists who drive for days to spend five minutes gasping over the canyon. And the contrast of our fire crews, hiking in to a remote fire, off road and trail. Knowing that in their isolation no other human eyes have seen those distant places for a hundred years or more. I think of what I personally know about, the secret meadow that appeared behind the ridge blackened by the South Fork fire. The bobcat that sprinted across the road as I struggled with the gears on the chase truck. The hidden hollowness of aging aspen, which rot from the inside out. And the way they can pinch down your saw, freed only by a long afternoon of pulling and prying, ropes and wedges.

I would not have seen or experienced any of this, this new and thrilling landscape, without my privileged access. Tourists hardly ever make it off the three paved roads on the North Rim, and only a handful of others travel off the dirt roads at all. My place on the fire crew has given me an amazing opportunity; the uniqueness of my experience surprises me at every turn, burning itself into my memory. And I revel, realizing that my intimate familiarity with the North Rim has been explicitly shaped and carved by my access to it. It may be a simple thought, that one's awareness of a situation is correlated to experience. That is, after all, how one learns. But this summer, I have exceeded this basic tenet. I realize that I view the North Rim, the Grand Canyon, even the surrounding Arizona desert, as if I were peering through a firefinder: looking for bearings and distinct landscape features, following the weather's tracks across the sky. For it is the nature of my access to the landscape, that of firefighting, that has shaped my consciousness. What I learn, and why it is important, how it is connected to other bits of information, have all been determined by the fact that I am a firefighter. And because I learned this landscape, the North Rim, as it relates to fire, I can never see it in a vague way, just seeing the stark scenery, the contrast of plateau against desert, of canyon and rim. I'll never casually notice trees; they will always be specific to their kind, their fire resistance. Just as the clouds will indicate the type of front moving through, and tell me from what direction I can expect the winds, and when they'll change, pulling the fire with them.

The firefinder accompanies me on every walk and every workday. I examine a side gully that drains into the mammoth canyon, and I see a quick fire run. Fire could whip through here, fed by updraft winds and the flashy quick-burning fuels of scrub oak and locust. I glance upward, noticing the vertical buildup of cumulus clouds over the South Rim. The potential lightning storms, and then the fires, they may bring as they move northward. I march through the woods, hiking into a fire, and I listen for the telling crackle of pine needles and small twigs beneath my boots, a sure sign of low fuel moisture. I know that white fir reestablish themselves quickly following a fire. We call them "regen," short for regeneration. I see a jumbled weave of fallen logs, vines, and prickly black locust, and I know that the choking forest needs to burn. That the remaining dominant trees are suffering with all the competition around their feet. I call standing dead trees "snags." I know that they are dangerous. I measure brief hours of needed rain against its effect on 10-hour and 100-hour fuel moisture. I unconsciously scan for evidence of past fires in catfaces, or firescars, on the older ponderosa. I carry this firefinder with me everywhere. It is in my eyes and ears; it has wedged itself into my memory.

I think of the fires I have seen this summer, how they have guided me through tangled forests and wrinkled topography until I recognize each ravine and ridge, each shrub and tree. These pieces form a puzzle, an interlocking collection of facts and objects that I use to make sense of the North Rim. For I can examine the pieces, their qualities and characteristics, and predict how they fit together to solve the problem, to fight the fire. I remember that Scott insisted we haul in two chainsaws for the Thunder Spring fire because he knew that area, between Swamp Ridge and Fire Point, was a jumbled mass of jackstrawed timber, huge matchsticks that would slow our progress and hamper an escape. Finding the Imperial fire, smoking on a distant ridge top, we were armed with triangulated bearings from the helicopter, the roadside departure point, the fire tower. But we actually found the fire with our knowledge of the terrain; we hiked in through the Bright Angel Creek drainage until the fourth ridge tilted up to the south. We have all learned the daily weather pattern. The morning inversion that clouds the inner canyon, the haze that burns away by noon, and the bright, blue skies that lead to afternoon buildup and evening lightning storms.

All of us took special care with the Lancelot II fire, perched on the edge of Lancelot Point, and subject to the furious canyon winds. Still, a near-miss, as over thirty firefighters had to be evacuated when the fire made a midafternoon run, crashing up the slope, consuming a half mile in ten minutes. We returned later to find abandoned firepacks and rations melted, charred. I use the skies, the lay of the land, even the type of tree, to guide me to a fire, and through a fire. Those details can dictate how to find a wildfire, how to fight it, how to survive it. My access to this land has given me the awareness and ability to understand it, to predict it, to live and feel it.

I wonder about those before us and what relationship they shared with this land. Theo, who constantly points out the fragments of Indian pottery around our firelines, tells us stories of those people. Anasazi ruins and cliff dwellers' caves appear in our binoculars; ancient fragments of black and white pottery and arrowheads surface in our shovels. We fly high over the Havasupai Reservation, nestled within the canyon walls. Still thriving, a patchy green beneath our helicopter. More recent, a crooked shack, once used by Teddy Roosevelt's hunting expeditions, sits astride Muav Saddle, bridging Swamp Ridge and Powell Plateau. Theodore Roosevelt, credited as the founder of the park system, shot more of the now-absent mountain lions than any other man in canyon history. And now the mule deer population has exploded, no predators left to curb their growth.

Did these people realize the value of fire? The rejuvenating force it possesses? The way it lets a forest breathe anew, black and ash only temporary? I've heard tales about how Indians used to set their forests on fire, to clear the underbrush, to flush out the game. And I know that fire is natural. It is as much a part of the ecosystem of a forest as the seed of a maple or the fungus on a rotting log. Temperate forests evolved under the pressure of fire; the trees and soil depend on its life-giving properties. I also know it is my job to extinguish fire. And that it is the modern tradition of firefighting that gives rise to unhealthy forests, choking on the shrubs and seedlings that would have been eliminated in a forest fire. This is why the fires get worse, and burn hotter, every year. It is because there is more fuel accumulating every year. It is never burned when nature intends. This is the conflict I live with: fighting fire in a forest that needs to burn. And quietly hoping for a place with the prescribed fire crew next year, the program that reintroduces fire into a natural landscape in a controlled manner, a job that eases my conscience.

After three months here, learning and living, fire now serves as my reference point. I drive the main highway, scanning the woods to the south. I was told to pick up our abandoned tools at "mile two," but I know it's closer to the orange flagging that led us to the Fawn Spring fire. A tourist asks me why ponderosa pine are so special, aren't they famous for something? All I can think to reply is that they are fire resistant—their hardened sap-rich bark shields against excessive heat—and fire dependent—the cones will only release seeds when they reach a certain temperature well above 400 degrees, possible only in a scorching forest fire. I explain the topo map to a visiting friend. "This is Rainbow Plateau. We had a two-acre fire there." "This is the Dragon. It gets hammered by lightning all the time." "See this drainage? It leads to the Kanabownits area, and the

Big Springs fire was right on this ridge." "This is called the Elephant Bogs road. It's closed, but we can still hike on it to get to fires."

I have found that wildland firefighting lends a significance to natural details, to Nature, in a way we have forgotten. It is a way I never knew. How to read the weather to predict and plan, to be aware of one season's shortfalls and next season's gains. No spring rain, so fewer mosquitos, but more yellowjackets. Little snowfall last winter, so less wildflowers and more wildfire this summer. There is a way to be more alert, to notice what Nature is telling you. It is a heightened perception, looking for causation and reason behind and within the landscape. Farmers and hunters of my grandfather's generation know what I mean. My parents and brother do not. This intimate sensing of the land is not possible from behind a car window, or even a short hike. It is in the daily, regular interaction with the land. Letting the dusty soil creep beneath your fingernails, the morning dew coat your boots. The sunburn on your face, the smell of cactus flowers in monsoon season. This is the way to read Nature, to understand the stories she has to tell us. Be aware, and make sense of the world around you.

Today, viewing and reviewing the North Rim, scanning and re-scanning the eye-level canopy, I think of how differently I relate to other landscapes, distant terrains. I can look at the skies of upstate New York every day and never see the signs of coming storms or of atmospheric disturbance that I see in Arizona. I can hike the Appalachian Trail in Pennsylvania and have no idea how fast or slow the yellow birch and striped maple would burn. I can hear rain on the roof in Atlanta and wonder what shoes I will wear, not how moist the fuels will be at the end of the day. I did not learn those landscapes as a firefighter; I cannot see them as they relate to fire. Our knowledge is so encased in our experience, and access so greatly shapes our experiences. I cannot help but wonder how happenstance it all is. How the tiny turns in our lives can so greatly affect how and what we know. Why we think the way we do, how we relate to a situation. And how the choices that lead us down certain paths can shape us as people.

I know I view the North Rim as it relates to fire. I also know that my actions, my character have been shaped by my firefighting experience. I can make decisions and act on them quickly; I work well under pressure. I can orient myself and survive in almost any situation; I work well on a team. And the land and the fires that I have manipulated and controlled have also molded me physically. Just as I dig line, cutting a swath through the groundcover baring mineral soil, the land has subtly influenced and sculpted me. It is in the calluses on my hands, the blisters on my heels, my hardened biceps. My tanned forearms and blonding hair. Ours is a persuasive, give-and-take relationship. Handing off influence, impressing upon and compelling each others' form.

In reflecting on this, I think how everyone could tell a similar story. How they had a job, or an encounter, that influenced the way they thought about, or acted in, a situation. My story has this element in common with everyone else's. The backbreaking nature of firefighting, the solitude of the desert plateaus, the isolation of the North Rim. It is no coincidence that I crave hard work, being alone, and sparse company. Like this, we have all been shaped by our own experiences; we have all learned to internalize what we are taught. It is within this incorporation of knowledge and incidents that we grow and learn. We must combine new acts with old ones, constantly juggling information and purpose, in order to apply what we learn. And it is this assimilation that teaches us how to look at, and understand, the world. We are what we come from, and where we have been.

My season is coming to a close. I leave in two days, only halfway through the fire season, to return to college, one last year awaiting me. I realize that this summer has been a privilege, a unique chance to see the canyon, the North Rim, and Arizona as a firefighter, looking through a firefinder to explain and understand a remarkable natural wonder. As one of the fire crew, I have enjoyed access to the

North Rim as few have. I know this land because I have lived it, I have cared for it, and, like the time I had to nestle beneath the branches of a white fir for warmth, a brief rest from cold nighttime fireline patrol, it cares for me. I have learned to read this landscape, perceiving the canyon and the rims in an intense and intimate way, just as a blind woman runs her fingers over a page, feeling and sensing her way to a better understanding.

As I prepare to leave the tower, I take one last look in every direction. I will not see these views, these vistas, again until next June, when I return to the North Rim. I take one last peek through the firefinder, horsehairs centered over the southeast, where although I cannot see the rim from here, I know the canyon opens wide. Shades of brown in every direction but up, swifts darting beneath and through the late afternoon thermals. Hawks and ravens the only contrast to the deepening sky. My day is over, and I must leave the firefinder in the tower, a motionless brass ring, to guide other people's eyes, other people's lives. As the slivered moon rises in the east, I think one last time about the direction my life is taking, and how I will never be able to look at this land, or my life, without seeing them as they relate to fire. My own firefinder now rests beneath my skin, buried in my heart and mind. Content, I make my way down the steps to the truck, to the half-hour drive that will take me home.

Barry Lopez

Searching for Depth
in Bonaire

from *The Georgia Review*

I

The last day I spent on Bonaire, a Catholic Sunday, I drove most of
the small Dutch island's few dirt tracks and undivided asphalt
roads. This short traverse—the island is only twenty-four miles long
—took me south to rows of refurbished slave huts standing alongside towering, blistering-white mounds of sea salt; out to a wind-
ward Caribbean shore to look at pictographs made centuries ago by
indigenous Caiquetío Indians; then to Gotomeer, a lake on the
northwest coast where at dusk flamingos rise up in a billowing sheet
of pink, flecked with carmine and black, and roll off south across
the Bonaire Basin for the coast of Venezuela, sixty miles away.

That dependable evening Angelus of departing birds deepened
the architecture of the sky, and it resolved, for a moment, the emotional strain of my brief, disjointed conversation with this landscape. No longer Caiquetío land, no longer Spanish, provisionally
Dutch, Bonaire has become an international hinterland. Five hundred years of complicated cultural history have produced a subtle,
polyphonic reality here, full of striking temporal hitches. At a fruit

stall an elderly woman in a thirties-style print dress pops a button of
dirt off a fresh cantaloupe with her thumb and waits for a young
man in J. Crew casuals adjusting his earphones to see that he's in the
way. Not long after deplaning, one easily feels embarrassed for having come here, as I had, with but a single idea: to dive the pellucid
waters of the place Vespucci named *la Isla de Palo Brasíl.*

Bonaire is the second largest of five islands in the seemingly in-
definite Netherlands Antilles. Sint Eustasius, Saba, and Sint Maarten
(which the Dutch share with the French)—three very small, densely
populated islands clustered 500 miles northeast of Bonaire, to the
east of Puerto Rico—compose one geographical element. Bonaire
and its larger neighbor, heavily populated Curaçao, compose the second. (Nearby Aruba, long a sixth member of this political archipel-
ago, seceded from the Dutch Antilles on January 1, 1986, resolving
a fractious sibling rivalry with Curaçao but sharply curtailing its own
access to financial assistance and technical advice from Holland.)

Sophisticates on Curaçao regard lightly populated Bonaire as
hopelessly bucolic; a promotional brochure says foreign investors
will be pleased by its "progressive and cooperative political climate."
Lying safely south of the track of Caribbean hurricanes, its mildly
humid air cooled by persistent trade winds, the island is a rocky,
desert place, crooked like a dog's hind leg. Its landscape rises gently
from green, red, and lavender salt ponds in the south through a bush
plain to low, brush-covered hills four or five hundred feet high at its
northwest end. It is without a permanent river (residential freshwater comes from a desalinization plant and a few natural springs),
although brilliant fairweather clouds regularly stream west over the
island, even at night, obscuring the Southern Cross and other familiar constellations.

Before an impatient eye, Bonaire appears stark and bony. Its early
cover of brazilwood and lignum vitae forest is gone, sold to Europe
piecemeal, centuries ago. Its dry, meager vegetation, rooted in
bleached coral rubble, lies trampled and tattered by generations of

donkeys and bark-stripping goats. Its coarse headlands of volcanic ironstone, irradiated by a tropical sun, scorch and nick the hands.

Starkness of a different kind arises from a contrast between the genteel manner of Bonaire's residents, entering and exiting (light as sparrows) the innocent pastels of their stucco homes, and the island's two modern, rigid, metallic edifices: Bonaire Petroleum's brightly lit oil transfer terminal in the north and Trans World Radio's antenna park to the south, a powerful transmission facility operated by a fundamentalist Christian sect.

A fevered search for mineral wealth and the religious acquisition of souls, of course, form the beginning of Bonaire's engagement with the Old World; these subjects—spiritual salvation and the control of resources like oil—are old ones on Bonaire. In 1513, Diego Colón dismissed Aruba, Curaçao, and Bonaire as *islas inútiles* (useless, meaning without metals). The Caiquetíos were brusquely sold off to hidalgos in Hispaniola, where they soon perished working in Spanish "gold" mines. In 1634 Bonaire—the name apparently derives from a Caiquetío term, *bajnaj*, meaning low land—was acquired by the Dutch in their search for sources of salt and wood. Two hundred years later slavery was abolished; open to settlement, Bonaire stabilized as a sort of sprawling hacienda. People independently grazed cattle and sheep, grew aloe vera and divi-divi pods, evaporated seawater for salt, burned coral to make chalk, raised horses, and made charcoal, all for export. This diverse subsistence economy, augmented later in this century with wage labor off-island —in oil refineries on Aruba and Curaçao, aboard fishing vessels, and in the cane fields of Cuba—persisted relatively unchanged until the 1970s, when real estate development and tourism began abruptly to alter the island's tenor.

This latest economic wind blows with a vaguely disturbing odor —the forcing pressure of big, fast money, the entrepreneur's heat to create wealth in "undeveloped" lands. (From an older Spanish perspective, perhaps it's only *plus ça change, plus c'est la même chose*.) A modern visitor from the United States like myself takes wry note of the fact that Bonaire Petroleum and Akzo Salt, the great bulk of the island's economy, are US-owned businesses, as is the fundamentalist station. You see all this—a strangely beautiful landscape, attractive people, a kind of praying mantis economy—more or less quickly, in the first few hours. But I did not travel here to nurture a ready cynicism. I did not make the long flight through Denver and Miami to idealize whatever threatened virtue there might be in rural Bonairean life, or to feed any sense of irony over the fate of the Monroe Doctrine in postcolonial America. I came with a single intention: to become intimate with the island's undisturbed realm— its fringing coral reef.

Bonaire's reefs are among the most astonishing in the Americas. Patient divers can find nearly every one of the western Atlantic's seventy or so kinds of coral here. Schools of horse-eye jack, swift as tuna, bolt into the dimness. Starfish and white anemones pearlesce in the lugubrious shadows cast by Atlantic manta rays. Blizzards of tropical fish swarm over and through fields of exotically shaped sponges, some tall as barrels. Four-foot-long tarpon, predatory fish whose ranks of scales resemble chain mail, routinely rise at night from Bonaire's near depths to swim alongside divers in the dark. Most days, one can see farther than eighty feet in the limpid, sunshot water. Among the rare local creatures I hoped to find were a cryptic, ambushing hunter called a frogfish; pistol shrimp; glowing fluorescent sponges; and an animal emblematic of the Jovian peculiarities of these waters, the ethereal sea horse.

I would eventually make seventeen dives, over eight days. I would lie awake those nights, a trade wind blowing through my room, trying to understand where I was. The contrast between a desiccated land and the rococo display of life in the sea, between hardscrabble existence on tenuous farming landholds and the burgeoning growth of condominiums to provide housing for divers like myself made sleep difficult. As we sometimes seek to hide ourselves in dreams, so

I focused those nights on the beauty of the world into which, come morning, I would fling myself.

Like many scuba divers I had made my initial dives (after those for certification) in a tropical sea, in warm, clear, currentless waters on the Great Barrier Reef in my case, east of Cairns, Australia. In the years following I saw more of the tropics but dove, too, in steep-walled fiords in southeast Alaska, in subtropical Galápagos' shark-filled waters, in kelp forests off the coast of California, and under the sea ice in McMurdo Sound, in Antarctica. Diving regularly on the Northwest coast of the United States, near my home, in strong currents and cold water and wearing a bulky dry suit has made diving in the tropics seem an unencumbered, almost rarefied experience. The ornate patterns and brilliant color of tropical reef life, displayed like Persian rugs in glycerin hues, and the sometimes overwhelming number of living forms in lucent, tranquil water, are enough to make some cold-water divers, like myself, speechless. The visual impact of Bonaire's reefs is further intensified by the fact that they have changed very little since Vespucci's ships passed overhead. Only large conchs and lobsters and the larger grouper have been hunted out. Here is a welter and diversity of life still comparable to what once stunned the first Europeans to enter the Americas.

In 1971, as a precaution, Bonaire closed its nearshore waters to spearfishers, to collecting for the aquarium trade, and to commercial fishing. The same terrestrial barrenness that once caused the island to be disparaged (and so left undeveloped) has, oddly, contributed directly to the preservation of its reefs. Elsewhere in the tropical world coral reefs are significantly endangered—a blight little known but comparable to that on tropical rain forests. (Because coral reefs occupy less than one percent of the ocean floor but harbor close to twenty-five percent of ocean species, marine scientists regard any threat to them as alarming.) An unspecified amount of reef destruction in the past decade, all over the world, has been attributed to a rise in ocean temperatures, one debated cause of which is global warming. Less debatable causes of coral-reef destruction include coastal logging and intensive agriculture. Sedimentation from eroded, clear-cut slopes and pesticide and herbicide runoff from farmlands may have damaged many coral reefs in Central America and Indonesia irreversibly. In the Philippines, cyanide flushing used to stun fish bound for pet shops and restaurant aquariums and fishing with dynamite are major problems.

One is not reminded of these troubles in Bonaire. Before coming here I had read several intriguing papers about Bonaire's healthy waters. One discussed the shelter offered by seagrass beds and saltwater-tolerant mangrove swamps in an embayment called Lac Lagoon, a highly productive nursery for yellowtail snapper, great barracuda, stoplight parrotfish, schoolmaster, French grunt, and dozens of other species of fish. Another paper described cryptobiotic marine communities, so-called hidden neighborhoods established beneath natural coral rubble in Bonaire's shallow waters, ensembles of life in which the authors counted 367 species of sponges, tunicates, bryozoans, and other small aquatic creatures. These communities were vigorous, varied, resplendent.

Provoked by such wonder, or driven by curiosity, the ordinary diver in Bonaire finds this complex seascape nearly impossible to penetrate with any degree of certitude. With a concentrated effort (an enthusiasm admittedly at odds with the relaxed atmosphere of the resorts), one might sort out the differences among several dozen fish or learn to distinguish between corals and sponges. But even for a conscientious diver the task is enormous. The descriptive vocabulary—crinoids, ctenophores (TEEN-ah-fores), nudibranchs (NUDE-i-branks)—offers relatively few images or names easy to recall. Of the thirty-three or so body plans, or phyla, into which all life is routinely sorted, only two arrangements are at all familiar to land-habituated divers: arthropods (insects and spiders) and chordates (all fish, amphibians, reptiles, birds, and mammals). Representatives of *every* phylum are found in the ocean, arthropods and chordates minor among them. The specific arrangements of biological architecture, metabolism, and propulsion are so counterintuitive here, so strange to human senses, they seem extraplanetary. Moreover, many animals—sea fans, hydroids, wire corals, for example—look like plants. Other animals, such as encrusting corals and scorpionfish, look like rocks. Even fish, the easiest animals to identify, can be perplexing—juveniles of various species of reef fish frequently look nothing like their parents, and other species change shape and gender over time. And a *single* organism, such as a sea nettle, may look no different from a *colony* of animals, such as a Portuguese man-of-war.

A diver in sixty feet of water, checking to see how much air is left and how long she or he has been down and where dive partners may be, does not readily hit upon any good approach to these mysteries.

Most scuba divers at Bonaire's dozen or so resorts—about 13,000 a year fly in, slightly exceeding in number the island's indigenous population—anticipate balmy, hospitable weather and plan to make two or three dives a day for a week or so. Developing a refined sense of what one is actually looking at underwater doesn't seem called for; to be able to talk about it in any detail seems, for many, to run vaguely counter to the idea of a vacation. The experience, principally, is to be thrilled by. The reefs are to be genuinely appreciated and, perhaps over cocktails, are conceivably meant to provoke. One is prompted to wonder, for example, what's happened to this kind of profusion, this density of life, in the rest of the world? Aside from enclaves of birds in the jungles of Ecuador and Peru or wildlife in isolated parts of Zaire, few undisturbed terrestrial spots remain for any late twentieth-century observer. But then one might also be moved to wonder a little about Bonaire. Sections of its reefs have recently been closed to diving in order to "rest" them. They have begun to show the scrapes, breakage, and fatal smears of small animal life associated with intensive tourist diving. (Barely fifty years old, scuba diving has already had a marked effect at some localities. Reefs in the Florida Keys, for example, have been severely damaged in spots by thousands of dive-boat anchorings, by the snatching and impact of divers unable to control their buoyancy and drift, and by divers carelessly kicking out with their fins.)

When I emerged from Bonaire's waters each day, I would enter in my notebook the names of the fish I had seen on Leonora's Reef or in one of the other places where ten or twelve of us dove at a time: cornetfish, smooth trunkfish, yellowhead wrasse, longspine squirrelfish, balloonfish, midnight parrotfish, honeycomb cowfish, whitespotted filefish, lizardfish—and then the crabs and snails, the eels, the sponges, the corals, until I was worn out, paging through the reference texts and enquiring among the divemasters who supervised our excursions.

One afternoon, walking back to my room from the boat dock, I stopped next to a frangipani tree in which a single bird, a bananaquit, was singing. I imagined the dense thicket of the tree's branches filled with forty or fifty kinds of singing, energetic birds, and that I had only a few moments to walk around the tree, peering in, to grasp some detail of each to memorize. I had no paper on which to write down a name or on which to sketch. Then, I imagined, they flew away. Who were they? How could I know where I was, really, if I didn't know who they were? It was like that every day underwater—an unknown host, confounding and esoteric as the nine choirs of angels.

The reflexive habits human beings must develop to stay alive underwater with scuba (self-contained underwater breathing apparatus) are inherently risky. They have largely to do with controlling the rate at which pressure on the body's tissues changes. Divers who are physically fit and diving under supervision in a benign environment like Bonaire, and who possess even amateur technical diving skills, rarely experience a problem. Still, diving is dicey, strange. The stress the human body is subjected to by the change in pressure at a depth of only sixteen feet compares with the effect of a change in altitude of 18,000 feet on land. Releasing the increase in pressure too quickly can be fatal. In holiday circumstances like those prevailing on Bonaire, one can be lulled into thinking nothing will ever go wrong—with the salubrious weather, the magnificent reefs, or one's own dive technique. It is the feeling, of course, one vacations in search of.

The divemasters on Bonaire cautioned us repeatedly, in a friendly way, not to dive deep, not to go below 100 feet. It is not only inherently dangerous (four atmospheres of pressure at that depth is enough to precipitate nitrogen narcosis and disorientation), but for most, unnecessary—the density of marine life drops off quickly after about sixty feet. As much as anything, their cautions were a reminder to pay attention to air consumption, to the time you spent at each depth, and to your rate of ascent to guard against decompression sickness, the so-called bends.

Few scuba diving accidents occur at depth. Most happen at the mysterious surface, a wafer-thin realm where air bounds water, where light suddenly changes flux, ambient sound changes register, and the body passes through a membrane fraught with possibility or, coming the other way, with relief. When water closes over a diver's head, a feat that once had seemed implausible, to breathe underwater, seems suddenly boundless with promise. There is often little indication at the undulating, reflective surface, the harrowing transition zone, of the vividness, the intricacy, the patterns unfurled below.

Something, most certainly, happens to a diver's emotions underwater. It is not merely a side effect of the pleasing, vaguely erotic sensation of water pressure on the body. (Doctors subjecting volunteers to greater atmospheric pressure in hyperbaric chambers don't find the increased flow of plasma beta endorphins—the "buzz" hormones—that divers frequently experience.) Nor is it alone the peculiar sense of weightlessness, which permits a diver to hang motionless in open water, observing sea life large as whales around him; nor the ability of a diver, descending in that condition, to slowly tumble and rotate in all three spatial planes. It is not the exhilaration from disorientation that comes when one's point of view starts to lose its "left" and "down" and gains instead something else, a unique perception that grows out of the ease of movement in three dimensions. It is not from the diminishment of gravity to a force little more emphatic than a suggestion. It is not solely the exposure to an unfamiliar intensity of life. It is not just a state of rapture with the bottomless blue world beneath one's feet, what Jacques Cousteau calls "*l'ivresse des grandes profondeurs*."

It is some complicated run of these emotions, together with the constant proximity of real terror, exhilaration of another sort entirely. I have felt such terror underwater twice, once when I was swept away in a deep countercurrent in the Gulf of Mexico, and another time beneath the ice in Antarctica, when a piece of equipment froze and a sudden avalanche of events put me in a perilous situation. Afterward, I was not afraid to go back in the water, but I proceeded with more care. The incidents made me feel more tenderly toward anything at all managing, in whatever way, to stay alive.

II

One day, walking into town from the resort where I was staying, I saw a man making a wall of coral stone, three feet high, two feet wide, and hundreds of feet long. The wall would separate the grounds of a new resort condominium from the public road, Kaya Gobernador N. Debrot. He controlled the definition of this stretch of space by fitting randomly shaped stones in a ruler-straight wall with its edges perfectly square. We didn't speak. I did not stare while he worked but came back in the evening to appreciate the lack of error in what he'd engineered. He had the firmest grasp of this reality.

No such attentiveness marked the resort meals available where I was staying. They so lacked imagination in their preparation that after one or two dinners one had experienced the whole menu. Nothing was to be found under the surface. Seeking an alternative, I began to walk into town with my dive partner Adam Apalategui, an American Basque, to see what we could find. Kralendijk, meaning "the place of the coral dike" in Dutch, is the largest of Bonaire's two towns, and locally more often called Playa. We located a good spot there, a small pub and restaurant named Mona Lisa. One evening, after the chef had elaborated in English for us on his French-language menu of the day, he suddenly offered to make something special, a medley of local wahoo, barracuda, and dorado, brought in fresh only an hour ago. At an adjacent table he went over the same menu again, speaking Dutch. The meals he served were set out beautifully on the plate, distinctively flavored, punctuated and savory. His appreciation of the components of the meal that night intensified for me moving images of the three species of fish. As we ate I imagined one thread of succulence tying the Dutch chef, our dives, and the indigenous fishes together. The chief, lingering with us as he had in his initial description of the meal, meant the connection to be made, to enhance the experience of Bonaire.

In most every settlement or rural village I've visited in Africa, in China, in Australia, I've taken a long walk in the late evening air after such a pleasant meal. Sudden bursts of domestic noise, the sprawl of sleeping dogs under a yard light, the stillness of toys on pounded earth, the order in wash hung over a line—all compel a desire to embrace the unknown people associated with these things, as if all the unwanted complication had gone out of life. One evening, as Adam and I strolled north along the main road back to our resort and rooms, I ruminated silently, and quite presumptuously, on the Bonaireans.

In a book I was then reading called *Politics on Bonaire*, Ank Klomp describes the evolution of a system of political patronage that characterizes the island. (The Netherlands Antilles are autonomous within the kingdom of the Netherlands. The five islands form a parliamentary democracy, with parliament sitting in Willenstad, Curaçao. Each island also has its own legislative and executive bodies.) Among the more interesting things Klomp discusses is the curious history of egalitarian society here. Because it could never support banana, sugar, coffee, cotton, or tobacco plantations, Bonaire never developed either a class of gentlemen planters or an agrarian working class. As a result, social distinctions based on ownership of land, on race or ethnicity, remained relatively unimportant, as they did not in the rest of the Caribbean. (The building of oil refineries on Curaçao and Aruba early in the twentieth century brought an influx of North American and European managers and divided those previously analogous societies more sharply along racial and class lines.) Bonaire exports very little today save salt (much of it bound for the northeastern United States, for use on winter roads); and it is without an agricultural or manufacturing base. Since all goods must therefore be imported, and because government is the major importer, politicians on Bonaire are in effect, in Klomp's phrase, "'gatekeepers' par excellence." Further, since Bonaire's population is small, the imposing personality of a single politician can have a major impact on political expression on the island.

Where this has led and how patronage operates on Bonaire are the central subjects of Klomp's book. Observations in her introduction, however, cause a reader to reflect on the ethnic and racial accord apparent today in the streets and shops of Kralendijk and Rincon, Bonaire's second town. And to wonder what changes have come since 1983 when *Politics on Bonaire* was written. The number of resorts and condominiums to accommodate divers has greatly increased since then; and, to hear local people tell it, the conspicuous wealth of North American and European visitors and their abrupt, suspicious public manner have subtly altered the unconscious atmosphere of equality that once characterized Bonaire.

The situation, of course, is more complex than this worry. One gains some insight into social subdivisions, and into the island's history, by listening to where and how people speak. English, the language of tourism, is spoken at the airport, in gift shops and resorts, and in many of the restaurants. In the schools and in banks and government offices it is Dutch. On the street and in homes throughout the island (as on Aruba and Curaçao) it is Papiamentu, a creole developed from the Portuguese pidgin of slave traders and influenced by Spanish, Dutch, and West African dialects. In the open-air vegetable market near the Kralendijk docks, and on a popular radio station, it is Venezuelan Spanish. Bonaireans politely and easily compliment each other by saying so-and-so speaks three or four languages, lending the island a cosmopolitan aspect, but this is rarely true. What some people learn in addition to the language they are born to, which of course they may speak poorly, is almost always the "supermarket idiom" of another language, a tropeless speech of commercial transactions and declarative conversation—unengaged, impersonal, pleasant. It is the language of international air carriers, phatic and anemic. To listen closely to its banalities, or to hear no other, fuller language spoken in place of it, is eventually to become terrified. It is the language that matches the meals served at my resort.

One evening, after Adam and I had walked back from town, after the silence of my room had replaced the night drift of human voices along the road, I grew restless and went out again. I stood on the resort's plank dock by the water, near an open-air restaurant where the last patrons were throwing pieces of bread to schools of fish racing frantically back and forth beneath the illuminated surface of the water. Forty miles to the west the lights of Willenstad glowed on the horizon. Above the penumbra of that glow, Venus sparkled in a deep Prussian-blue sky. Higher overhead huge cumulus towers scudded west.

I watched the enormity of the clouds for several minutes. What I wanted to experience in the water, I realized, was how life on the reef was layered and intertwined. I now had many individual pieces at hand—named images, nouns. How were they related? What were the verbs? Which syntaxes were indigenous to the place? I had asked a dozen knowledgeable people. No one was inclined to elaborate— or they didn't know. "Did you see the octopus!" someone shouted after a dive. Yes, I thought, but who among us knows what it was doing? What else was *there*, just then? Why?

I wanted to know in the way, sometimes, you want to know very much more than a person's name.

On the way back to my room, just as I was passing an open

window, I unconsciously raised a hand to brush my forehead and glanced in. Moonlight filled the interior of a bedroom. A woman in a sleeveless cotton nightgown lay wide awake beneath a single sheet. She waved at me tentatively, as though I were someone walking by in a dream she was having.

III

Our last day on Bonaire, Adam and I drove a small Japanese rental car south of Kralendijk to see the salt flats that had once drawn the acquisitive attention of the Spanish and then the Dutch. The salt ponds here were actively worked from about 1624 until 1863, when the Dutch abolition of slavery rendered the operation unprofitable. In 1972 a United States and Dutch concern began exporting salt again on a regular basis. A few of these shallow ponds also now serve as a fortuitous refuge for a once endangered population of greater flamingos. (Their numbers have increased tenfold since this nesting ground was closed to egg collectors, hunters, and low-flying aircraft.) The nearby rows of slave huts—each a carefully restored, peak-roofed, work-week domicile for two—are an anomaly, too comely a reminder of this malign human proclivity. Out of curiosity I began to sketch and measure the huts to see what I might learn. I didn't know whether they had been accurately restored, but standing inside them it was apparent they had been designed to take astute advantage of cooling trade-wind breezes, to shed downpours, and to insulate against tropical heat, like tile-floored adobes.

As is sometimes the ironic case with such shadowed places, they have attracted lovers in another age, people who have drawn hearts and scribed their initials or written their names in chalk and ink all across the whitewashed walls, inside and out. Here, also, was "The Criminal gang is the best so fock [sic] the rest," a sentiment about life on the island that hadn't yet registered at the resorts.

At a place called Onima, fifteen miles away on the east coast— because of heavy surf and strong currents there is no diving on this side of the island—we found several sets of Caiquetío pictographs in unprotected shelters. Early chroniclers describe the Caiquetío as tall, honorable, "*una gente muy pulida y limpida*," a clean people elegant in their manners and movement. Many of the pictographs had been gouged by vandals or written over with graffiti. It took several minutes to spot, higher up on the undersides of overhanging rocks, other drawings in apparently perfect condition. Fascinated, I began to draw some of them, including a strikingly accurate rendering of a species of angelfish. As I did so, a woman approached in a rental car along the dirt road. Who was this? A companion, someone like us? Driving slowly, she rolled down her window and scanned the limestone bluff where I was standing, as though searching for an address; then, gathering speed, she drove quickly away. I imagined her indifferent to the site, to the history it contained. Then I realized she was alone, that two men were standing around, and that this was an unfrequented part of the island. We had closed it to her.

The paintings and drawings were similar to ones I had seen in northern Spain, in Arnhem Land in Australia, at Brandberg in Namibia, in canyons on the Colorado plateau. The evidence of humanity in each place is tantalizing, replete with meaning, but finally elusive, inscrutable.

An hour later, within Bonaire's relatively large Washington/Slagbaai National Park, Adam and I located a watering hole called Poos de Mangel. Numerous birds flitted through the thicket of its trees crowding a small, dust-and-algae-covered pool. I got out of the car with my binoculars and a locally published guide. Whenever I visit a new country, I buy as soon as I can a guide to its birds. If often proves to be the most accurate and least political survey of life in the region. Its pages, frequently written in a tone of appreciation, urge a reader to do little more than share the author's regard. In Kralendijk I had found Peggy Boyer's *Birds of Bonaire*, a guide in English and Papiamentu with black-and-white line drawings by Carl James Freeman. Opening it, I immediately recognized a half-dozen birds

I'd seen around the resort but had not known names for, like the bananaquit.

I stood back in the trees by the pool for half an hour, watching red-necked pigeons, yellow warblers, smooth flycatchers, and black-faced grassquits angle in warily, branch to branch, finally hopping down to sip the water.

Turning back south, we stopped at several spots along the coast where Adam hoped to photograph flamingos and where we saw great white egrets, brown pelicans, and least terns. Late in the afternoon we halted for cool drinks at a small inn on a cove near the island's northwest tip, a place called Boca Bartól, a stunning dive site. Spokes of coral radiate seaward from the beach, the canyons between them floored with pale sand—a formation called spur-and-groove. Inviting as it is, few divers travel to this site. The currents are often strong and the drive up from Kralendijk can take more than an hour on a winding, pitching dirt road. Adam and I sipped our drinks and watched with mild envy as four divers prepared to go in. (Nitrogen gas remains in solution in a diver's tissues after he or she surfaces, the result of breathing normal air at depth. It may take twelve hours or more for this gas to completely diffuse into the bloodstream, the circulatory system carrying it to the lungs where it is exhaled. Prudence dictates divers stay out of the water during the twenty-four hours before they fly to guard against decompression illness, the gas-bubble-related maladies that can set in when an aircraft gains altitude and cabin pressure drops.)

The four divers before us glinted like seals in sunlight glaring from the water and then were gone. We knew how ethereal, how quiet, how consolidating to the spirit such a stray kingdom as this could be. It might launch you past many forms of melancholy.

In Rincon, at a filling station across the street from a branch of Maduro & Curiel's Bank, we asked which road would take us back to Kralendijk via Gotomeer, the lake where flamingos mass in the evening. Rincon seems an amiable town. Its streets meet at casual

angles, like footpaths in a mountain village, and many of its house
doors stand ajar. With the heat of the day now past, a group of boys
was changing clothes in an open field at the edge of town for a soc-
cer game. As we merged with the main road I saw a statue briefly in
the rearview mirror, a man in a suit and tie and hat, striding. I
guessed at who it must be—José Gregorio Hernandez, a Venezuelan
physician who died in 1919. Gregorio Hernandez is said to have
ministered to his patients diligently and compassionately, often
without charge. He is regarded by many today in Bonaire, Aruba,
and Curaçao as an intercessor before God on behalf of the sick. You
spot his picture in taxicabs. Statues of him in that black suit, a dark
vest, and a fedora are found beside sickbeds.

The fact of Gregorio Hernandez (his admirers continue to peti-
tion the Catholic Church to have him beatified), like the clouds that
pass majestically over Bonaire each day, makes the ordinary venality
and inevitable shallowness of so much in human affairs—the coarse-
ness and greed of life, the failure of ideals, the withering of our
aspirations—seem forgivable, even inconsequential. The memory of
Gregorio Hernandez's work on Bonaire, as his admirers describe it,
filled Rincon in that moment with grace and made its every element
—watchful dogs, paving stones, wild parrots—transcendent in the
afternoon light.

I wanted to go back and look at the statue, but Adam hoped to
see the flamingos gathering at dusk, so I drove on. As the car picked
up speed, we passed a middle-aged man with hand tools walking
home from his kitchen garden in trousers caked with mud. I wanted
to see the vegetables washed and firm on his dinner plate. I wished
to know more about Gregorio Hernandez. I wanted to come back
to dive between the pale green coral spurs at Boca Bartól. I wanted
the exquisite flamingos just ahead to ferry each heart's anguished
speculation about who we are, the knowledge of our beautiful and
infernal complexity, across to the shores of Venezuela tonight,
where, in another language, the endless deciphering of what we are
up to would go on.

Terry Tempest Williams

To Be Taken

First publication

The revolutionary question is: What about the Other?...It is not enough to rail against the descending darkness of barbarity....One can refuse to play the game. A holding action can be fought. Alternatives must be kept alive. While learning the slow art of revolutionary patience.
Breyten Breytenbach

Tortoise Steps

Tortoise steps.

Slow steps.

Four steps like a tank with a tail dragging in the sand.

Tortoise steps—land-based, land-locked, dusty like the desert tortoise himself, fenced in, a prisoner on his own reservation

teaching us the slow art of revolutionary patience.

It is Christmas. We gather in our grandparents' home: aunts, uncles, cousins, babies—four generations wipe their feet at the holiday mat.

One by one, we open the front door. "Hello," "We're here," glass panes iced are beginning to melt from the heat of bodies together. Our grandfather Jack, now ninety, presides. His sons, John and Richard, walk in dressed in tweed sportcoats and Levi's; their polished boots could kill spiders in corners. My aunt Ruth enters with her arms full of gifts. Jack's sister, Norinne, in her eighties, sits in the living room with her hands folded tightly, greeting each one of us with a formality we have come to expect.

Tradition.

On this night, we know a buffet is prepared: filet mignon, marinated carrots, asparagus and cauliflower, a cranberry salad, warbread (a recipe our great-grandmother Mamie Comstock Tempest improvised during the Depression when provisions were scarce and raisins plentiful), and the same silver serving piece is obscene with chocolates.

The Christmas tree stands in the center of the room, "the grandchildren's tree," and we remember our grandmother, Mimi, the matriarch of this family whose last Christmas was in 1988. We remember her. We remember all of our dead.

Candles burn. I walk into the dining room, pick up a plate, and circle the table.

"What's new, Terrence?" my uncle asks, ribbing me.

"Not a thing, Rich," I respond. We both look up from the buffet smiling.

I take some meat with my fingers. He spears vegetables. We return to the living room and find a seat. The rest of the family gathers. Jack sits in the wing-backed chair, his hands on both armrests. My father sits across the room from his brother.

"So how did the meeting go last week?"

"Terrible," Rich says.

"What did they decide?"

"Simple," my uncle says, "tortoises are more important than people."

Heads turn, attention fixes on matters of the Tempest Company, the family construction business that began with our great-grandfather in the early part of the century, a company my brothers all work for, cousins, too.

"What are you talking about?" I ask.

"Where have you been?" my father asks incredulously. "We've been shut down eighteen months because of that—" he stops himself in deference to his aunt—"that *stupid* Endangered Species Act."

I look at my brother Steve who nods his head who looks at our cousin Bob who looks at his sister Lynne who shakes her head as she turns to Brooke.

"I attended the public meeting where they discussed the Habitat Management Plan," Rich says to us.

"And?" Lynne asks as she walks over to her father and offers him a piece of warbread.

"They ruled in favor of the tortoise."

"Which job is this, John?" asks Brooke, who at the time is working for the governor's office of budget and planning as the liaison between environmental groups and the state.

"It's the last leg of the Information Highway," Dad says. "Seven miles of fiber optic cable running from the town of Hurricane to St. George linking rural Utah to the Wasatch Front."

"We're held up in permits," Rich explains. "A construction permit won't be issued until US West complies with federal agencies."

"The government's gone too far," my great aunt interjects.

"Too far?" my father says, his voice rising like water ready to boil. "Too far? We've had to hire a full-time biologist at sixty dollars an hour who does nothing but look for these imaginary animals. Every day he circles the crew, singing the same song: "Nope, haven't seen one yet."

"The guy's from BYU and sits in the cab of his truck most of the day reading scriptures," adds Steve, who is the superintendent.

"Thou shalt not kill a turtle," someone mutters under their breath.

"Sixty bucks an hour," Dad reiterates. "That's twice as much as our foremen make! It would be cheaper to buy a poolside condominium for each mating pair of tortoises than to adhere to the costs of this ridiculous act."

"The government's gone too far," my aunt restates like a delayed echo.

"And on top of that we have to conduct a 'turtle training course—'"

"Tortoise, John," his granddaughter Callie interrupts. I wink at my niece.

"A turtle training course for our men, OUR MEN, so they can learn to identify one and then remember to check under the tires and skids for tortoises looking for shade before turning on the backhoes after lunch."

Rich stands up to get some more food.

"One hundred thousand dollars if we run over one," he says, making himself a sandwich.

"Is that worth a hundred grand?" my father snaps.

"From the tortoise's point of view…" Lynne says, pushing.

"What's St. George now, the fourth fastest-growing community in the country?" Brooke asks.

"Not if the enviros have anything to do with it," Rich says.

"What do you kids want? To stop progress? You and your environmentalist friends have lost all credibility. One local told us a bunch of radicals actually planted a tortoise in the parking lot of the Wal-Mart distribution center just to shut it down."

"How do you know it didn't walk onto the asphalt by itself?" I ask.

"They had its stomach pumped and it was full of lettuce," Rich replies.

We all roll our eyes.

Steve asks his cousin Matt who is a first-year medical student, "Have you performed an autopsy on a desert tortoise yet?"

"Not yet," Matt responds. "Just human beings."

"Can I get anyone anything?" Ruth asks, holding her granddaughter Hannah on her hip. She looks around. No response. "Just checking."

"And you wonder why people are upset," my father says, turning to me. "It's easy for you to sit here and tell us what animals we should protect while you write poems about them as a hobby. It's not your pocketbook that's hurting."

"And is yours?" I ask, fearing I have now gone as far as my father has.

I was not aware of the background music until now: Nat King Cole singing "Have a Merry, Merry Christmas."

"I don't know," Jack says, clearing his throat, pulling himself out of his chair. "Why don't you boys tell them the real story?"

John and Richard look puzzled.

"What story?" Rich asks.

"Hardpan," Jack says.

"Never mind," my father says, grinning. "Just keep that quiet."

Richard starts giggling like a little boy.

"Tell!" We beg our grandfather.

He places his hands on the back of the lounge. "We had twenty-two crews during the war, put all the piping in the airbases at Tooele, Salt Lake, Hill, and Ogden. I never went to bed for five years: 1941, '42, '43, '44, '45. Just dropped dead on this lounge from exhaustion every night. We even had work in Las Vegas putting in a big waterline to the north. I was away for weeks, missing Kathryn and the boys. Then one day, I was walking along the trench when I spotted what I thought was a helmet. I bent down. It moved. I realized it was a tortoise. I picked it up—its head and feet shot back into its shell. I put him in the back of my truck and brought him home for the boys. We named him 'Hardpan.'"

He looks at his sons, smiles, and walks out of the room.

"Everybody else had a dog," my father says. "German shepherds, Doberman pinchers, black Labs. We drilled a hole in his shell and tied a long cord to it and walked him around the block."

We all look at each other.

"No kidding," Rich says. "Every day we walked him."

"Hardpan?" I ask.

"You know, the desert without rain—hardpan, no give to the sand." Dad's voice is tender.

"He was reliable, old Hardpan, you have to say that about him," Rich adds.

"Until he disappeared," Jack says, returning to his chair.

Gopherus agassizii. Desert tortoise. Land turtle. An elder among us. Even among my family. For some of us he represents "land-locked" like the wildlands before us. Designate wilderness and development is locked out. Find a tortoise and another invisible fence is erected. The tortoise's presence compromises our own. For others, tortoise is "land-based," a sovereign on Earth, entitled to his own desert justice. He is seen as an extension of family—human and nonhuman alike—living in arid country. His presence enhances our own. The tension tortoise inspires calls for wisdom.

These animals may live beyond one hundred years. They walk for miles largely unnoticed, carrying a stillness with them. Fifteen acres may be home range and they know it well. When they feel in their bodies that it is about to rain, they travel to where water pools. They wait. Clouds gather. Skies darken. It rains. They drink. It may be days, weeks, months before their beaks touch water again.

If native mythologies are true and turtles carry the world on their backs, the carapace of the desert tortoise is designed to bear the weight. It is a landscape with its own aesthetic. Three scutes or plates run down the vertebrae, hexagons, with two larger scutes on top and bottom. Four plates line either side of center. The shell is bordered by twenty-four smaller ones that seem to hold the animal in place. The plastron or bottom of the shell fits together like a twelve-tiled floor. The desert tortoise lives inside its own creation like a philosopher who is most at home in the mind.

In winter, the desert tortoise hibernates but not in the manner of bears. Hibernation for reptiles is "brumation," a time of dormancy where cold-blooded creatures retire, rock-still, with physiological changes occurring independently of their body temperatures. Much remains mysterious about this time of seasonal retreat, but brumation among turtles suggests it is sparked by conditions of temperature, moisture, photoperiod, and food supply. They stir in their stone-ledged dens when temperatures rise, dens they inhabit year after year, one, two, maybe five individuals together. They leave. They forage. They mate. The females lay eggs in supple sands. Two dozen eggs may be dropped in a nest. Buried. Incubated. Hatched. And then the quiet plodding of another generation of desert tortoises meets the sands.

It is a genealogy of evolutionary adaptation until *Gopherus agassizii* suddenly begins bumping into real-estate developers after having the desert to himself for millennia.

1996: A long desert tortoise stands before a bulldozer in the Mojave.

My father and the Endangered Species Act. My father as an endangered species. The Marlboro Man without his cigarette is home on the range—I will list him as threatened by his own vulnerable nature. I will list him as threatened by my emotional nature. Who dares to write the recovery plan that regulates our own constructions? He will resist me. I will resist him. He is my father. I am his daughter. He holds my birth story. I will mourn his death. We face each other.

Hand over our hearts, in the American West united states do not exist even within our own families. "Don't Tread on Me." The snake coils. The tortoise retreats. When the dust devil clears, who remains?

My father, myself, threatened species.

I recall a statement made to me by another elder, a Mormon General Authority who feared I had chosen not to have children. Call it "Ode to the Gene Pool," a manipulation of theology, personalized, tailored to move me toward motherhood, another bulge in the population.

"A female bird," he wrote to me, "has no options as to whether she will lay eggs or not. She must. God insists. Because if she does not a precious combination will be lost forever. One of your deepest concerns rests with endangered species. If a species dies out its gene pool will be lost forever and we are all the lesser because of the loss.... The eggs you possess over which your husband presides [are] precious genes.... You are an endangered family."

I resist. Who will follow? Must someone follow?

Clouds gather. It rains. The desert tortoise drinks where water has pooled.

Who holds the wisdom? My grandfather, the tortoise, calls for the story, then disappears.

Tortoise steps.

Tortoise tracks.

Tracks in time.

One can refuse to play the game.

Across from where I sit is a redrock ledge. We are only a stone's toss away from the city of St. George. I am hiking with my father. He has gone ahead.

Today is the spring equinox, equal light, equal dark—a day of truce.

I have followed tortoise tracks to this place, a den. It is cold, the air stings my face, I did not dress warmly enough. Once again, the desert deceives as wind snaps over the ridge and rides down valley.

The tortoise is inside. I wish to speak to him, to her, to them about my family, my tribe of people who lose money and make money without recognizing their own threatened status, my tribe of people who keep tortoises, turtles, as pets and wonder why they walk away.

"Have you heard the news today?" I pull the clipping from the local paper out of my pocket, unfold it, and read aloud:

> If you're a desert tortoise living in Washington County, take this advice: Start crawling your way toward the hills north of St. George, Utah.

Come March 15, any tortoise living outside a specially designated "desert tortoise reserve" could become subject to "taking"— a biological term for the death of an animal or the destruction of its habitat.

State and federal officials on Friday signed an interlocal agreement that will set aside 61,000 acres of prime tortoise habitat as a reserve that wildlife biologists believe will secure the reptile's recovery.

On the flip side, the agreement also provides permission and means by which developers and others may "take" some 1,200 tortoises and develop more than 12,000 acres of tortoise habitat outside the reserve without violating the Endangered Species Act, under which the tortoise is listed as a "threatened species."

Friday's signing ends six years of battles over the slow-moving animal, whose presence around St. George has created headaches for land developers and local governments.

"We feel confident that we're going to be able to work together and have a permit that provides for the recovery and protection of the tortoise," said Bob Williams, assistant supervisor for the Fish and Wildlife Service.

Senator Bob Bennett, R-Utah, agreed. "This is clearly a very major step toward getting the endangered species issues resolved short of the trainwreck of the spotted owl."

...Between 1980 and 1990, Washington County's population increased 86% from 26,125 to 48,560. It is projected to have between 101,000 and 139,000 people by 2010. Implementation of the Habitat Conservation Plan is scheduled to last twenty years and cost $11.5 million.

There is no movement inside the den.

"Tortoise, I have two questions for you from Neruda:
    'Quién da los nombres y los numeros al inocente innumerable?'
    Who assigns names and numbers to the innumerable innocent?
    'Cómo le digo a la tortuga que yo le gano en lentitude?'
    How do I tell the turtle that I am slower than he?"

The desert tortoise is still.

I suspect he hears my voice simply for what it is: human. The news and questions I deliver are returned to me and somehow dissipate in the silence.

> It is enough
> to breathe, here, together.
>
> Our shadows lengthen
> while the white-petaled heart of Datura
> opens and closes.
>
> We have forgotten the option of restraint.
>
> It is no longer the survival of the fittest but the survival of compassion.

Inside the redrock ledge, the emotional endurance of the tortoise stares back at me. I blink. To take. To be taken. To die. The desert tortoise presses me on the sand, down on all fours. The shell I now find myself inhabiting is a keratinous room where my spine is attached to its ceiling. Head, hands, feet, and tail push through six doors and search for a way home.

Tortoise steps.

Land-based. Land-locked.

Land-based. Land-locked.

Learning the slow art of revolutionary patience, I listen to my family.

Rick Bass

Metamorphosis

from *The Book of Yaak*

DEAR BILL,

I'm sorry I missed you when I called two days ago, the day of the summer solstice. I left a message saying that I was going to take a hike for you. This may have sounded puzzling or imprecise but I didn't want to leave a long and windy message. Instead, I went up to the mountain that I climb every time I hear a friend is sick. I have been climbing it for eight years now and it has a success rate of 50 percent. I don't know if it was a holy mountain to the Indians or not. It is to me. Let me report to you what I saw on your hike.

It was a damp, rainy, foggy day. In clear weather you can see Idaho to the west and British Columbia to the north from the mountaintop, but I knew that would not be the case this day. I started up the trail midday. I had not been on the mountain all year —not since early last winter. There had been waist-deep snow, then; now the trail was overgrown with ankle-deep ferns and flowers. Seeps and springs glistened from the sides of the mountain, as if it were leaking, or bleeding, life.

I wound my way steadily, quickly, up the trail through old cool forest, anxious to get into alpine country—the steep grassy places where the mountain tips sharply skyward. Up there, I'll find the avalanche fields, where most tree seedlings get swept away by each year's snowslides—the mountain sheds the snow, and its trees, like skin, which leaves behind its core and essence: bare gray slickrock that shines in the sun. Clumps of rich soil—and tall grasses—cling wherever they can beneath the bright rock. This is the part of the mountain I am always most anxious to get to: the part where I feel things begin to happen.

The sky was slate-purple, luscious with rain—the clouds still bulging with storm, though it had been raining steadily for seven days already. It's the greenest I've ever seen the valley.

I hadn't been hiking for more than two or three minutes when I heard the chain-saw sound of an approaching plane—a small single-engine plane, such as the biologists use to chase and keep tabs on the grizzly bears they've live-trapped and fitted with radio telemetry collars. There are ten or twelve grizzlies in this valley—and four of them have collars. Ten or twelve doesn't sound like very many, and it isn't—there used to be one hundred thousand of them in the West, or even more. The bears in this valley are generally considered more valuable from a genetic standpoint due to their unaltered wildness than those few hundred bears that are left in Yellowstone and Glacier National Parks.

There's a big monster of a bear that hangs out on top of this mountain: a sweetheart, terrified of human beings, but big as a dinosaur. He *is* a dinosaur, holding on to his world with all four paws. I've seen him but once though I've seen his tracks often. His feet are as big as snowshoes. I was discouraged when I heard the tracking plane, not so much for the disruption of my solitude, but for the bears'. This big bear isn't radio-collared, but there must have been one up here that is—maybe a female. It's about that time of year when they get together.

A wonderful thing happened, though, before the plane could reach the mountain. The purple, silver-streaked storm clouds that were lingering on the back side of the mountain came drifting—*rolling*—over its crest, just as the little plane came near, so that it had to turn around before it reached the alpine fields where the grizzly often grazed.

So I knew he, or he and another one, was up there. But now it was just he and I, or he, his radio-collared paramour and I; we had the mountain to ourselves.

I don't know what it is about this mountain that makes it special. And I don't want to know.

The pitch of it, once up into the avalanche section, the swept-clean slopes, demands everything your lungs have got. The slope sets your calves to burning, and after a while turns your upper legs to quivering jelly rather than sound muscle. It's an alchemical transformation. When you stop to rest, your heart feels like thunder. Even on a cold day, you're bathed in sweat by the time you're halfway up.

It's so damned good to be healthy.

I've seen almost every species of mammal in the valley up on this mountain, at one time or another. Often I see them in conjunction with each other.

None of this has a direct bearing on my report to you: this explanation of past trips. This hike for you was taken solely in the context of the present: only the present. I shall try to confine my remarks to what I saw, that day—not to what I didn't see, or had seen in the past.

I moved up into the clouds. My God, the names of all the flowers—hundreds of species, it seemed, all of them spangled with rain. Each summer I tell myself not to take them for granted; each summer I promise myself that I will learn all of their names.

But each year, I learn only a few. It's a gradual process. Still, I have to believe that it will all add up. That one of these days, I'll know them all. Glacier lily, mariposa lily, penstemon, bluebell. Bellflower, lupine, paintbrush, aster. Tiger lily, phlox, lady's slipper, balsam-root. Canadian violet. Northern bog rein orchid.

I moved carefully into the fog, grateful for the cold mist against my face: grateful it had chased the clattering plane away, and grateful for the steaming beauty it brought to the landscape, the grass- and rock-scape, now that I was out of the forest. It was good to be on a mountain that had a grizzly on it—one of the very few grizzlies living outside a national park—though I worried a little that the plane might have pissed him off, and that the bear might not at the moment be feeling goodwill toward men.

The fog got thicker near the mountain's crest. A spooky white fog—not swirls and whisps of vapors, but a near total whiteout. It was like being in the belly of a cloud, which I suppose I was. Ordinarily it would seem like I was at the edge of danger, pushing beyond the prudent edge of a thing—past respect—but I figured that I had some kind of permission or authority—yours, perhaps—and that, well, whatever happened was meant to happen: was meant to be relayed to you, in this report.

Still, I have to say, I'm glad I didn't see the bear.

Not that anything on this earth could remotely compare to what you're facing: you're at the edge of all there may ever be. Maybe your illness will reverse direction, through either reasons known or unknown, like animal tracks across new snow.

If I were to come upon a grizzly bear, high up in this cloud, walking down the ridge toward me, he or she would probably only stop, squint and sniff at me, from whatever close distance we encountered each other—grizzlies can see about as well as humans, but have a sense of smell that is about a hundred times better than ours—and then he almost certainly would have turned around and gone the other way; as would have I—as would have I.

Things are far less certain, for you. Things are far more dire.

So I was relatively unworried; only curious to see what the mountain would show to me to report back to you.

A ghost-shape galloped past me, moving from right to left, just at the farthest range of vision: a dark young bull elk, his antlers in June velvet, running in a curious, steady, circus-horse canter. A yearling; maybe a two-year-old. An adolescent. I thought of your son, and your daughters, and pushed on. The elk slipped into the timber below.

Aside from walking a small circle for luck around the old stone cairn at the crest, I didn't spend much time there. It was my notion to cut a transect from east to west across the whole of this mountain, which runs long and narrow north-south; to dig deep, to reach into it not for all that it had but for all that it was willing to give you through me. I'd started at the headwaters of the creek on its east flank, climbed to the top, and now would drop down to the creek on its west flank—actually a high hanging hidden valley, almost like some place of the imagination; a perfectly green and serene spot. And then I planned to climb back up the steep west side, go over the top again, and down the east side, back to where I had started.

It would be like going fishing—like trawling with a wide net. I didn't know what I'd find or see for you.

It was raining lightly on the back side. Wood thrushes were singing. This reminded me of a book your company published, *Birds of Texas*, and in turn reminded me of another book you published, *Back Roads of Texas*. I remember us joking about doing *Back Roads of Montana*, and my horror at such an idea. It makes me laugh to think that now I am sending you a report and a description of my favorite place-without-a-road. An even deeper baring of the soul.

Descending the western side is especially refreshing because of all the deciduous leaf litter underfoot. There's still the Pacific Northwest coniferous overstory—larch, fir, spruce, lodgepole pine and white pine—the giant cedars lie farther below, where the water accumulates—but on this near-vertical descent there's an incredible abundance of not only ferns and forest flowers, but broad-leafed deciduous trees as well: maple, aspen, buffaloberry, huckleberry, alder, ceanothus, even sarsaparilla. It's a place where two worlds collide—or if not collide, where they get pressed tightly together right here at this edge, to form a new world.

The deciduous leaves seem to rot easier—seem, in their broadness, to trap and retain moisture more readily between themselves and the soil—and because of this, the soil is rich, thick and black. This is a young valley, just-sprung-up yesterday from the glacier's retreat; the trees, because of the Pacific Northwest weather systems, are huge, but the soil is thin: you cut the trees once, and they won't come back like they were before. Not until a new bedding of soil forms. Which—if the trees are left alone—might take a few thousand years.

This is the richest soil I've seen in the valley. The healthiest. Perhaps the way this side of the mountain faces the west-approaching storms causes it to catch more moisture: causes it to even create its own moisture. Perhaps the west-setting sun, warmer than the rising sun, has over time more thoroughly weathered and disintegrated the rock—dissolving it like geological fertilizer, to add to the mystery of the forest below. Perhaps...

It is a healing mountain.

Yellow warblers and yellow tanagers fly past like creatures escaped from a lifetime of imprisonment, singing and swooping. The needles of the coniferous trees do not break down and return to the earth as easily, as quickly, as do the leaves of the deciduous trees. There's a beetle that helps chew up the waxy coating on some of these coniferous needles, however, thereby enabling the rotting process to get started, where otherwise it would not. They're vital to the process of soil formation, these chewing bugs—vital to the forest, vital to the sky, to life. They're one of the rare leaf-eating insects in the forest. I remember a friend telling me how most insects in this forest were predators—that they ate each other—because there were so many billions of them that if they ate plant matter, they would quickly strip the entire forest bare.

As we are now doing. But that is another story, and is secondary to the story of immediate life—though it is not secondary to the longer view of things.

It's like looking through binoculars, or a telescope; like looking through them backwards, where everything's tiny, and then looking through them frontwards, where everything—even the moon—is huge.

What this trip today is about is to just try and look at things the way they are.

An attempt to make a walk without a thought of tomorrow.

I make this hike when people are well, too; the beauty of these woods—these untouched woods—has plenty to offer me when all is well. It's not a place I come to only in times of the sickness of friends. But it—the walk, and the woods—takes on, or seems to imbue—as with the pulse of a breathing thing—even more meaning, and deliver more understanding, when experienced in the context of illness, the context of sorrow.

The woods provide.

Going down through the lush dripping understory, trying to pick a path, and barely able to see ahead through the chill fog-clouds, might be akin to your present grasp of things. Everything on this walk reminds me of and amplifies your condition. I want to tell you about it all. Though I have made this transect on numerous occasions, no one path is ever the same as the one before it, and this time I discover one of the most amazing larch trees I've ever seen.

It's not amazing in size, and especially not for a larch; some in these woods are almost like redwoods—three- and four-hundred-year-old trees large enough to drive a car through. What's amazing about this one—it's about fifty years old, is my guess—only five or six years older than you—is that it metamorphosed into three separate trees. It's not at all uncommon for a larch to have twin trunks, but I've never noticed one before that has three trunks.

More amazing still, these three trunks, each as thick as a man's waist, spiral around each other as they rise vertically toward the canopy, so far above. They coil not so much like a great tree trunk, but like a vine, or DNA; like a corkscrew, like serpents around a staff.

Ordinarily such an unusual tree would not survive in the chaos of the forest—or what we call chaos, but which is of course a constantly changing state of unrelenting order and complexity, unrelenting grace.

Ordinarily, a tree like this one—so out of the mold for a classic larch—would have been pruned by insects, lightning, ice storm, or wind. It would not have been allowed to channel that energy—frivolous energy—all that sunlight, all that photosynthesis!—into such a seemingly whimsical and most decidedly unlarchlike design.

But I looked at what surrounded it, and I saw how it had survived.

Trees of different species formed a circle around it—fir, aspen, lodgepole, even cedar. Their branches, as it was growing, must have helped to shelter and stabilize it, hold it up, as though they were friends, or at the very least—and in the sense of the word that I think we must turn to the woods to relearn—like community.

There was no way to look at the tree and not think of you, and of all the other things that mattered.

I guess I'm not a hard-core pagan yet—and may never be. I still like to stop at the edges of realism, and not travel too far over into the world of the symbolic. I still sometimes cannot help but hold on to the notion that what we see and understand is all there is: that we have run out of mystery. I know in my heart that's wrong, but still, nearly forty years old, I have trouble shaking that stone wall certainty, the milieu in which I've grown up—the idea that we've got it all figured out. "It" being everything.

If I believed—if I dared to believe—more deeply in the power of symbolism, and the immeasurable, unknowable power of myth and ritual, perhaps I would have climbed that DNA-twisted tree and sawed or chopped down one, or two, or all of the spiraling trunks—a strange effort, 2,000 miles away, to bend back the spirals of your own DNA—to make them change course; to divert the path of destiny, the genetic markers laid out in your beginning cast-of-dice, charting in advance, so long ago, the path of your flesh.

Or perhaps not: perhaps even if I believed, or knew, that a tree in Yaak could be connected to a man in Texas, I would have left it alone, as I did; believing, as I do, that there can be just as much power, or more power, in restraint as there can be in the desire to shape, manipulate, alter, and impose.

I walked on.

There were mushrooms everywhere and of every color dazzling the eyes, and vibrant lichens, on the wet boulders: lichens that were hundreds, even thousands of years old. The undergrowth of *vaccinium* — huckleberry bushes — already had their swollen green berries on them, just waiting to turn purple in August, to transfer their chlorophyll to straight high-octane sugar; waiting to be eaten, in August and September, by the birds drifting southward, and by the bears drifting back up to the high north slopes, as they prepared to crawl down into the earth for their deep winter's sleep.

It all reminded me of you. The bears—your life. The bull elk— your son. The birdsong—your heart, our hearts, all hearts, hoping. The sound of the spring creeks trickling down the steep walls of the mossy, forested mountains—your life, again, and all lives.

Sometimes they build roads into the virgin forests up here under the pretense of getting into trees—lodgepole pine, usually—that have been infested with mountain pine beetles, for which lodgepole is a host. It's an intricate, highly evolved cycle about which entire books have been written. Basically, though, pine beetles attack overmature lodgepoles, killing them, sometimes in large numbers, which then sets that dead or dying stand up for a fire—usually lightning-caused —the heat of which the lodgepole's cones can then use to be cracked open and reproduce.

Through the ashes of the fire, all of the forest's nutrients are returned to the soil—the flames open the seed cones for the next forest—and so its goes. The fire destroys large numbers of the beetle "epidemic," as well. The cycle of the forest rises and falls, in that manner, like piston-and-valve, or calliope music. Like the hands of a potter working clay.

What's strange about this forest is that none of its lodgepole pines—though they're mature ones, even overmature—have beetles in them. By any account, this mountain is a place of unsurpassed health, from the soil all the way up to the tips of the treetops. These lodgepoles are eighty-five years old, and without a pine beetle in sight. These lodgepoles have the genetics, and the magic, that future land-managers—though, good God, not the current crop, it seems—will be interested in.

I pick my trail downward through the thick forest toward that backside creek in the high green hanging valley. I've never been in that valley without seeing a cow moose. I don't know if it's the same moose every time or not.

I keep thinking about DNA—about the bends in it, the alterations, that can yield or summon cancer—a meltdown of the flesh. The paths that are charted for us from the beginning, versus those that are sometimes chosen for us by others: by pollutants, contaminants, carcinogens. I'd recently read a newspaper column by a timber industry lackey who was pooh-poohing the dangers of dioxin. Never mind that it's the second-deadliest carcinogen known to man, next only to plutonium (another element for which the timber spokesman had kind words). The largest emission of dioxin, he said, actually comes from the forest itself when it burns. Dioxin, he said, was something trees inflict upon us.

I guess he ran out of space in his column, or in his mind, maybe, or just forgot and left out the part that forest fires release dioxin because the dioxin has settled on the needles of conifers as a result of chlorine precipitation from industrial emissions.

God, I hope you can turn this thing around.

As I get lower and lower, closer to the creek, it begins to rain again. Massive larch trees, giant burned-out skeletons, stand sentinel-like and tell the story of the 1910 forest fire, which burned, off and on, for a distance of 250 miles, from Spokane to Kalispell, and whose smoke was visible as far away as Chicago. It was this fire—redepositing all of the forest's nutrients, rather than trucking them off and putting them on a ship bound for Asia—which laid the foundation for the immense forests of this valley. Not all the trees burned—some in the valley are five hundred years, even a thousand years old—but those that did burn gave birth to an incredibly rich and blessed place. They left more behind than what they came in with.

In the valley, we talk about the 1910 fire—the magnitude of which is probably a two- or three-hundred-year event—as if it occurred back in the most ancient corner of history; and in some ways—in the scale of you and me, for instance—I guess it was.

In 1910, you wouldn't have been born yet. In 1910, perhaps even your father and mother wouldn't have been born. Your grandfather would have been a young man then, strong in the world.

So much green, everywhere, lush and dripping and wet.

The rain falls lightly on the broad leaves of false hellebore, a plant that the Indians of the British Columbia coastal tribes hold in highest esteem for medicinal purposes. You can't eat it—it'll make you sick—but the smoke from the burning green plant can heal both your body and your spirit. I snap one off above the base, leaving the roots to regenerate, and put it in my daypack to mail to you. The rain makes a pattering sound as it strikes the broad leaves all around me—I'm standing knee-deep in a helleborine garden. The sound itself—unusual for this valley—is healing. As the rain knifes through the conifers' needles it makes a steady hiss. I'm very near the creek now, muddy and wet to my waist. A ruffed grouse is drumming nearby, courting, perhaps, working toward his second clutch of the summer, following the freak blizzard only two weeks ago, which extinguished a fair number of the spring's hatchlings, the first clutch.

Life, go on, go on. Go on.

Through the forest I catch a glimpse of a faraway mountain—four, five miles upstream, in the headwaters of this secret valley. A little road was built into the edge of this roadless country, farther up in those headwaters, during World War II—it was thought that we'd need to cut more wood for building more ships—but the war ended before those trees could be reached, and the road is invisible now, completely grown over with alder and pines as big around as your thigh. Up at the headwaters, there is one smallish clearcut, up at the source of things, like a blemish, a nick or a cut one might have gotten while shaving. The rest of this green forest—despite the nick's relative tininess—seems somehow poised against it; suffering it quietly, absorbing and absolving the tiny sight of it—but not unmindful of it: not forgetting that it is there.

I'm in dark, dense timber close to the creek now. It's wet, and I slip. I hear the thunder of something large running away from me, or toward, I can't tell which, at first.

Away.

More 1910-charred giant larch skeletons. They were several hundred years old before they burned. That's a rule of the West, and a rule of the world: if it doesn't rot, it burns.

If it dies, it's born again—as long as there's a soil base for it to return to. Orange mulch or gray-black ash, it makes no difference; it lives and dies in its home and then lives again. Even when the soil is washed away, it is not the end of things, because then the sun and frost and snow and rain begin to work on the exposed bedrock, crumbling it and kneading and pulverizing it through millennia to make soil again.

It's good soil, here, in this back-side valley. I'll send you some. It feels good to be standing on it. There are a lot of stories buried within it. It supports so much life.

Over on one of the other mountains earlier this summer—up on one of the burned mountains, scorched black in places from last autumn's fires—the bluebirds and flickers were swarming in search of all the remaining insects. The birds' songs were beautiful in that black landscape of birth, and the bluebirds were flying chips of color and song. It all has to rot or burn, and there's only so much in the bank. Forgive me if I keep repeating the obvious: it just seems like such a revelation to me that in the end it is all the same, and that it is really the part leading up to either of those two ends that makes life so sweet for us.

Here is a feather from these woods. Here is an antler. Here is a stone, still light years away from becoming soil.

The ranger I talked to last year, when I went down to the Forest Service office to protest a road being built into this last forest, said, in response to a direct question by me, that no, he didn't consider this mountain any different from any other. They'd tried to come in here and cut last year, but a court appeal ruled against them.

Didn't matter. They came right back and proposed the same thing this year, only bigger.

The ranger said that no, he wasn't aware of any particular magic hiding out in this little valley, that it was no different from any other mountain in the valley.

He was full of shit.

"I'll put it into the record that your comments were considered," he said curtly, glancing at his watch.

Here is the creek, then: you emerge into a glowing green place—holly, maple, water-drip, moth-dance. The scent of roses. Mayflies rise from the virgin creek. Cedar trees 200 feet tall shade the still waters of a beaver pond, drinking the clear water with their almost-ageless roots. A giant cow moose and her calf, seemingly no larger than a small dog, stand in the bright healthy lime-green of the marsh grass farther downstream. Sunshine illuminates them.

The creek is narrow; in some places you could vault across it. And across the creek lies more unroaded country, and the beginning of another mountain.

I dip my hands in the creek and splash its water on my face. I turn and start back in the direction from which I have come.

If you make it—if you pull out and turn this thing around—you and I will have to take this hike next year, or the next.

If you don't, I will send the map—the rough sketch of it—to your family, so that your children might someday see it.

This is the thing I wanted most to share with you.

The moose and her calf—frightened by my presence—splash across the creek and go into the forest on the other side. I start the climb back into the rainclouds.

The swatch of gold shining on the marsh remains, waiting, like the light of hope itself. Not like anything come down from the sky, photosynthetic life from the sun, but like something deeper and more permanent: like hope from the center of the earth, hope from the soil.

The hope of fallen, rotting trees.

Lisa Couturier

Walking in the Woods

from *Iris: A Journal About Women*

I know a woman who lives alone in the woods in a wooden house with lots of windows and no curtains. I house-sat for her once. Before she left on her trip, she told me a story about men who twice had broken into her home and robbed her of her food.

At night, alone in her house with no curtains, I didn't move from the couch. Outside was pitch black. No street, no street lamps. No neighbors, no porch lamps. Still, there could be *someone* out there, and I didn't want them to see me walking through the house, alone. During the next two weeks I prepared daily by staying in the woods while it was light, convinced that from there I could get away fast if anyone unknown showed up.

The woods were a source of fear and a source of safety; men might come out of them, but still I went in, isolated yet rarely feeling alone. Wonderfully red and orange salamanders, who turned green and brown when I talked to them, stared at me from tree trunks. Sometimes I followed the woman's cat through the woods while she hunted. We searched for the flutist melodies of wood thrush and heard deer crash through the bush. I never saw the men. I never saw anyone.

I had been in such woods before.

I had thought about men and woods before.

I had been a different person before I knew men.

I had, at that house, been a woman alone in nature: loving woods, fearing men.

I am reading *Pilgrim at Tinker Creek* by Annie Dillard, and as I follow Dillard over the mountains and through the woods and fields, in summer, in winter, out into night, the big question I have is this: When will she write about being afraid? Not of the land or animals. Surely she would be attentive to nature's signals—the colors of poisonous snakes, the behaviors of bears, the fluctuations in temperature. But does she not fear men?

In Anne LaBastille's *Women and Wilderness*, I read about women who are strong and independent, self-assured, in the woods and backcountry. They touch the land and the trees, live with animals every day. How did I come to fear land beyond fences and gardens and roads when I feel so strong a love for it, when I want nothing more than to walk into it, alone?

There was a time I walked alone. I suspect many girls did. It was before I consciously knew my body; it was a time when the knowledge of what was between my legs didn't keep my legs from walking into the wild.

When I was young, my father's job transferred him from our home in the Maryland suburbs to Winchester, Massachusetts. In Winchester, we rented a house near the rim of an abandoned gravel pit that was in the process of becoming a forest once again. Along the west and south rim, grasses grew so long and full they fell over, forming soft green moguls in the heat and brittle bisque-colored ones in the cold. The walls of the pit below the moguls balanced rocks, seedlings, and wildflowers. On the north and east rims were patches of the forest that had once covered the entire area, and from the north flowed a skinny creek that long ago ran the land. Now, when it reached the top of the pit it tumbled down—a waterfall in my eyes—and became a pond in the belly of the beast, down at the bottom, where bushes tangled over one another and saplings reached through the gravel and sand that the tractors and road crews had left behind.

The pit. I went there every single day to meet up with black racers and box turtles; butterflies, blue jays, and robins; and blue and purple dragonflies that might sew shut my mouth if I didn't quiet myself when they flew by. I fell through thin ice, lollygagged in the sunshine. I knew it was a special place, magical. And I imagined: There was a troll who guarded the cave near the pond, and I rode camels in the sand. The pit. Kid culture. Wildness.

In New York City, where I now live, I am pulled toward anything that "speaks pit"—trees, birds, rocks, water. I move toward small unnoticed lives around me. On my fire escape I feed house finches. I grow millet in a ceramic planter; the birds eat the seeds and the plant. They bring their babies by. On my way out each day, I touch the leaves of the white ash growing in front of my building. Its roots reach below the street and into soil that was once home to Jones Woods, a 160-acre forest that in the mid-1800s ran from the East River to Third Avenue between 66th and 75th Streets.

New York is not my pit. But I am not in Winchester, and nature is not always somewhere besides here. I take what I can get.

On the west side of town I ride the A-train with my husband Kirk to Inwood Hill, a 196-acre forest and salt marsh oasis on the northwestern tip of the city. Zipping underground like a mole through the dark tunnels of Manhattan, I envision this island, my home, just over three centuries ago: completely forested, ringed with tidal marshes, walked on by the Rechgawank, the last Native Americans —a part of the Algonquin Nation—to live here before being swindled out of the land by Europeans. I am heading for the remnants of that land; I'll be lucky if I see the one muskrat a friend told me built a lodge in the saltwater cordgrass of Inwood's marsh. My husband talks to me about the glacier that covered Manhattan 15,000 years ago with a wall of ice more than 2,000 feet high. At Inwood there are boulders the ice left behind. He talks of Inwood marble, the rock below the Manhattan schist where the skyscrapers he designs are anchored.

Mostly, though, I think about the beauty of the woods—maples, tulip trees, oaks, black cherries, birches, ferns, wildflowers, songbirds, insects; light ribboned around leaves.

We are there. In the marsh one great egret, glowing white fire in the spring sun, skewers an invertebrate with its bill. The muskrat? Could be—certainly there's an entrance to something in the cordgrass. Twelve mallards, four Canadian geese, and two snowy egrets linger by the pond. We hear an oriole and look for it in a London plane planted near the marsh, which is fenced in to protect it from park visitors chasing misdirected footballs. At the southwest tip of the marsh we take a left and walk south through the manicured lawn where fathers wrestle with sons and a mother ties pink birthday balloons to a tree.

The woods: We enter holding hands, as lovers will. Tall trees, lush, unkempt, and un-parklike darken the path, which is a dying human artifact stabbed by weeds, moss, grass. The soil is cooled chocolate. The air is breezing. Here I can hear trees.

It is the small patch of paradise I envisioned until I hear the voice. *Don't go into the woods.…*It is my mother, protecting me from the place I want to be most. It is society saying, *You shouldn't have been alone.*

Because even with a man, I am not safe—women are usually raped by men they know. Because even with my husband, whom I trust completely, I am not safe from other men. I know this.

One out of four women in the United States will be raped. A frightening statistic, though I also know that the odds are against anything happening to me anywhere. Still, the fear can be strong in a woman's life, in my life, no matter where I am, whom I'm with. There are warning stories all around—the woman in New Jersey a few years ago, riding her bike in the country; then, off her bike, taken into the woods by a man. Raped and tortured. There was a woman near my university, dragged into the woods by two men. Raped repeatedly and then burned to death. There is my best friend's sister—she was raped and left in the woods near a creek, mouth taped, feet and hands bound.

There was me with an esteemed biologist last spring. We spent a long day together in the field, talking of Canada geese, woodchucks, falcons, sun rays, animal communication. During a meal, I took an aspirin. Said the biologist, "I guess that's your way of telling me you're not going to bed with me tonight."

I left.

It is second nature for me to be alert to non-point source sounds —footsteps, whistles; to be aware of shadows, movement; to have keys in hand long before I get to the car door, the house door. It's a necessary instinct.

My husband does not have this instinct. I suppose the women in *Women and Wilderness* may not either. Nor Annie Dillard. But there are others like me, other girls who couldn't walk into the woods— not because they didn't *want* to but because without cougars or grizzlies in Northeastern forests the biggest threat to anyone is the male *Homo sapiens*.

Boston raised my mother as much as her parents did. She was a city girl, dancing, hanging on street corners, riding subways. Nature is not her forte. Bless her, she tries protecting me long distance: *Don't go alone…Be home before dark; I'll call you at ten*. I asked her recently to tell me why I wasn't allowed in the woods that graced the edges of our suburban Maryland home.

"There were older boys in there. You shouldn't have snuck down there like you did. It wasn't safe."

Defying my mother was easy. At nine and ten years old I trusted the woods. In them I ate wild strawberries; raced with the creek; made huts out of fallen branches; rested against the bark of birch, maple, oak; searched for salamanders, frogs, tadpoles. Branches and vines challenged my body, strengthened my biceps, toughened my palms, and taught me to endure. I was a persistent player, and the woods were a preeminent partner. Older boys? Hey, no problem.

But problems came up, as they do in girls' lives when we experience the paradox of primping to attract boys while simultaneously learning to fear them.

Boys. I first feared them when I first bled. Menstruation sexed me. No going back. My tomboy blood poured out. Surely, I thought, others could smell me, could see the awkward way my legs straddled that sanitary napkin while I walked home from school. I felt exposed, vulnerable. The older boys drove by and slowed down, yelling about my new breasts, my hair, my behind; whistling, hanging out the windows and panting like dogs. My mother's warning finally made sense.

It still does. Yet the fear is frustrating. The more I try to leash it the more it runs away with me.

Violence against women undermines my trust in men. Which in turn undermines my trust in myself, alone, in nature. Still, I am drawn to the trees, the creatures, the land. Nature reminds me that talking to salamanders or following a cat on its hunt are acts of boldness necessary to help me thrive and keep alive my wild feminine. The woods are hated by those who have never been in them, by those who would burn them, log them, build on them. By walking through woods, through wild areas, forests, I stand up for them. I stand up for myself.

Dan O'Brien

Dog Days

from *Equinox*

You have to wonder what goes through a dog's mind. There are those who say, Not much, but I'm not one of them. When I was a boy it was popular to believe that animals were incapable of thought. Of course, that idea has its origins in some nonsensical, anthropocentric, Christian notion about the hierarchy of animals. Anyone who has seen a pointing dog lock up on a skittish pheasant, glance impatiently over his shoulder as the shooter hurries to get into position, then take off in a sixty-yard arch that puts him in a position where it is impossible to smell the bird might question the dog's intelligence. But you've got to be as smart as the dog. What he's done is put the running bird between himself and the hunter. He's pinned the bird so the shooter will get his shot and he's proved that he can reason—perhaps better than any who might doubt his intelligence.

A veterinarian at the University of Iowa once told me and some friends that the old saying "Dog is a man's best friend" is more than a cliché. This was late at night and there had been many beers in the preceding hours but the old doctor held forth with a professorial gravity that made me believe. "There's a special connection," he said. "They have a much stronger bond to humans than any other species, stronger than horses, or cats, or even falcons." He held a hooded falcon on his fist as he spoke. He was a big man with a beard, a booming voice, and bifocals. He swayed in the firelight with his two golden retrievers looking up at him like they were afraid he might fall. He projected his voice to the assembled group of young falconers. "After all," he said, "they are the only animal to have volunteered for domestication."

The inspired veterinarian claimed dogs were never caught and tamed like other domestic animals but that they followed the camps of early man, drawing closer and closer, until finally the two species were joined in an unprecedented interspecific alliance that has lasted ever since. His speech exhausted him and he sat down between the retrievers and fell silent. The dogs put their heads in his lap and thumped their tails on the floor in canine applause.

The combination of dogs and alcohol prompted another memorable late-night soliloquy years later on the plains of South Dakota. It was a New Year's Eve in the late seventies and I was camped in the snow with Bill Heinrich and Dan Konkel, two old falconer friends from Colorado. The wind had been blowing thirty-five miles an hour all day. It is rightly considered very bad form to drink alcohol while actually flying a falcon. But our birds had been grounded and it was New Year's Eve. We fried up the two pheasants we had caught earlier in the week and ate them along with the pinto beans that had been simmering with a ham bone for three days on the woodburning stove. We had a big wall tent, but with three people and four dogs it was a little close. We started to bring in the New Year as soon as the sun set. In South Dakota, on the last day of December, that's about four o'clock in the afternoon.

By midnight we were ready to hear each other's New Year's resolutions. We sat on our cots with our dogs curled as close to the stove as they could get without getting off the cots. I can't remember what Bill or I promised to do in the coming year but Dan's resolution is forever embedded in my memory. He's a big, blond, wild ex-wrestler who is known for his low tolerance for alcohol. He had two dogs on that trip: an old, glassy-eyed setter bitch named Jessie and a pup named Lark. He loved these dogs with a passion that was hard to believe of a guy with such rough edges. They were both draped over him and he stroked them as gently as his big hands allowed. When it came his turn to make his New Year's resolution, he didn't look up at us until he had thought it through. His eyes were a bit blurry but his hands never stopped stroking the dogs. He spoke earnestly and twice his voice threatened to break. "This next year," he said, "I want to live my life more like a dog."

We stared at him dumbly. "No really," he said. "Look at them." He gestured to the dogs in his lap. "Not a phony bone in their bodies. They always have a positive attitude. They live for what's real. Huntin', eatin', fuckin', and fightin'." Dan paused. "But they're loyal. These dogs would do anything for me."

Dan made perfect sense to us that night and I still find truth in what he said. It was certainly true that his old dog, Jessie, was loyal. An hour after we let the Coleman lantern die out, Bill and I heard Dan having trouble keeping his dinner down. The wind was howling and Dan was too incapacitated to leave his bunk. We heard the pheasant and beans splattering on the tent floor. Bill and I wanted no part of this. We pretended to be asleep. There was a heavy silence in the tent as Dan's foggy brain tried to sort out what to do.

Finally we heard his whisper. "Jessie. Here, Jessie. Jessie. That a girl. Good girl." Any doubts we might have had about dogs' desire to do anything for their masters were dispelled when we heard Jessie's reluctant lapping.

My first bird dog's name was Lucky. He had another name when, without parental permission, I brought him, his doghouse, chain, and sack of dog food home. He worked on a hunting preserve and I figured I'd gotten a lot of bird experience for twenty-five bucks. He was a seven-year-old German shorthair. My dad pretended to be outraged by my stupidity; there was obviously something wrong with a twenty-five-dollar dog. That was when Dad started calling the dog Lucky. He figured the preserve owner had bilked me out of twenty-five dollars and saved himself the price of a bullet. Secretly, I think he was pretty proud that his thirteen-year-old son wanted a bird dog bad enough to make such a pitiful deal. I think he also hoped to shoot a few pheasants over old Lucky.

My dad was a dog nut and we had always had dogs. Even though we were pheasant hunters, we'd never had a bird dog and I watched my dad studying Lucky. He was intrigued by this tough old veteran of six seasons of hard pheasant hunting. The dog was big and solid and by July I had him minding as well as any dog my dad had ever seen. But there had to be something wrong with this dog, and it was just a matter of time until it showed itself.

Dad told me the dog probably wouldn't point, that he'd go crazy as soon as he smelled his first bird and that would be the end of it. But when I planted a pigeon for him like I'd seen dog trainers do, Lucky slammed to a stop and stood there while I scared the bird up. He watched it intently as it flew away; he didn't offer to chase it. "Can't be," my dad said. "Got to be something."

I have two brothers and every year, the night before the first day of the hunting season (which was an excused absence from school in those days), we would ceremonially sleep on two sofa beds in a guest bedroom with all the windows open. Since it was the middle of November the nights were often cold, but that was part of the tradition. To this day, I associate the feel of cold air against my face as I sleep with the excitement of the night before the season opener. The night before we tried Lucky out was even more exciting than usual. He was my dog and I knew from the beginning that having your own dog made an already fantastic experience unfathomably better.

Early in the morning our dad came into the room. "Rise and shine. Hit the deck. Jesus Christ, it's colder than Billy Hell in here." We loved it when my dad swore. It was strictly forbidden by our mother, so when he did it we felt somehow closer to him. The idea of being grown up someday didn't seem quite so impossible. We piled out of bed and into our hunting clothes, which meant our old clothes. We were downstairs in the kitchen in time to see Dad bring the first batch of burned pancakes out of the oven.

Only on rare occasions was Dad not at work by the time we got up, and on those mornings my mother stood aside. Only one pheasant opener morning do I remember my mother cooking our breakfast. That year, my dad had to work and, since it was unthinkable that we kids wouldn't go hunting, she took over. It's not that unusual now but in the fifties there weren't many women in the field. Now, every time I see Kris dressed for the hunt I think of my mother, a lady with dungarees tucked into rubber boots and wearing a sweatshirt from my father's college days. She didn't know that much about guns and almost nothing about hunting—she was there to be sure her three boys were safe. She was beautiful.

My mother is renowned for her wisdom, so there probably were several reasons why, on opening day, she would leave the kitchen entirely to us. I wonder if the main reason wasn't the pain of watching my dad cook. She was a bit of a gourmet for those days and there was always plenty of wonderful food around when we were kids. But sauces and soufflés can't hold a candle to breakfasts cooked by your father on the first day of the pheasant season.

To say the least, those meals were unusual. They consisted of stuff we wouldn't have eaten in a million years if our mother had fixed it. There were runny eggs and burnt French toast, hot Italian sausage, lumpy oatmeal, cornmeal mush, and—if dad had done the shopping—buttermilk and head cheese. I cringe to think of it now, though at the time we loved it, gobbling everything put in front of us. Our favorite was the greasy fried potatoes. I still use Dad's recipe. He started with one yellow onion fried in the grease left from a pound of bacon. In those days all potatoes were peeled before they were cooked but my dad had a certain pioneering flair. Every season opener he committed an act of unheard-of culinary daring by throwing sliced, unpeeled potatoes into the sizzling grease. Just before they were done, he sliced a second onion into the whole mess. We used lots of ketchup and ate every bite.

The rules of engagement were designed for safety. They were simple: only two guns, one shell for each, my older brother got to carry the 12-gauge, my younger brother and I traded off the 20-gauge, Dad was the full-time field marshal. No one knew where Lucky would fit into the scheme, but it was hoped he knew something about hunting and would, at least, kick a few birds into the air. Till that point Lucky had been an easygoing old dog. He slept a lot and didn't get excited about much. But that morning, sitting between me and my younger brother in the backseat of the station wagon, his personality changed. He watched attentively out the windshield. He trembled and whined. He refused to be calmed by ear scratching. My dad glanced at him in the rearview mirror and raised his eyebrows.

It took a few minutes for us to get organized, and Lucky barked from the backseat the whole time. But once the skirmish line was formed and we began to advance through the weedy corn stubble, Lucky started to quarter like a pro. We hadn't gone a hundred yards into the field when his gait went soft. He turned into the wind and pussyfooted to a solid point. After an instant of disbelief, my dad took over. "Scott, move up on the right. Be ready. Mike, leave the gun on safety, move to your left. No, no. Left. That way." He pointed out the exact spot for my little brother. "Handle your dog, Dan. Everybody be careful. I'll flush."

Nobody really believed there was a bird in front of Lucky, so when the rooster pounded from under a crumpled cornstalk there were four exclamations of surprise preceding two completely wild shots. The pheasant sailed, unscathed, across the cornfield. Lucky followed him for thirty feet, then stopped. We all watched the pheasant disappear into a distant grove. "I'll be dipped in shit," Dad whispered.

It took a few minutes to rally the troops. Some strategic changes were made: Scott was given two shells for the 12-gauge pump, Mike was demoted to dog handler, and I was given the old side-by-side 20 and two shells. "All right," Dad said, "let's bear down." He turned to Lucky. "Find the birds, boy."

A hundred yards farther on Lucky slammed onto point and we fanned out into position. The bird came up perfectly. A shotgun roared once—twice. The rooster lined out. A third shot. A fourth. And we all watched the bird follow his buddy into the trees. "Well, for Christ's sake," Dad said.

Then there was silence. We all looked up at him and his gaze moved slowly from face to face. When he finally spoke again his voice was flat and determined. "Give me a gun," he said.

The next two points were hens and Dad held up on them expertly. Scott, Mike, Lucky, and I watched them go and prayed the next would be a rooster. Dad shot left-handed and we figured he was about the best shot in the world. Only now do I understand the pressure that was on the man, and only now do I appreciate his coolness when a rooster did come up. I can see it in slow motion: Lucky pointing again, Scott moving in to flush, the cackle, and the elegant shape catapulting skyward. The gun came up easily, following behind the bird as it leveled off. Dad swung through just as the stock touched his cheek, and the rooster crumpled. I don't remember hearing the shot, but I can still hear the cheers.

The crowd went wild. It was the most fantastic shot ever made and my dad hammed it up, finally raising his hands in a show of false modesty and to ask for calm. When we settled down, Dad sent us out to pick up the pheasant. It had clearly fallen dead and no one thought there would be any trouble finding it. "Right there," Dad said. He pointed and walked right to the spot. But all he found were a few feathers.

"Hey," Mike said. "Where's Lucky?"

We all looked around. No bird and no dog. Then I saw Lucky,

running toward us from the far side of the field. He bounced with happiness and came right to my feet for a pet. He didn't look sheepish but his muzzle was covered with dirt.

"The rotten cur," Dad said. "He buried my pheasant." Silence settled on us. We looked at Lucky, who panted and wagged his stubby tail. His front paws carried evidence, too. Everyone stared at him, and he realized that we had found the fault that had made him a liability at the shooting preserve.

We never found that first pheasant. But we ended up taking three birds home that afternoon. It just took a little creative hunting. We divided our efforts into three basic jobs, two shooters, one flusher, and one dog tackler. If the shooters did their job, then the tackler had to do his. And tackling a determined German shorthair in the open field is no easy task. But we got good at it, and even though breaking up the hunting day with wind sprints was frustrating, we came to love that old dog. He certainly made bird hunting more interesting and helped set the course of my life. I haven't ventured into the field without a dog since.

Since the days of Lucky there have been many dogs. Though it has been a while since I've had a dog with a vice as severe as bird burying, I've never had a perfect one either. The one thing you can say with certainty about dogs is that every one is different. The summer Kris was getting ready to head east we had three dogs that proved that point.

Idaho Spud was ten years old that summer. He's a black and white English setter from a big running strain in the Northwest. To date, he's the best bird dog I've ever had and has gained some fame in falconry circles for his brains and his ability to find birds. A few people have thought enough of him to have him sire litters, and that spring he had hosted a nice little bitch from Wyoming for a romantic weekend. Since then he had been feeling pretty frisky, but he was no pup and there was a hitch in his gait that bothered me.

He had never been a dog to take care of himself. He's a sweetheart, always ready for a pet or a cuddle, but he's tough as rawhide. He'll run in ice and snow, sandburs, swamps, through barbed wire and broken glass. He's been lost overnight in below-zero weather, been stomped by cows, fallen off cliffs, killed coons, cats, badgers, and one coyote. He's pointed every North American game bird, including wild turkeys. In ten seasons I'd never seen him quit or even slow down. So even though he might have earned that little hitch in his gait, it surprised me. I guess I never thought he'd grow old.

Taking a closer look, I saw that his hindquarters were no longer like Christmas hams, his muzzle had grayed, his coat had lost some sheen, and there was an incipient clouding in his eyes. I still thought of him as the hard-headed puppy he had been until his third year. He had been a nightmare to break, a happy, playful dog, with a fantastic *way of going*, but a bird-chasing maniac. Even at ten, you had to talk tough to him if you wanted him to hold his birds. But boy, could he find them. When it soaked in that Spud might not be around forever, I took a good look at his backup.

Way of Going. The quality of a dog's gait; the way he carries himself.

Old Hemlock Melville is a big, goofy, slow-moving setter from one of the most famous lines in the world. He was just coming on four that summer but in many ways was still a puppy. Even though his lack of speed made him something of a mismatch for our big rolling grasslands, he had won a solid place in our hearts.

Mel thinks that Spud is the greatest dog on earth, his hero, and he will *honor* Spud's points from any distance. I had high hopes for Mel as a falcon dog; so far, however, he was finding only half as many birds as Spud. Though he had only a fraction of Spud's drive, he was a gentleman, a natural *backer* who made few mistakes. While Spud found lots of birds, he mishandled many of them. Mel didn't find as many but he was careful, smart, and, above all, hunted with you. Because Mel looked at hunting as a team sport, he was a piece of cake to handle. From his first year on, he was Kris's buddy and favorite hunting partner.

Honor. The action of a dog when it freezes upon seeing another dog on point. Usually only the first dog scents the birds.

Back. The action of a dog when it stops behind another dog that is on point. Generally, both dogs can scent the game.

On our annual woodcock hunt in New Brunswick the fall before, Mel had come on strong. Again, he hadn't found the birds that some of the other dogs had; when he found one, though, he found it within sight of the hunters and held it. His long feathering, massive head, sad eyes, and old-fashioned low tail can't help but make you feel like part of an oil painting as you walk in front of him with your double-barrel held high. When you hunt with Mel, there are no extended expeditions deep into unknown woodcock swamps in search of the distant signal from a beeper collar. No yelling is necessary, no discipline. He's a pleasure to hunt with even if you aren't shooting birds. He moves at his slow pace and saves himself for the cocktail party afterward. The classic Old Hemlock head and shiny orange *Belton* coat look great in front of the fire at the lodge. If we'd allow it, Mel would drink single-malt Scotch and smoke a pipe. He's an amiable dog who enjoys the company of other hunters. He seems to have trouble understanding why the rest of the dogs are too exhausted to join the party.

Belton. A color phase of dog, usually an English setter, in which the black or orange is distributed in very small spots over a coat of white.

Mel's saggy face surprises some people. To those used to modern setters he might look more like a thin Saint Bernard, but he is a gun hunter's dream, especially if the hunting is done in the close *cover* he was bred for. Sharp-tailed grouse live in 5,000-acre fields with no trees in sight, however, and Mel had not proved himself in that terrain. At his New Brunswick pace it would take Mel a month to hunt 5,000 acres. His brains and biddability might make the difference, yet when I looked at him in light of Spud's advanced years, I got nervous. If Spud pooped out on me and Mel wasn't yet ready to come off the bench, what would I do?

Cover. An area that is likely to hold birds, usually woodcock or ruffed grouse. Sometimes called covert.

There was one other possibility. For the past four years our woodcock hunt had included a guide who specialized in close-working springer spaniels. His springs are small and attentive and can be tucked away, by the half dozen, in a setter-size dog box. Though they're energetic and happy, they're short-legged and dumpy compared to the tall, feathered setters around which the hunt revolves. They look like dwarf setters with bobbed tails, the kind of dog Danny DeVito might own. They snort and wiggle in an ignoble way and have been tagged with the affectionate nickname of the trolls. The banter between the springer and the setter folks goes on the entire week. While it's agreed that setters bring a certain quality to the hunt, it is also the overwhelming opinion of both sides that the springers are more efficient for bringing birds to the bag. They're little machines; it's like turning a pack of Hoover vacuums loose in a cover. Whatever's in the bushes comes out, and it comes out within shotgun range. If it gets shot, it gets retrieved. You don't lose birds when there is a troll along. And you never lose a troll, either. In fact, they're forever underfoot wanting to know what you want them to do next. Over the years I came to love these little monsters and thought they might have a tremendous application in the kind of falconry we do on the Great Plains. The British use similar dogs to flush ptarmigan that have been pointed by other dogs, something I'd always thought made sense. I've encouraged some of my setters to flush, and that, of course, softens their points. But if you flush yourself, the quarry makes the decision when to go. Whether you're forty feet or two inches away, a grouse will wait until the falcon is in less-than-perfect position. We also fly at a lot of grouse and partridge that are not pointed—a flock settles into a grainfield ahead of us, a few heads are spotted in the grass. I thought situations like this cried out for a troll, so when I heard that our guide had a new litter, I told him to pick a small, smart, active bitch and send her down.

We named her Moose, not for her size but in honor of her home province of New Brunswick. The name is versatile and can serve as a nickname for *mus musculus* (the scientific name for house mouse), or the more feminine Moose-Anne. She is exactly what I ordered, small, smart, and unbelievably active. She never stops moving. From the day she arrived she's been flying around the house and yard, her front feet hitting the ground with half the frequency of her hind feet. There is always something in her mouth—her coveted slipper, a ball, a stick, a chunk of firewood, a deer bone, a stone, a dead mouse, a horse apple, a screwdriver. She must have slept in the first six months we had her but I never caught her at it. By the time Mel has gathered himself to jump into the back of the pickup, Moose has sailed up and down a half-dozen times. She is a 45 RPM dog in a 33⅓ world. I had no idea what might happen if I had to elevate her to a starting position on the grouse team.

A sobering thought was that all my worry about having a good dog to use on sharptails that fall might well be moot. The falcon I hoped to get back from the hack was no sure thing. First, the chances of losing her at hack were great, and second, few first-year birds are really good grouse hawks. I figured I'd be lucky to catch a dozen partridge with her. That left me with the old intermewed falcons.

Little Bird was a fourth-year Barbary *falcon* that we had flown almost exclusively at release Hungarian partridge. She was a beautiful bird with a light slate back and a buff front with a few delicate horizontal flecks of black. Her manners were perfect, and she was easy to hood and pick up off a kill or the *lure*, and tame as a house cat, if she liked you. If she didn't, though, or if you wore a hat or were a dog she'd never seen before, she lost her mind. Erney had a special relationship with Little Bird; I was just tolerated.

Falcon. Purists follow the ancients' lead and use the term falcon to refer only to the female peregrine falcon. But it also can mean a female of any species of falcon. A still more general usage applies to any of the long-winged birds of prey, male or female, as opposed to the short-winged hawks.

Lure. The usually leather pouch garnished with meat and swung to call a falcon to the falconer. Falcons are fed on the lure.

She flew at just under twenty ounces, and could put on a show. When she was on her game, she flew as well as any bird I've ever seen. Her normal pitch was in the realm of "just a speck," and from that height partridge had no chance—unless, of course, she decided not to drive through them the way the really good ones always do. When Little Bird was *cast off*, you could be sure she'd go up high and *wait on*, but that was about it. In the three years we'd flown her she'd caught a lot of release partridge, many of them in great style, but she'd never looked at a duck and she'd bounced off grouse like a tennis ball. She had gained a reputation as a temperamental sandbagger. I didn't have a lot of hope for making her a first-rate *game hawk*, but my plan was to try.

Cast. A pair of falcons flown together. Also, to hold a falcon or haw, as when jesses and bells are being attached. Also, to launch a bird into the air from the fist; to cast off.

Wait On. To go to a height above the falconer and dogs and stay there until the game is flushed.

Game Hawk. This term does not usually refer to hawks at all but to a falcon trained to catch game birds from a pitch.

Dundee was a second-year, fully hacked Australian peregrine tiercel with an unusually sweet disposition. We flew him at about eighteen ounces, but weight didn't seem to matter. He was the kind of bird that was always happy to see you. He would *bate* at you even with a full *crop* and would crawl onto your fist when you were tying another bird to the perch beside him. When you raised the hood to him, he would stand on tiptoe to get his head inside and anyone could handle him. But those endearing characteristics don't make a good game hawk and, in fact, he was a lousy hawk: the only bird I know of that never did learn to wait on.

Bate. To fly from the fist or a perch and be brought up short by the leash. This is to be avoided.

Crop. The membranous pouch in the gullet of a bird where food is stored before it is digested.

His poor showing as a game hawk was, no doubt, my doing. I had made him a *mar-hawk*. For decades, I have harbored a desire to fly falcons "out of the hood" instead of the more traditional "waiting on" style of flying. When a falcon waits on she is allowed to gain altitude over the quarry before it is flushed. When a falcon is flown out of the hood, the quarry is flushed when the falcon is still hooded and on the fist. At the flush, the hood is struck and the chase begins. It is admittedly a more basic approach, but natural, and very demanding. It's the kind of falconry practiced in Arab countries, but because we in North America are so heavily influenced by British falconry, we look down on flying out of the hood, even though much of our terrain and quarry are perhaps better suited to that style.

Mar-hawk. A bird that has been spoiled in some way by the falconer.

I did it seriously one year when the grouse population around the ranch crashed and the white-tailed jackrabbit population skyrocketed. I had great fun that winter with a gyrfalcon, a sharpshod cow horse we used to rope calves in the spring, and a muzzled Saluki given to me by a Canadian falconer friend. Galloping over the treacherously icy prairie in pursuit of falcon, dog, and ten-pound rabbit whetted my appetite for that kind of falconry. (It also, incidentally, confirmed something I always suspected but didn't want to admit: that things are even more interesting if there's a chance you'll get killed.)

I thought flying a falcon out of the hood would be easy compared with training it to wait on. And it might be, if you know what you're doing. But I didn't and Dundee suffered for my ignorance. Even though he had spent thirty days flying at hack, he never really caught on to flying birds down. By the time I decided to give up, it was too late to get him back on track for waiting on.

Erney and I agreed that we had ruined him. Because he'd had a lot of air time, was in great physical shape, and had had his hack, we tried to turn him loose the spring of his first year. He wouldn't go. He hung around and picked off our homing pigeons using a variety of ignominious methods, until we brought him in and kept him. I think it made everyone happy. Dundee was glad to get back into his mews, and Erney and I were glad to have such a cheerful little guy around.

Erney had given up on making him a hunting hawk of any kind for good reasons. Now with this chance to devote full time to falconry, I believed it was possible to get him catching birds. In fact, I thought the stars might be right to get a falcon performing on doves, and that Dundee might be the bird.

But my main hope for a successful season was in the hackbox. The day before I left to drive Kris to New Hampshire, Erney and I sat on the deck planning just how we hoped the hack would go. The three falcons would stay in the box another five days. That would give me time to drive Kris to New Hampshire and the falcons time to mature to the point of being able to be fledged. I'd fly back from Boston the evening before we opened the box and let the birds free. All Erney had to do was check on the falcons and feed them, skipping the last day's feeding to ensure that they'd be hungry enough to stick around long enough to at least get the lay of the land before they tried their wings. We'd both be on hand for those critical first days of liberty.

We sat at the picnic table sipping our coffee and trying to think if we had forgotten anything. We stared out to the east and watched as a mule deer doe herded her twins out of the draw and into some distant plum bushes. In the summertime we spend a lot of time on the deck, looking out over the big draw that is continually offering up natural phenomena like the doe and her fawns. We use the deck as an observation platform and I have no idea how we ever got along without it.

Erney and I built it and put a pair of sliding glass doors on the east side of the old house five years before. As with almost all our projects, there was grave debate over construction philosophy. Erney is a minimalist. He believes it's a waste to build anything bigger or stronger than absolutely necessary. I, on the other hand, tend to overbuild. Too often I have seen South Dakota weather twist and smash structures that were underdesigned. Discussion about size of foundations, distance between joists, even number of nails per board, can get heated. But in the end things do get built.

The deck has a great view to the east and south and would give us a clear view of the hackbox if the Russian olive tree at the edge of the deck weren't doing so well. Growing trees on the Great Plains is like growing cactus in Alaska. They're not meant to be there and it takes ingenuity and tenacity to get them to survive, let alone thrive. The reason for the Russian olive's health is that when we built the deck, we ran the downspout from the roof under the deck and into the tree's basin. It gets twenty times the normal rainfall and as a result is the fastest growing tree in the county. We're pretty proud of it but it does make it hard to sit at the picnic table and see exactly what's going on at the hackbox.

As Erney and I sat talking, we periodically glanced among the branches of the Russian olive and sometimes caught the movement of one of the birds behind the protective bars of the box. We weren't paying much attention; there was some movement, a bird was flapping. Then there was *kakking* and Erney and I shot to our feet. It was the noise used to ward off trespassers. We immediately thought of the golden eagles who were nesting on the east side of the ranch. They could be deadly to falcons, so I jumped to the deck's lowest level, intending to reveal myself fully and scare off whatever might be harassing the falcons. There was no eagle, but I caught a small brown flash as it disappeared around the barn.

Kakking. A noise made by excited falcons.

"What was it?" Erney asked.

I shook my head. I wasn't sure. "Had to be an *accipiter* of some kind."

Accipiter. A genus of raptor with short wings and a long tail, known for short bursts of speed. *Accipiters* are the true hawks, represented in North America by the sharp-shinned hawk, Cooper's hawk, and goshawk.

"Yep," Erney said, as if that was what he expected. "There was a baby Cooper's hawk trying to catch the pigeons yesterday."

"Great," I said. A Cooper's hawk is smaller than a peregrine and probably wouldn't hurt them, but it could cause all sorts of trouble during a hack. "Well, we may have to do something about him," I said, though I didn't know quite what could be done.

Kris and I left the Black Hills on a Tuesday. I had a flight out of Boston on Saturday and the falcons would be released on Sunday. The plan was to drive through Minnesota, across the Upper Peninsula of Michigan, cut across Ontario to Montreal, then travel straight down to Hanover, New Hampshire. The drive was over 2,000 miles so there wasn't much extra time, but if Jim Harrison was going to be at his cabin in northern Michigan, we wanted to stop and visit. If it was possible, we wanted to view him in his native habitat.

Jim is a well-known writer, hunter, fisherman, gourmet, and gourmand, connoisseur of all manner of earthly delights. I first met him in a motel in Rapid City, South Dakota. He was passing through with another writer, Dan Gerber, and called to tell me he had read one of my books, *The Rites of Autumn*, and liked it. He wanted to meet me. I'd never heard his gravelly voice and assumed someone was playing a trick on me. All my friends knew he was something of a hero of mine. Kris and I both half-expected a gang of people to jump out of the motel room and have a good laugh on us.

But it really was Harrison. He roared for us to come in. The first thing he did was to offer us a glass of whiskey. "Sorry," he said. "We don't have any mix. There might be some ice, if you want it."

That was a good start and things warmed up from there. The evening culminated at a Chinese restaurant, where Harrison ordered for everyone. "We'll take page two," he said to the waitress. "And don't bring any of those little boxes. We'll eat it here." It was a grand evening. Kris and Jim hit it off and kept up a continuous chatter about food and cooking techniques. We made plans for Jim and Dan to come out to the ranch the next day to watch me work a very young falcon.

Jim is a big guy. He really does remind me of a bear. He's built like a bear and talks like a bear would talk. There is also a genuine wildness to his face due, in part, to a glass eye that is permanently fixed on the horizon. He claims to have lost the eye in grade school, in his first encounter with a woman. Jim's looks belie the man underneath. He is generous, curious, and sensitive to all sorts of animals. With the possible exception of English setters—he is the one who recommended Melville's line to me—birds seem to be his favorite, and he was fascinated by the falcon we flew that morning.

The bird was just a beginner and I was trying to encourage him to go up high and wait on. I had brought one of our homing pigeons to toss out for him as a reward if he did happen to go up even a hundred feet. He was not experienced enough to catch a pigeon, unless it did something stupid, but he loved to chase them.

Jim watched the falcon leave my fist and circle us as we stood in the middle of a 1,000-acre flat of wheat stubble and grass. His functional eye followed the flight and a grin came across his face. The falcon was going up and I knew that when I threw the pigeon, Jim's grin would explode into a smile. I flipped the pigeon out and when the falcon started his stoop I turned to watch Jim.

There was this block of a man, a mile from the nearest cover of any kind, with his legs spread and his hands on his hips. Were it not for the glass eye, the look on his face could have been that of a joyous and innocent child. But as I watched him, the smile began to fade. I looked back toward the birds and saw that the pigeon had turned. The falcon was right on its tail and it was heading for the only haven in sight, Harrison.

Jim's face went ashen. The shadow of the plummeting birds came over him and he looked like a heavy, one-eyed Wile E. Coyote about to be leveled by an anvil. But Jim can move a lot faster than you might think. The instant the pigeon took refuge behind his left leg and a split second before the falcon piled in talons first, the big man dived to the right. He landed on his stomach ten feet from where the falcon and pigeon rolled in a feathered tangle. The earth shook and a small puff of dust rose.

I was doubled over with laughter and even Jim had to smile. He rolled into a sitting position and spit out some dirt. "I thought the little son of a bitch was going for my good eye," he said.

When we called Jim, he said our timing was good. He was just heading up to his cabin to get some work done. He added that his wife, Linda, had been after him to lose some weight for the upcoming bird season, and he thought isolation might help. We could meet there, spend the night, and get out early the next morning. That was perfect. It took us most of the day to cross the top of Wisconsin and run almost the entire length of the Upper Peninsula. We passed through hundreds of miles of woodcock and grouse covers and threatened to return some day to check them out. The sun was low over Lake Superior when we took a thirty-second tour of the tiny town closest to Jim's cabin.

Ten minutes later we came to a dirt driveway angling off into the Northwoods. From our written directions, this had to be the place, but there was a big sign telling us to keep out. Maybe this wasn't right. We drove on down the back road but found nothing and returned to the sign. With reservation we began our winding descent into the bush. It looked like a good ruffed grouse cover, just the kind of place I expected, but there were more discouraging signs. KEEP OUT. GO BACK. NO TRESPASSING. But we pushed on and slowly the signs began to take on a certain Dantean ring.

We were on the right track and two twists of the road later we pulled into an idyllic clearing with a trout stream moving in front of a small but substantial log cabin. It had to be the right place. It was like stepping into Jim's book *Sun Dogs*. A Land Cruiser was pulled up beside the house with its back door flung open. What looked like a medium-sized black bear in Bermuda shorts and flipflops was rooting through boxes and books piled in the back.

Jim turned to give Kris a hug and to shake my hand. "Good to see you. I just got here myself. I was thinking about dinner."

"I thought Linda had you on a bird-hunter's diet," Kris said with a little ribbing in her voice.

"She packed a box of food for me," Jim said, and turned back to the car. Kris and I leaned over his shoulder as he pawed through the box. He checked everything out closely, then let his head drop. "Just as I thought," he said. "A fucking whole-grain nightmare."

Then he reached deeper into the car and brought out another box: "Good thing I stopped on the way and did some shopping." He led the way into the cabin, and in the box he carried I could see at least two bottles of wine resting on a bundle of white butcher's paper.

The cabin's kitchen was functional but small. I, being unskilled labor, was chased out to start the charcoal while Jim built the salad and Kris peeled and crushed garlic. When I came back inside for a second glass of cabernet, Kris and Jim were happily slicing away at twin cutting boards and talking about the virtues of jicama. I looked over Kris's shoulder and saw that she had already crushed a handful of garlic. She took one more head from a brown paper bag, held it up, and asked Jim if he wanted her to do another one. Jim looked at the pile on the cutting board. "Oh," he said, "might as well do them all." He reached over and dumped out the bag. There were at least ten more heads.

When Kris and I looked at him in disbelief, he shrugged. "It's not a seasoning," he said. "It's a vegetable."

The plan was to rub all the garlic into the meat he'd bought. When he pulled the bloody package from the box, I couldn't believe my eyes. It looked like a mastodon steak, but Jim assured us it was beef. It had to weigh six pounds and when he rolled it, encrusted with a half-inch glaze of garlic, onto the grill, I worried it would put my fire out.

But it cooked just fine, well done for the outside quarter-inch and cooling to a full inch-and-a-half center strip of cherry red Black Angus. The garlic was perfect, the salad and sugar peas just right. There was plenty of good red wine and we talked about books, politics, and brook trout. I had done most of the driving that day and so I faded first. I crawled up into the loft and flopped on the bed. The reflection of the fire played on the ceiling and I rolled over to point my good ear to the conversation about the philosophy behind a novel Jim was working on, then about Kris's fellowship. The last thing I remember hearing was a discussion about the ethics of critical-care medicine: When do you pull the plug on a terminally ill patient? The voices sounded wise. The people below, sitting in front of the fire, sounded mature and responsible. They were engaged in the vital organs of life and I couldn't help but wonder if the same could be said of me. Could a passion for grass and falcons be compared with concern for human pain and the philosophies that might explain such suffering? Maybe it was the wine, but stretched out on that bed, knowing what the next four months held for me, I felt trivial, like a stevedore who works the deck but knows nothing of how the ship is run.

There was just enough garlic steak left for a grand breakfast and as I slid into the driver's seat I joked that I'd have to hold my hand over my mouth every time we stopped for gas. Jim was shaking my hand. "If they don't like garlic," he said, "fuck 'em."

After clearing customs at Sault Sainte Marie, we began the long, mostly single-lane trek to Montreal. I have always liked Canada and Canadians. The people have a great attitude about life, like Australians, only coherent. A higher percentage of Canadians hunt than Americans and they drink more beer. They have more wild country than just about any other place on Earth. But parts of the diagonal across Ontario, from the Sault to Montreal, are not pretty.

There was heavy summer traffic, and everything—bridges, roads, gas stations—seemed to be under construction. It took half again as long as it should have, and were it not for the ripe blueberries being sold cheap along the road, it would have been torture.

Mining had made a moonscape around Sudbury, but the bushes that were struggling back were purple with blueberries. To add to the poor traffic conditions, the cars of local pickers were stopped haphazardly at every imaginable turnout. Because we were already behind schedule, we didn't even try to pick our own. We pulled to a halt at a rickety stand and bought the smallest basket for sale. That was two kilos of blueberries, enough to give an entire Boy Scout troop terminal dysentery.

We were careful and Kris meted out the sweet berries as if they were prescription drugs. It was a fine fruit experience. That was all we ate until we crossed back into the United States. There were still several pounds of blueberries in the basket and we had to make a special stop and bury them in the back of the Explorer under the stereo, where we couldn't get at them. We couldn't bring ourselves to throw them away.

Our last night on the road was spent in Burlington, Vermont. The plan was to get into Hanover the next morning, find Kris's rental house, and get things moved in. The next day we'd be off to Boston, and I'd catch a plane to South Dakota.

The house had been billed as a country place where we would be able to keep a couple of dogs when I finally came out to stay. The roads in South Dakota are straight. If you miss someone's place by a mile or two, you are usually in sight of it. You just go to the next road and head back in the right direction. I learned pretty quickly that New England is not like that. It took a while to find the house, but finally the country opened into a five-acre field and there it was, a nice, little yellow house surrounded by ruffed grouse woods and within twenty minutes of Dartmouth-Hitchcock Hospital. When I saw a tree, bigger than anything in front of the house, the feeling that had been just under the surface throughout the drive came out. I was gripped with regret. Suddenly, I wasn't sure I wanted to leave.

The no-nonsense New England landlady met us in the driveway. She went through the operation of the house like it was the preflight checklist for a Phantom jet. As I listened to her explanation of how the electric heat worked and when the recycling would be picked up, I thought she would be relieved if she knew what it takes to maintain a place where humanity's grip on the land is still tenuous. The stone wall that separated this pleasant front yard from the cultivated forest beyond was almost two hundred years old when the first white settler laid eyes on the land that is now our ranch. She was worried about her house deteriorating. When I think about taking care of a place, I think in terms of keeping it from disappearing altogether. It didn't look like there was much danger of that happening here, but we listened to all her warnings and feigned close attention to her suggestions.

It was not yet noon when we were left alone. We unloaded most of the car, then went to town for lunch. Ten years before, Kris had been a medical student here and a few of the good restaurants from that era survived. She took me to a charming Italian place on the main street of Hanover and we ate a lunch you simply cannot find in Rapid City, South Dakota.

After the meal we went to a café down the street and sat watching the Dartmouth summer students pass outside the window. The café was called the Dirt Cowboy for reasons I still don't understand. I'd be willing to bet that I was the closest thing to a cowboy that had ever scarfed a scone in that establishment. There were no shitty boots, no sweaty hatbands, no puckered Copenhagen lips. Everyone who came in the café or passed the front wore frumpy L.L. Bean clothes and pale New England complexions. Sitting at the window table in new Patagonia shorts, enjoying a double latte mocha, I had to smile. It was that luscious feeling of getting away with something, like being mistaken for the groom at a high-society wedding.

It was after dark when we finished settling Kris into the house. The day had been warm and humid and the night didn't cool the way it does in South Dakota. I didn't sleep well. It was impossible for me not to be reminded of Kris's old dog, Jake.

For ten years Kris has carried a photograph of me in her wallet. In the picture, I'm kneeling in front of a reservoir not five miles from where I lay sleepless that night. I'm wearing a heavy coat and looking very young. My arms are wrapped around a big black dog. The dog has a red bandanna around his neck and we are both clearly happy. Kris claims it's her favorite picture.

Kris's affinity for dogs is nearly paranormal. She has a knack for knowing what they're thinking and what they want. But when we first met, her attraction to dogs was indiscriminate, embracing schizophrenic Pomeranians as passionately as it did finely focused English pointers. This, I was sure, was because she had never seen a dog doing what a dog does best—hunting. I like to think that it was my influence that created in Kris an understanding and love for hunting dogs, what they do, and how they can enrich your life. But lying there trying to sleep that sultry New England night, I understood that the real credit had to go to Jake. He knew her long before I was on the scene.

Kris was raised in Southern California. She never had the chance to see a trained dog locate, point, or retrieve a bird. But she had a good companion when I first met her. Jake was an eighty-pound Lab–golden retriever cross that had been with her since she started medical school. One of the first serious things she ever said to me was that she wouldn't have made it through if it weren't for Jake.

He was with her the whole way, bounced around from city to city, keeping her company when she was studying, and sometimes waiting indoors for sixteen hours at a stretch until she could get home to walk him. She told me that some nights, when she got home, the combination of long hours and sub-zero temperatures conspired to depress her to tears. But Jake was always there to greet her and they walked every night, and that's what gave her the strength to get up the next morning and do it again.

That she had learned the restorative powers of a relationship with a dog told me she was special. And that Jake had been the one to teach her made him special, too. I had always dreamed of finding a woman who would enjoy being afield with me and a dog, and those two gave me hope that that might not be too farfetched.

Jake got his looks from his Lab side. Except for slightly longer hair, you'd never have known he wasn't pure Lab. He had one of those heads that could have been carved from granite, and a gentle way of looking at you—as if he felt vaguely sorry for you, being human and all. Like so many of the really good ones, Jake seemed to know how he could best support the people with whom he lived. After Kris moved on to her internship and residency, when she had even less time, and I started hanging around more, Jake shifted a portion of his allegiance to me. I'm sure he knew it was what Kris wanted, and I was grateful to be included.

After medical school Kris engineered a two-year residency in Denver, and since it was only 300 miles away from the ranch, I took to spending a lot of time there. I was used to sleeping alone, and while sharing a bed with Kris was a welcome change, sharing a bed with Kris and Jake was not exactly what I had had in mind. I remember coming face to face with Jake one of those first nights. He stared at me unflinchingly and I realized that it was I who was the inter-loper here. I was infringing on the unity of a serious, well-function-ing team, and so Jake stayed on the bed.

During residency Kris was putting in fourteen-hour days with every third night on call. Jake and I were thrown together and it was good for both of us. Her house was on a busy street. The traffic was confining—something new for me—and Jake and I used it as a good excuse to escape the city.

We began going on extended walks in more remote places than Jake was used to. Kris was a little protective of him, suggesting, for example, that he wouldn't eat dog food without cooking oil on it and that November water was too cold for him to retrieve sticks from. She made it sound as if Jake preferred tofu to T-bones. But after I started taking him to the ranch and he met Spud, who was just a pup then, and an old basset hound named Morgan, I came to know something about Jake that I had suspected all along.

Morgan had been an ace-high rabbit-hawking dog, but was retired by then. He was like an old demented pensioner returning to the office out of habit. He got up early, had a little drink of water, and usually struck a trail about seven-thirty. He'd work that rabbit until about noon, come into the house for another drink, and snooze until about four o'clock, when he'd get drowsily to his feet, stretch, amble to the door, and let out one assertive bellow. He'd run another bunny for the rest of the day. A little while after dark he'd come in to eat and sleep and it would start all over again the next morning. When I think of Morgan I think of James Gavin's descrip-tion of scent in his book *The Meadow*. He saw it as a vaporous blue contrail that fades with time. I love to imagine being able to see those streaks and watching old Morgan sorting through them to find the brightest one.

He was slow and inefficient but he'd had hundreds of rabbits caught by hawks in front of him. To my knowledge Morgan never caught a rabbit on his own. When he came baying up on the jumble of fur and feather at the end of the trail, he would simply turn and go find another track. I'm not sure he ever even saw a rabbit without a red-tailed hawk stuck to it. He must have thought he was trailing some sort of griffin-type beast, part hawk, part rabbit.

Morgan took his work seriously and didn't pay much attention to this big, black, city dog who stayed in the house. But several times I caught Jake watching Morgan from the kitchen window, studying the old-timer as he snooped through the overgrown haying equipment, and it wasn't long before the black ears came up and the eyes danced at the sound of Morgan's strike.

Jake acted indifferent when he saw me picking up a falcon and heading out to hunt, but he couldn't help glancing at Spud and me as we went through yard training. The whole ranch scene, with its cacophony of bird noises and new smells, made him a little nervous and though he disdained close contact with Spud and Morgan, he couldn't help being interested. When Kris came out to the ranch and made a fuss over these two ruffians, it threw Jake into a tailspin.

It was about that time that Kris began to take an interest herself —in me, I suppose, but more specifically, in the elements of my life. She asked about the falcon hoods, the electric collar, the dog boxes and hawk perches built into the back of the pickup. She watched Spud point a grouse wing and was fascinated by the way this little moron puppy went deadly serious over a game. She watched steady old Morgan going about his appointed rounds and began to see how important it all was to me.

After about the third visit, she wondered if, the next time, she might try shooting a shotgun and I, of course, bent over backward to comply. I planned to let her shoot my side-by-side 20 but Erney shook his head. "That's a mistake," he said. "She won't hit anything and a light little thing like that will kick her silly." When Kris arrived at the ranch for her first shooting lesson, I had a brand-new Remington 1100 12-gauge with open choke and a shortened stock waiting for her—ugly, but no kick and maximum chance for success.

Before there was any shooting, however, we had to put Jake in the basement. Though he'd never seen a gun before, he was apparently shy of explosions. Kris said he spent most of every Fourth of July trying to get under the refrigerator.

I had a hard time believing it. With little Spud pistoning in his kennel and poor old blind Morgan limping out to investigate every dead clay pigeon, it was hard to imagine that a dog like Jake wouldn't want in on the fun. But it was clear he did not.

After shooting practice, Kris and I came into the house full of good thoughts about the possibility of Kris joining me on a pheasant hunt. The season was half over by then but there might be a way to get in some sort of hunting. She was delighted with the shotgun and the shooting. I was delighted that she was delighted. She even mentioned the idea that Jake might go with us on the hunt.

But when we went into the basement, we found Jake quaking in a corner. It was a terrible sight and my ebullience drained when Kris put her arms around Jake and apologized for shooting. I felt the plans for a pheasant hunt and a woman to share my days in the field slipping away. But it was a dream worth fighting for and I vowed right there that I would.

Thank God Jake loved cheese more than he feared anything.

Kris was skeptical, but after Jake figured out that the sound of a cap gun wrapped in a towel meant cheddar, it wasn't long until the towel was discarded. Another week and you didn't want to be between him and the kitchen when the starter's pistol went off. Finally he'd come full bore across any field for a 12-gauge shot—and a quarter-pound of Gouda.

We at least had a chance. Dog over his gun-shyness, new shotgun, first-time hunter—this had the potential to be fun. But there was another catch. On a picnic during a rare medical school break, when Jake was just a puppy, he had wandered off and been caught in a chicken coop, knee-deep in fresh-plucked chickens. It was the first time Jake had ever seen birds up close but the owner of the chickens wasn't in a forgiving mood and whacked him across the nose. "He hasn't shown much interest in birds since," Kris said.

She swore the punishment had been extremely mild—only a

crisp thump across the muzzle—and I assured her that there would
be no problem. Jake didn't mind gunfire anymore and he loved to
retrieve. His natural instincts would take over and he'd do fine.
That's what I told her. But I'd gotten to know Jake pretty well by
then and knew he learned lessons for keeps. I was worried that his
desire to do what people wanted him to do might extend to that
New Hampshire chicken farmer. In an attempt to avoid a bad day in
the field, I took a Hungarian partridge a falcon had killed the day
before to where Jake and I normally played fetch with tennis balls
and sticks.

He leaped and twisted with joy when I held the stick over his
head and sat, trembling with anticipation, when I gave the com-
mand. I threw the stick twice and he pounded after it, delivering it
to hand when I asked. The third time I surreptitiously substituted
the partridge from my pocket for the stick and sent him off after it
with an encouraging "Fetch." He bore down on the partridge like a
hungry goshawk, but never laid a tooth on it. As soon as he recognized it as a bird he pulled up like it was a cow pie and trotted
quickly back to my side. He looked up at me as if I'd pulled the dirt-
iest trick in the book. I had a problem.

All I could think was that Kris was counting on a pheasant hunt.
I tried to reassure Jake by putting my arm around him. He turned
his head from me and I knew I'd better get him back into retrieving
quick. I got Jake's favorite toy—a green, day-glo Frisbee—and this
snapped him out of his paranoia. He did the happy-dog dance, complete with leaps and yips, and I sailed the Frisbee out for him to
chase. He was a Frisbee pro—a veteran of San Diego beaches and
Ivy League campuses—and made a long, graceful lunge, picking the
disk neatly out of midair. It dawned on me that this might be the
ticket.

I found a roll of duct tape under the seat of my pickup and, out
of Jake's sight, taped the partridge to the top of the Frisbee. Then,
in my most affected voice, I encouraged Jake in his excitement. I
held the Frisbee above him with the partridge safely on top and out

of sight. He again leaped and yipped. When I sent the disk wobbling out into the grass, he charged after it as usual. But when he came close he jumped back like he'd found a rattlesnake. Still, he knew the Frisbee was there and wanted badly to bring it back. He sat down and studied the problem. Finally, he reached out and, with lips curled delicately back, took the edge of the Frisbee in his teeth and dragged the whole works back to lay at my feet. Never did he, in any way, come in contact with the bird.

We had to start with a single tail feather taped to the Frisbee and work up through two feathers, a wing, two wings, and eventually a whole bird. But in a week he was over his dread of birds. I had to tape a pigeon's wings to its sides to get Jake to start putting moving birds in his mouth, but when he figured out what I wanted, he was a natural. In no time he was making seventy-five-yard, blind retrieves and doing them with enthusiasm.

While all this was going on, I was getting Spud ready for his first exposure to pheasants. I didn't expect much from such a pup but figured him to put a few birds into the air. He was such a go-getter I was sure he would hunt hard. Unlike Jake, his problem would be overzealousness, and that was a good kind of problem to have. My fear was not only that Jake might not retrieve, but also that he would just stick close to Kris and not hunt at all. I was afraid he might decide he didn't go for this rowdy life and quit without giving it a chance. I was afraid he might influence Kris to do the same.

All experienced hunters know that bad days happen. You can't let them get you down. Things will be better the next time. But a bad day could be fatal for a thirty-year-old, with high expectations, going hunting with her faithful house dog—both for the first time. If Kris's interest died, I knew my life would veer from its ideal path and I'd find myself hunting mostly alone.

The importance of the pheasant hunt took on cosmic proportions and by the time the day arrived I was a nervous wreck. I worried about Jake drawing a tough old rooster with only a broken wing for his first retrieve, I worried about Kris's shooting. I worried that I wouldn't be able to resist kibitzing.

By the time everything was ready it was late in the season and the wild birds had been worked over pretty hard. In an effort to control some of the variables, I chose a hunting preserve for the outing. Twenty dollars a bird seemed awfully high but we were sure of birds and I reasoned that our team was not exactly a well-oiled hunting machine that could run up a huge bill.

The day dawned gray and the low, flat clouds threatened rain or worse. It was not the kind of day I'd hoped for and I offered up a little prayer to Orion as I loaded the dogs into their boxes. Kris was nearing the end of her residency and we had begun to talk about what might happen the next year. There were job opportunities in California, Chicago, about any big city, but she didn't want that. She had come to like South Dakota and thought she might like the kinds of things we were doing that day. I looked at the sky as we pulled into the shooting preserve. There was a faint streak of blue directly overhead, but the horizon was still chalky and snow was still a possibility.

We drove to a half section of thick bromegrass with old, weedy milo fields along the edge of standing corn. There was a marshy spot where cattails grew thick below a large stock dam, from which we heard the sounds of geese and mallards. We unloaded near the corn and headed along the milo. I carried a gun but wasn't out to shoot. I hoped Spud would find a bird or two and maybe flash-point one. What I was really there for was to see to it that Kris had a good time.

It got off to a bad start. A rooster jumped at her feet before we were thirty yards from the truck and she fired twice before the gun touched her shoulder. She shot fifteen feet over the bird. Jake didn't flinch at the shots but didn't pay much attention to the bird, either. Spud chased it out of sight.

While we waited for the little imp to return, I tried to keep

Kris's mood light. But she's a competitive person and was used to breaking clay pigeons. She was instantly angry at herself—a beginner's mistake—and I was afraid it would affect her whole day. I seldom care if a bird comes to bag, but that day it seemed crucial. I laughed it off: "Everyone misses, forget it. Take your time. You've got lots of time." And the more I talked, the more I knew it was the wrong thing to do. I had to force myself to shut up. We waited in silence and Jake lay down at Kris's feet. When Spud finally returned, Jake got up and sniffed at the huffing little pup as if to ask what the big deal was.

We set off again, walking along the edge of the cattails, and the sky began to clear. The winter browns went rich with shadow and we both praised the changing weather. Suddenly it was pleasant just walking there with Kris. This was more what I'd hoped for. Spud was somewhere in the next county but I wasn't going to let that spoil the day. Jake pottered ahead, and it was possible that he might stumble onto a pheasant. Kris and I were both beginning to enjoy the day when Spud angled in from outer space and flushed a rooster twenty-five yards to our left. It was one of those tough, long, crossing shots. I didn't even pull up on it. But Kris brought her gun up and poked a shot. I winced when I saw the gun barrel stop just before she shot. The bird was forty yards out and going forty miles an hour by then. She missed it by a mile. "You got to keep the gun moving," I said before I thought to say it diplomatically.

Kris frowned. "I don't know about this," she said. It was in the tone of voice I had dreaded for weeks. I felt a touch of panic. It was me. I was driving her crazy.

"Look," I said. "Spud is running amok. I'm going to take him up into that bromegrass, where I can keep an eye on him. You and Jake walk up to the dam, then back through the cattails. There should be birds in the cattails for sure."

I gathered Spud up and headed out. I figured the only chance was to leave her alone and hope the improving weather would work its magic. As I started uphill toward the brome bench, I saw Jake watching me. He looked from me to Kris and back again. At the time I thought he was just confused about our splitting up. But over the years I came to realize that he sensed the tension in the air. Now, lying in that strange New Hampshire bed, it was clear to me that he had been evaluating things—trying to understand what was at stake.

Once Spud and I were alone, the day won me over. As soon as I started to concentrate on the puppy, everything mellowed out. He was wearing down and I stayed on him until he was quartering in front of me fairly well. We worked up through the brome for a few minutes and he bumped a hen. But he only chased it a few yards and seemed to hesitate just before the bird took to the air. After we made the turn and started back, he hit scent and stopped. He held it until I was in range. When it came up, I killed Spud's first bird.

We celebrated with a good petting in the dry grass and for an instant I forgot about Kris and Jake. But when we got walking again, the nagging feeling in the back of my head was still there. When we came to where we could look down on the cattail slough I was holding my breath, hoping Kris and Jake were not back at the pickup.

But they were still hunting the cattails. I resisted the temptation to join them. Spud and I sat down in the golden grass above them. It only took an instant to see that they really didn't know where to look for birds. They wandered to areas that seldom hold them. It was all I could do not to shout directions from the hill. But Jake was out front, quartering within range, and they looked happy enough. Spud was on a lead then and we settled in to watch the woman I love work her first cattail slough with her pet retriever. I was afraid it might be her last, but they didn't look too bad. Their demeanor had changed since I last saw them. They were concentrating on what they were doing, yet somehow casual and relaxed. Something magic had happened in my absence. There was an ease and excitement in Kris's walk I hadn't noticed before, but have seen a thousand times since.

They were certainly pushing birds in front of them. The way they were working the slough, they might just run into a herd of them where the cattails ended. There was a particular corner of firebush that looked good to me and Jake was leading Kris right to it.

I sat up a little as they approached the firebush. Jake's gait picked up. His tail was ringing! He began to bounce and up came a bird. Bang—and it folded. I couldn't believe it. It was beautiful. Jake charged into the brush and brought the bird to Kris. I could hear her whoop with delight.

But Jake didn't bask in the praise. He spit the bird into Kris's hand and dived back into the bushes. Up came another pheasant. Bang. Another perfect retrieve. Back into the bushes. Two birds. Bang. Bang. Kris stopped to reload as Jake searched out the birds.

Then birds were coming up everywhere. Bang! Bang! She had two more down before the rocketing pheasants turned into twenty-dollar bills in my mind. I struggled to my feet. "Wait."

By the time I'd hustled down the hill with Spud straining on the lead ahead of me, Kris had eight birds lined up on the ground. The gun was empty and she was kneeling with her arms around a panting, very happy retriever. She beamed up at me and I beamed back.

For weeks afterward all Kris could talk about was how great the hunt had been. Winter set in with a vengeance then and we didn't get a chance to hunt again that year. But Kris was hooked deep, and as a result we've spent hundreds of days in the field since. That first hunt became part of our history, part of what makes us what we are, part of what had led us to that rented house in New Hampshire.

Not long after that first hunt, old Morgan died, and though you always take the death of a dog hard, we knew it was his time and he'd had a good, full life. The real shock came early that spring, just after Kris and I decided to make our relationship official. It was the spring of Kris's last year of residency and we planned to get married and live in the Black Hills.

Jake had not been his old self for a couple of days, so we took him for a checkup. The vet wanted to keep him overnight for some tests. We really didn't think much about it. But early in the morning—it was a Sunday, because Kris was home—he called to say that Jake had died.

Kris was speechless and handed the phone to me. I listened dumbfounded while this perfectly nice young vet tried to explain. He was very upset and obviously had no idea what had really happened. I listened to him rattle on, searching for the explanation he never found. The cause of death was unknown. But I knew instantly why Jake was dead. It all fell into place for me and the knowledge of it has shaped my life.

Jake died because his job was done. He'd seen Kris through medical school, her internship, and her residency. He'd been there through rough and lonely times. He'd helped transform her from a college girl to a woman. He'd led her through a cattail slough and into a flock of pheasants. He'd eased her into a new, more vital life and he was counting on me to take it from there.

It was a terribly sad time in our lives. Most of the day I held Kris, rocked her, and tried my best to make her see what Jake had given her. But his gifts weren't only for Kris.

Lying in that New Hampshire bed I couldn't help thinking that I might be letting Jake down. He would not have left Kris alone. Every time I closed my eyes I saw his big square head, and the wisdom in his face was haunting.

But the falcons had to be released in less than forty-eight hours. If I lingered even a couple of days they would be too mature to stick around the hacksite long enough to learn the terrain. They might simply bolt from the box and never return. I had created other responsibilities for myself. The falcons and the dogs were counting on me.

Marybeth Holleman

The Heart of the Wind

First publication

A crested auklet flies in front of the boat, left to right, and then curves around and comes back, right to left. It weaves in front of us again and again, playing across the bow, close enough that I can see its round black body, the plume of feathers arching from its forehead, the bright orange thick beak. Looking back toward shore, I see the high cliffs of the island where this bird, and thousands like it, spend their summer raising their young. The treeless tundra makes anything—bird, boulder, bone—stand out in sharp relief. I can see the auklets constantly flying up in great clouds, circling around the immense field of boulders, then settling once more in perfect unison. Every afternoon, nearly all of these birds fly out to float and feed upon the rich bounty of the northern Bering Sea.

Sitting in the bow, the bird flashing across my line of vision, I wonder why this bird is out on the water now, at midday, rather than back with the others. I wonder, too, how it feels to the bird, this movement of boat and water and wind and wing.

"They do that all the time," Steve calls to me from the stern. "One time Warren's kid just reached up and caught one." And he demonstrates, arm up, hand grasping an imaginary auklet.

"What happened?" I ask, imagining this winged being in my own hand, in my fingers already clumsy with cold.

"Don't know. Guess he let it go."

As if understanding our words, the auklet soon ceases its dance. I turn my attention on that which holds me aloft. It's an aluminum boat, 22 feet long, with an outboard and steering column and no cover of any kind. There's only one seat, behind the steering column, and Denny sits in it to steer the boat. Rick, Steve, and I sit on narrow aluminum ledges around the sides.

I stare at the water frothing up toward me, so close I can touch it, and become engrossed in the movement of boat over water, wind in my face and through my hair, waves moving out from the bow. I love moving fast across water, love the freedom I feel, the embrace of the sea. But this is the Bering Sea, and even though it's a sunny day in July, I begin to chill. I put on a hat and float coat to cut the wind to my body, sorry to give up that feeling of wind enveloping me.

It's been about two hours since I arrived in Savoonga. I flew from Anchorage to Nome, and then to this tiny village on St. Lawrence Island, about as far northwest as one can go and still be in Alaska. Rick picked me up at the airstrip with a borrowed Honda four-wheeler, and we rode through town.

The wide, muddy road was lined with small one-story wooden houses and a few larger buildings set above the wet tundra on pilings. Most houses weren't painted but instead were the streaked gray of wood weathered by salt air and blasted by winter winds. Racks of seal and walrus meat hung to dry next to lines of laundry. On one roof lay a walrus skull and rib bones, bleached white. A few side streets led off the main road to more houses, the school, and the village store. At the end of the half-mile-long main road on a grassy bank, upside down on wooden platforms, sat several walrus-skin umiaks. Below on a storm berm lay a row of aluminum skiffs, a rocky beach, and the sea. The shoreline seemed to shape the town itself: roads led to it, homes oriented toward it, and boats huddled around it. It was the umbilical cord for the village.

We stopped at the fish-buying station. Two young Yup'ik Eskimo men in full rain gear greeted us as they continued washing off two long wooden counters with garden hoses. Beside them stood a freight container with an ice machine on it—where the halibut are kept awaiting shipping.

One of them, Orville Toolie, who manages the fish station, told Rick who had brought in halibut that day—*ivisa* in their language of Siberian Yup'ik. Rick is in Savoonga to help with this enterprise. He works with the Community Development Quota programs that allocate 7.5 percent of the huge Bering Sea commercial groundfish quotas to the 55 coastal villages to help support economic development. The idea behind the CDQs is that of sharing the wealth—the vast majority of the fleet that profits from these rich fishing grounds are based outside the area, outside, even, Alaska. So they give back a part of their profits to those who actually live where the fish live. This sharing fits with the Eskimo practice of sharing any wealth—be it dollars or salmon—with the family of village, of place.

Rick spends time in Savoonga each summer using this shared wealth to help them develop another way of providing. He has helped them to use longlines to catch halibut and to clean and package halibut for shipping and selling. He has helped them set up a buying station and a transportation route through Nome to buyers in Anchorage. For the last couple of years, the villagers have run the entire operation themselves, but Rick comes back because he likes this place and these people.

After talking with Orville for a few minutes, we climbed back on the four-wheeler and went to the house that was to be ours for a few days.

Rick had just fixed me a cup of coffee when there was a knock on the door and a man burst in. He was short and stocky with a round brown face and wide smile—clearly a Siberian Yup'ik.

"The weather's good, we're going out. Want to come?" he said quickly to us both.

"Sure," said Rick. Rick introduced me to Denny Akeya and we exchanged greetings, his small but broad hand surprising me with its strength.

"We're lucky to be going out with the biggest boat in the fleet," Rick said. And then they both laughed, for Denny's open skiff is only one foot longer than the rest. It's hardly a fleet of high-tech fishing vessels like the other fleets in Alaska.

Less than an hour later, we were on the beach. Denny and Rick pulled frozen herring from a cardboard box, sliced each one into three or four pieces, and then deftly stuck the pieces onto large hooks. Each hook was attached to a one-foot line with a metal snap on the end. Hook after hook they baited, laying each one over the edge of a five-gallon bucket. Hook after hook, hundreds of them. Transfixed by their quick, repetitive movements and lulled by the still, warm air and sound of waves, I stared at hands, fish, hooks.

Then I remembered the camera around my neck and took a picture of Denny cutting, of Rick pulling out a herring, of three boys throwing rocks at a herring gull enticed closer by the smell of fish guts, of six men pushing and lifting a fifteen-foot skiff over rocks and gravel and into the surf. The people of Savoonga keep to traditional Eskimo ways—men hunt and fish, and women stay on shore and shape the bounties of the hunt into food and clothing. Except for me, an outsider, only men were going fishing this day. I heard Denny calling me back, for I'd wandered down the beach, and we loaded up and were off, skimming across the waters of the northern Bering Sea.

I'd heard of St. Lawrence Island from Rick for two years, and he always spoke of it with such reverence that I had to experience it. I'd spent time in other Alaska Native villages, but this sounded different somehow. Perhaps it is the geographical remoteness of the island

—it lies closer to Russia than to North America. Perhaps it is the historical presence.

The Bering land bridge. I am just offshore of the backbone of the Bering land bridge, the only part not submerged, a piece of land that humans traveled over thousands of years earlier to inhabit the North American continent. During the Pleistocene glaciation, when most of the sea was frozen, the mountains behind Savoonga were the highest point of the land bridge. They must have been a reference point for travelers—bird, mastodon, bear, human. Now, only in winter does ice lock in the island, and the windswept, treeless mountains are still the reference point for the two small villages of about 600 people each—Savoonga and Gambell. From atop those mountains, they can see the Russian province of Chukotka, 38 miles from the island. The closest point on the American mainland is three times as far. And I was out on that sea below which the rest of the land bridge lay, with people for whom this isolated island was the point on which they stood to comprehend the world.

On the boat, Denny has a handheld GPS that's about the size of an old Texas Instruments calculator. He's constantly looking at it and telling us how far we are from the set, how far we've come, what our exact position is. Rick helped to introduce this bit of technology to the islanders two years ago in a winter snowstorm, showing them how it could point them toward home. Later Steve shows me on its tiny screen how they can use it to follow the exact line they scribed across the water when they set their gear two days ago. I can tell they are thrilled with this piece of technology. I think it's amazing in a mysterious way, much like the auklet's purposeful yet incomprehensible flight, but I can't fully comprehend how much easier and safer it makes things for them.

Before the GPS, some villagers might have gotten lost, but all relied on instinct and intuition, on knowledge of wind, ice, sun, and snow. They still do. They find their way by marking their boat's position relative to the mountains on shore. They keep an eye on the horizon, watching for change. At the fish buying station, we talked of whether the windless weather might hold for fishing that day. Walter Toolie, Orville's father and a respected elder, had pointed toward clouds on the other side of the island and said, "There is the heart of the wind."

We make it to the first set and, using a brand-new battery-powered winch to pull in the line, we begin. I learn later that this is the only boat in Savoonga that has a power winch; the rest still pull in every hook by hand. Too bad we can't go out with one of them, Rick tells me, pulling in by hand from a lighter, smaller, tippy Lund instead of this heavy stable boat. Too bad the water is so calm that I can't experience pulling lines in winds so strong and seas so high that the horizon dips and sways and the boat bobs precariously like a bath toy. A few days ago, he and Warren Toolie had been out setting lines when the winds picked up from flat calm to a gale-force 40 knots within minutes. They barely made it to shore. This calm water, this "big" boat, it's an uncommon thing for the islanders. But this small a boat is even less common for the commercial groundfish crews who fish farther out on factory trawlers the size of football fields.

Denny guides the line into the boat as Steve operates the power winch. I lean over the edge and see the line coming up, a thick white thread arising. Hook after hook comes up, hook after hook Denny takes off and carefully lays over the edge of the bucket. Hook after hook absolutely empty. No halibut, no bait. Nothing.

On the beach before we left, Denny and Rick were talking about how few fish the village was catching this year. Last year, they caught the entire quota of 40,000 pounds in three weeks. This year, they are six weeks into it and have only caught about a third as much. Boats are going out and coming back with nothing but cleaned hooks.

"There's a lot of well-fed crabs and sea urchins out there," Denny laughed as they baited. "They are the lucky ones."

Luck. I was to hear that word many times in Savoonga. Sitting in the washerteria, another day, waiting to take a shower, I spoke with a

Yup'ik woman about this new fishery. Agnes had just started working at the washeteria, where villagers come to bathe, wash clothes, and get drinking water. With no running water in the village, this was a busy place. Still, I was obviously a stranger in town, and Agnes wondered why I was in their small village so far from my home.

"I'm here visiting with my friend, Rick, who is helping with the halibut fishery," I said.

"Oh," she replied, "I hear some of them have been lucky, coming back with many halibut. That is good. It helps them provide for their families."

Newly widowed, Agnes was now even more aware of the difficulties of providing. No longer able to depend on the luck of her husband's hunting and fishing, she now depended solely on the luck of the village—and on the tradition of sharing good fortune.

At the buying station, too, and on the beach, talk was of luck, not of skill or competition. We came upon a man digging at an old village site for artifacts and asked him how it was going.

"Nothing yet," he replied. "But I hope I will be lucky."

This talk seems to run deeper than the "Have any luck?" question of the Sunday afternoon angler in Anchorage. Instead, it puts the focus clearly on the ebbs and flows of the place they inhabit rather than on their individual abilities. I sensed humility, acceptance, and respect.

Now, Denny is drawing up hook after hook. So much repetitive work. All the baiting, all the hooking and unhooking of lines, again and again. Repetition that requires care and concentration. Denny is quiet, intent, almost trancelike in his motions. I think of my readings in Zen Buddhism in which Thich Nhat Hanh, Vietnamese peace activist exiled to France, speaks of mindfulness—wash the dishes to wash the dishes, he says, and not to have clean dishes. I think Denny pulls the lines to pull the lines. Just to be here, doing this, is enough.

A couple of times, though, he pulls on the line and says, "Might have one coming," and we lean over the side, looking so expectantly that I can imagine a huge white cloud billowing up from the green depths, getting bigger and more defined, then thrashing over the side of the boat. We watch, but after a few minutes there is only bare hook after bare hook, and we sit back and talk of other things as Denny quietly pulls and pulls.

"So," I say to Steve, "how long have you been fishing with Denny?"

"About five years," he says.

Steve is not native to this island. He's a white teacher from the Midwest. But he's not typical of bush teachers who leave the island every summer to return to their homes, and who usually teach in a village only a few years before moving away for good. Steve stays here every summer; he is married to, and raising children with, a native woman from Savoonga. This is his home now.

"Those other teachers, they don't know what they're missing by not staying here for the summer," he tells me. "This is the time when things happen. This is what I live here for."

He tells me that this past April he was lucky enough to go whaling with the villagers. It's quite an honor for an outsider just to be invited to the whaling camp, but Steve got to go out in an umiak, the wood-framed walrus-skin boats used for whaling, and help bring in a bowhead.

"It was indescribable," he says, and so I have to rely on imagination to see a pack of white-skinned boats, light on the water, drifting among ice leads so quietly that they can hear the ice crack as it melts. Then the sound of that rush of spouting. I have to imagine the adrenaline rush of a single man holding a harpoon as long as himself standing up in that boat and aiming for the creature ten times the boat's size. I imagine black whale skin breaking through the surface of gray water, a slowly emerging mass like an island forming. I can see that one strike, how if the striker misses the whale is gone, taking with it their chance for a whale that year, too, since each village is only allowed a few strikes a year. How if he hits it, they follow in their skin boat, pulled by the line attached to the harpoon, and wait, wait, wait for the whale's life to ebb. Then they begin dragging that monstrous being of the sea to shore, where women and children wait, ulus ready.

Denny pulls the last hook into the boat. The entire set is clean, every hook. All we get is a few jellyfish stuck to the buoy line. He and Rick carefully untangle the tentacles and dip them back in the sea. He stands, stretches out his arms, and smiles broadly.

"I love doing this," he says.

Denny and Steve decide to move the set, since this spot yielded nothing. So we motor off, and as we near the next set, Denny throws out the buoy. It trails behind, looking like it's water-skiing.

"We like to drag our buoy," Denny laughs. And then, "Have you ever water-skiied?"

It seems a strange question out here in the northern Bering Sea, where in winter the ice pack brings them seal and polar bear, and in spring they hunt walrus and bowhead whales in the ice leads. Where the wind can quickly make the sea turn fatal. There's a memorial on a beach about five miles from town to five people who drowned last summer. They were coming home from fish camp, eight people, men and children, when the wind rose up. One of the two skiffs capsized, and though they were near shore and radioed for help immediately, only three survived.

Today, as odd as it sounds, the sun and undulating water make water-skiing seem possible. Today, with a dry suit, we might water-ski in the Bering Sea. Be the first one ever, make the Guinness Book.

I doubt that sort of thing holds any meaning here. In fact, they're struggling enough with things that most of us don't give a second thought. St. Lawrence Island embodies the subsistence economy. The cycle of seasons, the movement of the ice pack, the direction of the wind, these are what determine how well people fare, not the GNP or stock market. And nothing is certain here—not income or food source or transportation. The planes which connect them to the cash economy in Nome may be weeks in arriving during harsh winter storms. Their food sources are fish, seal, walrus, whale—either they get a whale, and everyone has plenty, or they don't get one, and everyone has little. And only a few jobs in town—the postal worker, the store clerks, the washerteria attendant, city workers, the electrical cooperative, and the airline dispatcher—pay regular salaries year-round. For most people, cash comes in small amounts through government subsidies, or in erratic windfalls from selling walrus ivory carvings and ancient artifacts. Providing—for the family, for the winter months—is always the topic of conversation.

Though the new halibut fishery, whose purpose is to boost the local cash economy, has been successful in bringing in a new source of money, some villagers are against it.

"We shouldn't be selling our food," they say.

Here, death by starvation is a very real possibility, and a pound of fish weighs more than a few dollars. In the late 1800s, over 10,000 people lived on this island in a half dozen communities. Then came the winter of the Great Starvation, when entire villages perished. The next spring, whalers found bodies everywhere, piled up in food caches, lying where they had fallen. Less than 2,000 survived.

What caused this? The Bering Sea is rich with food, but its abundance is seasonal and erratic. The walrus is a staple of food and of skins for whaling boats; if a village misses walrus, they can't hunt whales, either. Walrus come through on the retreating edges of the ice pack in the spring, once a year for a few days. Some say the men of the villages were so drunk on the alcohol introduced by Yankee whalers that they missed the walrus. Some say there weren't as many walrus because the Yankee whalers shot so many once whales became scarce. Some say it was disease brought by the Yankees. Some say it was all these things at once. Some say it was bad luck.

We reach a spot near the next set where Denny decides we should drop the lines. So we sit, Steve keeping the boat moving slowly backward as Denny feeds the baited line out the boat, dropping each hook gently into the sea. Then we motor on to the next set and begin the reverse process—pulling in the line.

Denny pulls and pulls, nothing but clean hooks again, until he says again, tugging on the line, "Think we've got one here." I'm struck by his optimism, wondering where it comes from, wondering if he's just one of those optimistic people, or if there's something he knows from living here that sustains hope.

But then, there it is, a dark gray sheet of fish coming up, and as it is pulled from its element, I see gills flayed out, eyes bulging, head and face distorted by the pull of line and the gravity of air. The huge gray mass of the 100-pound halibut, like a muscle with two eyes, thrashes alongside the boat and then slides awkwardly over the side. The strong tail, bigger than both of Denny's hands, splashes all of us as Denny and Rick pull it in. The fish thumps to the floor, filling the bow. Then Denny yanks out the hook, Rick stuns the fish with two blows of a stick, Steve cuts the gills with a long knife, and Rick and Steve together heave it over onto the white, eyeless side. All this happens in a matter of seconds. There it lies, shivering and flapping its tail.

Denny continues to work the set, pulling in more line, more empty hooks, and a couple smaller *ivisa*. These are laid next to the big fish. Then he begins again to set another line, hook by hook. My attention is riveted on these fish lying at my feet. One of them jumps around with the unfocused energy of my five-year-old son, and I wonder how old they are. I know that halibut can live to be at least forty years old. I ask Rick to guess their ages.

"The big one is maybe fifteen to twenty years old; these little guys, five or six years," he replies.

Denny finishes the set, and we head back to Savoonga. As the boat moves easily across still-calm waters, my mind wanders to the last time I went fishing on the ocean in an open boat. I was with my new husband and his father off the coast of Virginia. We were trolling, moving slowly forward as Andy and his dad played their lines. We caught some fish, but we also caught a little sand shark, no longer than my forearm. Andy's dad ripped the hook from its mouth, tearing the shark's face. He hit it on the head, cut off the head and threw it into the water, and cut the body into bait-size pieces. All the while he cussed the damned sharks eating his bait. Only my inhibitions at being the new daughter-in-law along on a traditionally father-and-son outing kept me from throwing up all over the deck.

This time, as I sit and watch these halibut at my feet, I do not feel the least bit repelled. I watch Denny and Rick and Steve gut them, pulling long strands of innards out and tossing them overboard. I help clean the deck and gear. The fish still flap about as they are gutted, spraying blood everywhere. Fish slime and blood, sun and wind. Still, with nothing inside their bodies, they thrash around.

One of the smaller halibut keeps thrashing so hard that it jumps around on top of the others. Rick reaches over and pats the white underside with his free hand the way people absentmindedly but lovingly pet their dogs.

"It calms them," he says to me.

And he's right. It does. They lie still all the way back.

When we're in sight of shore, Denny and Steve begin discussing unloading procedures. Evidently, it's quite involved. But first we motor around in slow circles, picking up each fish by its jaws, lifting one fish at a time over the side of the boat, cleaning them out with clean, cold sea water.

The way they hold the fish reminds me of the scene at the buying station this morning. Alex Akeya, Denny's father, had pulled up on his four-wheeler, a brown tarp strapped to the front.

"I had a bit of luck this morning," he said to us.

Then he got off, carefully untied the tarp and opened it up. There lay a single small halibut, probably no more than thirty pounds. He gently lifted it off the tarp and picked it up, holding it close to his body. He carried it, in both arms, to Orville. Orville accepted it and laid it carefully on the cleaning table. They took the kind of care with that small halibut I've seen in parents carrying a sleeping child. As it lay on the table, we all stood admiring it for several minutes.

With the four fish clean, Denny pulls the boat up to shore. Rick and Steve hop out, but I decide to stay on for the ride. I'd heard how they beach their boats. They have no harbor or seawall, but they do get some of the most ferocious storms in the world, so their boats must be beached as high up as possible—much higher than they can drag them.

"Okay, sit beside me and find something to hang on tight to," Denny says gravely. He finds places for each of my hands to hold onto the boat. Then he motors far offshore, turns and points the bow to shore. A crowd of men have gathered and stand on the rocky beach, facing us. Other boats lie scattered along the shore like driftwood. Behind them rise the mountains—the spine of the land bridge. We aim for a narrow space between boats and he hits full throttle. We're heading straight for the beach, going so fast things to the side—water, island, gulls, boats—are a blur. The force of air nearly knocks off my wool cap and pulls my hands from their anchors.

Then we hit the shoreline and skid fifty feet or more, almost to the top of the storm berm. We stop abruptly. I get out slowly, my legs wobbly on the loose rock. Denny's wife, Rosemary, and their daughter come down the hill to greet us. Rosemary looks in the boat and says, "Looks like you had some luck." Then the boat is circled by the other men on the beach. A dozen or more hands, broad brown hands like Denny's, grip the boat and lift, carrying it up above a storm's reach.

That evening, Rick and I sit atop the bird cliffs, looking back toward Savoonga. Huddled around the shoreline, it looks small, simple, neat, inviting. A slight wind sweeps up the grassy hills to where we sit on lichen-encrusted boulders. Deep in the rock recesses around us, a melodic clucking arises. It is the song of the young auklets awaiting the return of their parents. As we sit, the auklets begin to return from the sea. First a few come winging in, then increasing clouds of them move toward us like the wind.

David Petersen

What Abbey Was Trying to Tell Us
A Hunter's Credo

First publication

After we've lost a natural place, it's gone for everyone...a complete and absolutely democratic tragedy of emptiness. Richard K. Nelson

My late friend Edward Abbey wasn't much of a hunter in his final years—he was too busy writing wildly popular novels and life-changing essays and exploring and defending western America's shrinking wilderness. Yet he was supportive of his many hunter friends and a voracious eater of the venison and elk jerky we gave him. Today, some uninformed hunters put Abbey in the enemy camp because of his staunch environmentalism and outspoken criticism of some of the more egregious aspects of hunting. In truth, Abbey worked harder and accomplished more to ensure a future for hunting than any so-called "hunter's rights" group I know of. Let me explain.

I first met Ed Abbey in the early 1980s in his hometown of Tucson, where I'd gone to interview him for a couple of magazines. When I brashly inquired if he were an atheist, he sternly replied, "I am an *Earthiest*...I stand for what I stand on." And that was, and is, the meat of the matter.

Through a long slow process of maturing, in which hunting has played a significant role, I too have come to think of myself as an Earthiest. Like my friend Cactus Ed, I believe the wisest course is to live just one life at a time and as much of it as possible outdoors. Which is to say: Any afterlife that doesn't include bugling autumn elk, September aspens whispering in a mountain breeze, wild trout leaping for dinner and joy in clear running water, the explosive gobbling of lust-struck turkey toms, and the humbling aliveness that comes with the possibility of meeting a grizzly bear just around the next bend in the trail—any so-called heaven lacking these earthly blessings would be for me pure hell.

When I was a boy coming up on the windy plains of Oklahoma— I'm talking about the late fifties and early sixties—the only big game animals around were white-tailed deer, and even they were precious few and far away. I didn't see one, in fact, until I went deer hunting for the first time at age fourteen. Then I saw a few.

I was old enough to hunt but too young to drive, so my father who worked too much and had too little time to take me hunting and fishing made amends by chauffeuring a school pal and me 200 miles east to a place where clustered pines furred a bumped-up landscape and ghostly whitetails lurked. Dad hauled us and our little pile of primitive camping gear as far back into the woods as he could coax his old Ford wagon and wished us luck and turned around for home and another long day of work after the all-night drive. That week proved an epiphany and a blessing, and a week spent in the late November deer woods became a cherished annual ritual.

On those early hunting expeditions, I camped and hunted and explored and got terrifyingly lost and viewed it all as a spiritual pilgrimage—I'm dead serious about this: Those early hunting trips *were* pilgrimages, adventures of discovery and personal growth. The deer were magical alien beings, more ethereal than real, and the piney woods through which they ghosted were sacred groves. For that one week a year and that week alone I felt fully alive. One week, of course, wasn't nearly enough and I returned home each fall with a deep and poignant hunger brooding in my soul. I still do, though now I pursue deer, elk, pronghorn, turkey, and grouse across many weeks each year.

And so it was that my lifelong affinity for the natural world—for shaggy *wild* as opposed to natty pastoral nature—was born not as you might expect of a richness of early experiences afield, but rather of deprivation. Supply and demand. I had too little wildness in my young urban life, and I wanted and needed more. Still do.

Following a six-year career in the Marine Corps and various other wanderings that allowed for precious little hunting, I settled in 1980 in rural southwestern Colorado, where I set about reinventing my boyhood discovery of wild nature. But rather than the rolling hills of my youth, here are mountains that pierce hard-edged clouds. Rather than modest piney woods, here are vast dense forests of spruce and fir illuminated in autumn by incendiary clones of quaking aspens. And the beasts that lend magic to my life are no longer white-tailed deer, but beige-rumped elk and big-eared muleys and bears, lots of bears—which I do not hunt.

Owing to modern scientific wildlife management and vigorous game law enforcement, elk in Colorado, like whitetails in Oklahoma, have proliferated in recent years even as their habitat has been razed by so-called progress. In some parts of Colorado—Estes Park, a bustling tourist village adjacent to Rocky Mountain National Park over on the Front Range near Denver, is a piteous example— elk have become *so* abundant in winter that they're no longer viewed by locals as magical mountain spirits, but rather as giant rats with antlers. The same for whitetails, Canada geese, and other species elsewhere. Supply and demand.

But there are two faces to every coin, and for their part the elk of Estes Park probably have little good to say about the houses and roads and recreational developments and miles of old ranch fences that block their traditional migration corridor through Estes to lower wintering grounds, where they'd surely prefer to be. The elk of Rocky Mountain and Estes Parks in Colorado—as in Banff in Alberta and an increasing number of elsewheres across western North America—those unwillingly urbanized elk probably don't appreciate people usurping their traditional turf any more than some me-first yupster locals appreciate having elk in their midst to lumber out in front of their snobby Saabs and munch their designer landscape shrubs.

When I view winter-humbled urban and suburban wildlife I feel no magic, only an aching empathy and a deep sense of loss. Kentucky poet-farmer Wendell Berry captured the essence of progress when he wrote, "The thought of what was here once and is gone forever will not leave me as long as I live. It is as though I walk knee-deep in its absence."

Just so.

Yet (the beautiful irony!) these same animals for the bulk of every year—especially in late summer and early fall before the rifles of autumn haze them from the vastness of the contiguous national forests and into the crowded but protective bounds of Rocky Mountain and Estes Parks—these self-same elk are as elusive and ethereal as you will. The aloof majesty that's starved from them in winter flows back with the greening of each new spring. The same royal bull who lounges ignominiously in a condominium courtyard in January will call on millennia of natural selection to try and keep you from getting within a country mile of him in the autumn woods, and unless you're might good or might lucky, he'll win every time.

Tragically, this fecundity of wildlife and wildlands is under fierce and relentless attack—not just here in Colorado, but everywhere. And far too often with help from politicians who get themselves elected by professing to be defenders of sportsmen's rights while in fact being rapacious molesters of the habitat upon which wildlife—

and thus, hunting and fishing—depend. For the most dismal environmental voting records in Washington, year after year, look to the Congressional Sportsmen's Caucus (the name itself is a lie).

My most earnest Earthiest's prayers, therefore, are that sportsmen and sportswomen will learn to vote the big picture and the long run, rather than continue to be duped into electing enemies of hunting's future...that we as a species will find more and better ways to bring sanity and restraint to today's insane and self-destructive human population growth (time to confront that old taboo)...and that we "owners" (in fact, mere ephemeral custodians) of America's forests, fields, and streams will strive to evolve a wiser and farther-sighted paradigm for the development, or not, of rural "real estate." Soon. Before it's too late. Forever.

Not that nobody's trying. The conservation and education work being done by sportsmen's groups such as the Izaak Walton League, Ducks and Trout Unlimited, the Rocky Mountain Elk Foundation, and others, plus dozens of mainstream conservation organizations, is of critical importance and the gains are real if inchmeal. Likewise, the more literate, politically savvy, and ethical members of the outdoor media (of which there are far too few) are increasingly and courageously abandoning the standard paranoid harping, tired and tiring, against the vastly overrated "antis" in favor of striving to convert "just hunters" into hunter-naturalists and hunter-conservationists. For it is they, not the hard-liners, who stand the best hope of hushing hunting's critics—not with harsh words, but through necessary change, exemplary actions. This too is vital.

Yet, improving the ethics of *only* sportsmen is not enough. Unless all of humanity soon develops and sustains a significantly more charitable view toward the nonhuman world—we could call such a paradigm Earthiesm—this shrinking Eden, this heaven on Earth with which we've been blessed, will continue to founder and the quality of our lives sink with it until we and our children and theirs will be left to wander dazed through days gray as urban concrete, suffocating in the memory of what was here once is gone forever.

And among the first such casualties will be hunting: without large expanses of natural habitat in which wild animals can wander and hunters wander after them, the antihunting threat becomes superfluous. What Abbey was trying to tell us is that it doesn't have to be that way. And that is my hunter's credo.

SueEllen Campbell

On the Mountain

from *Bringing the Mountain Home*

When I went away to college, in one week's time I dropped from the cool silence of Skyland's 9,000 feet, where I'd spent the summer walking on mountains, to Houston's sultry, siren-loud sea level, and I immediately started looking for things to climb. A live oak by the library, where I spent hours reading and watching people pass underneath, hidden not by foliage but by the ground-gazing habit of walkers. The roof of my dorm, eight floors up, a bare concrete slab used mainly by sweltering sunbathers, where at night I could hear the roar of the lions in the zoo across the street. The library roof and the top of the astronomy building, locked doors and windows circumvented somehow in ways I can't remember, reached quietly at night with friends, the latter in October in hopes there'd be a usable telescope to see through the city's bright sky to the Orionid meteor shower.

And finally, late on a November night after physics lab, the most vertiginous point on campus: a construction crane set three stories deep in the ground and rising another three at least above. We started at ground level, crossing from solid earth over the enormous hold on a thin steel bridge, and then we took turns watching and climbing. My friend Jim went first but not very high. Then I climbed, all the way up, slowly, sticking close to the ladder, holding tightly with sweaty hands, weaving my arms through the rungs when I paused, testing each foothold before I shifted my weight. Under each step the crane swayed a bit, my stomach knotted, my heart quickened.

After that, I stopped pretending Houston's drained and paved-over swamps were like the Rockies. The top of a construction crane was not an adequate substitute for a mountaintop or a high ridge. It wasn't the adrenaline rush I was after when I climbed those peaks I was missing so much, but a collection of other rewards I'm still sorting out.

These mountains I'm talking about—they're not K2 and Denali and Kilimanjaro. Getting up one requires no porters or oxygen, no pitons or carabiners, no ropes or crampons or ice axes, no expensive permits or exotic visas, no headlamps for midnight starts. They're the everyday mountains you can just walk up with some time and energy and perseverance and a few pieces of simple equipment—jacket, rain poncho, hat, sunblock, water, a lunch, boots for ankle support. They need to be high, though, high enough to provide a really big view. Those old, soft, rounded, tree-covered mountains of, say, Virginia's Blue Ridge, those don't really count for me—evidence, I know, of my Colorado provincialism. You can't see far enough from the tops of those hills, and what you can see is mostly more trees.

Proper mountains need to climb above timberline. Out here these are common, several everywhere you look, rings of them, cirques, strings of peaks connected by high saddles, the occasional solitary giant, lots of colors and all shapes, the child's perfect triangle, flat-topped cliff-faced buttes, jagged spires and knife edges, hogbacks and palisades, huge rounded mounds, crazy quilts of miscellaneous mountain parts welded together inside the earth and then shoved upward into the thin high air to be cut and honed by glaciers. Every one of them is different, and on foot you learn their character.

Half my life has gone by since I first climbed this peak, the one I call Lupine for the intensely cobalt and sweet-scented flowers on the way down, one of the blue mountains I used to see across the lake at camp. And at least fifteen relatively sedentary years have passed since I last climbed it—years in which I've mainly been content with shorter climbs, to ridgelines, escarpments, high passes. It's a particularly alluring mountain, just under 13,500 feet high, standing alone above everything nearby, almost as tall as the 14,000-foot giants in the distance, some seven miles away across a map, several rugged days away by foot. Nearly the whole climb lies above timberline, too, most of it on loose, bare rock. We'd save this mountain for the very end of the summer when our biggest risk in trying it would be the weather, our muscles at their strongest, our blood thoroughly adjusted to the altitude.

I started thinking about going back up Lupine about a year ago, late last summer, idly at first, almost as a joke to myself about the gap between desire and reality—mediocre muscle tone and an allergy to working out, weak knees only partly improved by therapy, strengthening exercises abandoned some time ago, the energy and insouciance of twenty covered over by the moderation of thirty and the prudence of forty. Wouldn't it be good, I'd think, to climb Lupine again, a motive to get in better shape, an excuse to spend lots of time at high altitudes, just the right mountain to frame a big chunk of my life, a wonderful mountain, layered with translucencies of memory.

Slowly reality receded and desire took over. All winter I dreamed about being on the mountain.

I needed a companion, so I leaned on John until he agreed. Then my youngest brother, Bruce, stopped by with his family in Colorado for vacation, and on impulse I asked him, "Do you remember how to get up Lupine? Want to climb it with us a week from Sunday?" "Sure," he said. He'd been up four times to my three and thought he remembered the route. Conditioning? No problem, he took his tiny girls on walks around the Chicago parks. Knees? Bad, but we could go slowly, especially downhill. Altitude? Plenty of time. Desire? You bet.

Could we actually push ourselves to the top? I called a triathlete friend with a degree in nutrition and asked what to carry for a little extra help. Carbohydrates, she said. Forget protein and fat. No gorp, no Snickers, no cheese. Just bread, dried fruit, maybe one of those high-energy bars. Lots of water. And eat often, even if you aren't hungry. So I shopped.

And the weather? The driest year in a long time—lots of forest fires, not many wildflowers. But promising for us. Then the day after Bruce signed on, the summer monsoons hit the state, six weeks late, and we started watching the forecasts.

Though it sprinkled during the night, when we wake up the clouds are disappearing. Over breakfast I watch the sun hit the first ridge we'll climb, elation rising in me as the sky turns a bright, cloudless blue. Bruce arrives at about 7:30, and we stuff our packs, prepared, we hope, for anything. I squeeze all my gear into a fat waist pack and strap my bulky fleece jacket on top.

We're in no hurry. We cross the meadow and hop over a shallow creek on rocks; most summers this is gooey marsh. As we stroll up the valley Bruce and I talk about our route, planning to find our way by memory. The only trick is to avoid the rock faces and really steep scree slopes. An old mining cabin reminds us where to turn into the trees. We plunge into the dewy shadows and put our bodies to work.

We talk about knees. Bruce, who is a physicist and mechanical engineer, demonstrates torque for me, bending his leg at odd angles, holding his daypack straight out from his shoulder, then with his elbow sharply bent, arguing for short quick steps rather than the long slow ones I'm used to taking. We're both feeling stronger than we expected—it's the energy of excitement.

In about an hour we're at the top of the trees in a thin zone of sharply sloping meadow. More flowers than I'd expected are still blooming, but most have gone early to seed. I spot a bright green moss pond. A chunk of volcanic rock. A slab of slate with a layer of quartz-crystal teeth. A fresh elk print.

The ground becomes rock and steepens again, and suddenly the climb feels more like work. My knees start to twinge every few steps.

We stop to rest and think about our route. Two does move quietly across the slope above us, startled perhaps by Bruce, who's checking out the slope to our right. Then a crash, repeated, like breaking china, and a fawn, its spots nearly gone, bounds straight down the scree toward us and past, twelve or fifteen feet at a leap, a quick almost-stumble, a longer pause in the air to rebalance, feel in loose rock again, another leap, gone before I can catch my breath. Wild.

Another familiar old mining cabin tells us we're on track, we reach the ridge, and the view to the north opens all at once. Small valleys and big mountains as far as we can see, a wide vein of marble, a handful of persistent snow patches. A few small cumulus clouds cling to the horizon. It's just midmorning, rain's not likely before midafternoon, and the rest of the climb is all on spectacular ridgelines. I feel like I'm full of bubbles, transparent spheres of iridescence floating me up into the sky.

For a while the ridge is broad and relatively level, the rocks small enough to make easy footing. Two steps to every breath. I remember a friend from camp telling me that in such places he always wanted to ingest everything in view. I try to look at everything all at once. What I see is both simple and complicated—just space, light, and rock, but such a vast and figured space, so many subtleties of light, such intricacies of rock!

The ridge narrows and steepens. We're at about 12,600 feet. Step, breathe in. Step, breathe out. It's razor thin now, three feet wide or less, the rocks on top flattened slightly into a kind of trail, space falling sharply away on both sides. When the path veers a step to the right, the rocks on my left side are suddenly shoulder high. Breathing in, I see myself as space. Breathing out, I feel free. A single columbine, tucked in the rock—a rare sight so late and so high. Earlier this summer there'd been an abundance of them, whole hillsides full. So delicate, so rugged. A sudden roar, and we all stop. Thunder? Jet. But those distant clouds are growing and darkening. We speed up.

Suddenly it's much steeper. Now I'm leading. I step, breathe in, breathe out, step, stop to gulp some orange juice. The rocks are bigger and sharper. I put my gloves on, lean over to balance myself with my hands, test each step for stability. We measure our progress by the view. That's Frigid Air Pass, way down there. We're higher than the rim of Hummingbird Basin, the mountain across from camp, the mountain behind it. Soon only the fourteeners are above us. There's the lake at camp! Gleaming, so far away that none of the new buildings around it show—this view is the same as it was half my life ago. Home.

I know now I can make it to the top. But all the rewards are here in this moment. I'm stunned by beauty, breathless with it, heartstopped, afloat on elation. Bubbles pop and reform inside my head, my throat, my chest. For a magical instant, the world around me seems exotic, marvelous.

A deep rumble startles us to a stop. Big storm cloud to the north, wrapping two huge peaks in a dark sheath. We watch for a minute, see a strike, think the cloud is moving sideways, check that the breeze on us still comes from the sunnier south. But other clouds are building fast, several hours earlier than we'd expected, and we can't see to the northwest along Lupine's ridge, the most common direction for weather. We couldn't go down here even if we wanted to—it's way too precipitous—and the route back would be slow and very hard on our knees. A half-hour more and we'll be at what Bruce calls the Whale Back, a broad slope down to the south, covered with small, loose scree, good ground for a quick descent. We take off uphill, hoping the clouds will dissipate. John's just about decided to skip the peak, but Bruce and I are optimistic.

As the Whale Back comes into view, we talk about the way down —if we have lots of time, we'll follow that ridge all the way to the left; if we have to hurry, we'll go to the third snow patch and drop over the side. When we reach the point of decision, we stop, unpack sandwiches, and spread out to watch the speed and direction of the clouds. I drink from my red canteen, put my gloves away, switch from sunglasses to plain ones. Once, here, a golden eagle swooped across the ridge not 20 feet in front of me and just below. It's at least another hour to the top and back to this point—another 400 feet up, half a mile over, one more knife edge. I'd dreamed for months of sitting on top, drinking in the world, looking for ocean fossils in the palm-sized slabs of slate, basking in the sun. Reality and desire wrestle.

Desire loses. The sky above us is darkening quickly. We'll get wet, we think, even though there's no lightning nearby, and we won't be able to see much. We snap some quick photos: we made it this far, we will say, we could have done the rest, but look at those clouds! We step reluctantly toward our packs.

Crack! Out of the silence a lightning bolt, too close to think about, and then hail and rain. We grab the packs at a quick lope and start down, shouting directions to each other: Aim for the lighter patches of rock, they're softer, more recently disturbed. Crack! Land on your heels and you'll slide better. Don't twist an ankle or knee. Crack! If it gets really bad, dive over the left edge. John disappears in front of us. I turn and pause every few seconds to check on Bruce, a lone, stiff-kneed figure behind me, silhouetted against rock and charcoal sky. I review what I know about CPR, break into a run.

Bang! This one's so close I plunge off the edge and hit the steep slope with my seat, propel myself down with arms and legs, flailing like a frantic crab. John's below me. Will he come back up if I get hit? Bang! Bruce sees lightning hit the ridge below him, right where I'd just been, and dives off the side onto a snow patch, slides down until he hits rock. Once I know he's off the top I stop looking back, don't see the bolts, don't count for distance, just plummet down the side, cutting and bruising my hands, jamming knees, pure adrenaline, terror.

Maybe 800 feet down we find a little ravine and stop to regather. I pull my sunglasses from my pack, stick them in the pocket halfway down my thigh, and sit on the pack hoping it will provide some insulation against electricity. My knees are shaking violently, my glasses fogged almost completely over, my cap bill pulled low and dripping. I put on my poncho. I count between flash and boom: one one-thousand, two one-thousand, three! I scrunch lower. Bruce announces that the bolts are hitting everywhere around us, mostly on the ridge top, at least once below us. I squeeze my eyes shut, feel guilty about bringing us all here, about dawdling up higher while the clouds gathered.

Should we stay here, wait it out? There's zero wind, a bad sign, and we're clearly in the middle of this storm system. The gully feels a bit safer, but we're still high, 1,000 feet more down to the first trees, and the rocks are wetter by the minute, bigger and sharper, compacted by the rain, the footing harder, especially for Bruce and me. The ravine we're in is getting ominously deeper. Can we stay in it and keep going? Bruce walks over to see past the next bend: impassable. To move we'll have to climb back up on a small rib or two, feel even more exposed. I don't feel safe here, but the idea of moving tightens the knot in my stomach.

I try to remember every bit of lightning lore I've ever heard—and can't help remembering every story I've heard of people getting hit. The ones who survive unharmed. The ones who are stunned, then recover. The severe burns and long-term damage cases. The ones who die. Caves are dangerous, since the ground itself conducts. Would a ravine do the same? Should I try lying flat? But there was that man who was struck by lightning while he napped in his tent at the bottom of a valley. Should I keep sitting on my pack or squat on my boot soles? The usual folklore says soles, but my knees disagree, and only last week I read about some people who were badly burned after being struck in their *car*—a place I'd always thought completely safe. If tires don't help, shoes surely won't either. My niece Léa told me she'd been instructed to take off all her jewelry and throw it away from her. Right, I'd thought, the quintessentially useless action. A joke about helplessness. I check to make sure I'm not wearing earrings.

Now that there's time to think, I'm sure we're going to be hit. There's nothing we can do except hope and crunch ourselves into tight balls. The strikes continue, every half-minute or so, no farther away. Interminably. I'm not nervous or uncomfortable or apprehensive or worried; what I feel is plain *fear*. "Don't worry, Sis. Our odds are pretty good," Bruce says, and stands up until John barks at him to get back down.

John and Bruce decide we have to drop lower. I'm not about to stay here alone, so I hunch over and run with them across the rib into the next ravine, a shallower one, wincing with every knee bend, cringing with each slap of thunder, and turn to slide downhill. Here, near the water, just a foot wide but white with its quick fall, the rock is bare and slick. My heel slips, I slide several feet down, Bruce grabs and misses, I land on my pack, elbow, and palm, slide flat on my back into the water. The solid earth! Contact! Contact! I cradle my elbow and keep going, straight down the flow until I see enough loose gravel to hold my feet.

At last the lightning slows, moves a bit farther away. We can count to five, then six. Numbers that ordinarily would raise our blood pressure now signal reprieve. We reach the first willows, the ground flattens, the adrenaline slows, and Bruce and I can really feel our knees. We both start limping, trying to conserve what muscle and cartilage are left. I try to brush the gravel out of the skin on my hands. With every step I can see water bubbling out the toes of my new boots. I glance at a small pond beneath a tiny cascade and giggle at the thought that I'm carrying my own pair of pools. We check the time and can't believe it: it's been over two hours since the first bolt. No wonder it felt so endless! We swallow an aspirin each and start joking. "Good thing we had John along for emergency equipment." "Yeah, if I hadn't said we should go down, you two would be lying up there like charred chicken parts." "Lucky nobody sprained an ankle," I say, then twist mine, fall, and laugh. "Hey, we could try again tomorrow."

Finally we reach the road, barely paying attention to what's around us. I don't even notice whether any of the lupine are still in bloom or the late gentians have appeared. We take turns exclaiming: "It's almost flat! It's stopped raining! We're still alive!" And we trade stories—other brushes with lightning, hair standing on end, the smell of electricity, a friend of Bruce's who could see an aura around his ice ax, my next-door neighbor who watched a bolt shatter a nearby boulder, sending rock splinters everywhere. Our own story begins to take shape, each of us contributing details, sensations, making sense out of chaos, taming our fear. We'll keep telling it, nonstop for hours, frequently for days, every now and then for years.

Back at our tent we bundle everything together and throw it in the car. Not being masochists, we're heading for a hotel—drink, shower, dinner, hot tub. An hour later, when I start peeling off the sopped layers, black gravel sprays from my boots. My socks are dark gray—both pairs—and so are my feet. My pockets are full of soggy Kleenex and rocks. My pants and shirt are black, too, and my underwear. No blood on my palms, just scrapes, but I have to pick up my leg with my hands to get into the tub. I've brought the mountain down with me.

The next day we head home, delighted to be stiff and sore. I'm ready to retreat for a while, huddle among soft pillows. As he drives off, Bruce says, "That was fun. Let's climb another one next summer." I don't think he's joking. Within a week, I'm thinking the same thing, dreaming about being back up on the mountain.

John Daniel

Waist-Deep in Blackberry Vines

from *Looking After*

I'm waist-deep in blackberry vines looking for a cat who isn't here. Or if she is, she has an acre to be hiding in and she's ignoring me. It's my fault either way. When the carpet layers arrived at 8:30 I put her on the deck, harnessed and leashed, to keep her out of their way. I brought her food and water and stayed a minute to soothe her ragged nerves, then drove to Dixie's Café for breakfast and the newspaper. When I came back, the leash was wrapped around a rosebush, and the harness, still buckled, lay empty in the grass. She must have unpeeled herself into freedom. A feline Houdini. No sign of fur or blood. No sign of cat.

And so I'm wading the tangled, thorny biota of our new home in the country, calling *Here, kitty kitty kitty* in a falsetto voice—the only way I know how to do it—embarrassed that the carpet layers might hear me and worried sick that I'm singing to a long-gone cat. Maybe she's taking a nap, my head argues hopefully. But my heart has a mind of its own, and my heart knows she's gone. She's fled the noise and confusion of this unsettled place to find the home she remembers, the home on Princeton Street in Portland where she was raised and for which she jilted her owner to move in with us. The home she defended from every tom and puss in the neighborhood with fierce screeches and deep, vibrant, business-meaning yowls. If my heart is right, she has 100 miles to go and she won't make it. The farms around us all have dogs, many dogs, and around the fringes of the farms are coons and coyotes, and not much deeper in the woods are mountain lions.

And roads, of course. The instant I saw the empty harness I remembered in panic that I'd just seen a dead tabby on the way back from Dixie's—but it was two or three miles from here, and the body had already begun to bloat.

Here, kitty kitty kitty...I thrash ahead, listening for her odd, bird-like chirp.

Since her miserable, boxed-up trip from Portland, we've kept her mostly inside, letting her get to know the new house. As we cleaned and spackled and painted, she made her rounds. She sniffed meticulously, as high on the walls and lower cabinets as her hind legs would lift her. She rubbed her scent against corners and doorways of special cat significance. At a particular nail head along one of the joints of bare subfloor, something drove her delirious—she licked and pawed and rolled on her side in a frenzy of sensuous attention. She sharpened her claws on the subfloor and on the driftwood posts of my mother's old bed.

Once or twice a day, Marilyn or I would take her outside to let her acquaint herself gradually with the grounds. It was wonderfully absurd. A cat no more belongs on a leash than that French poet's lobster. She would creep along in slow motion, drawing out the retractable leash with no regard for the human at the other end, immersed in whatever intensities her eyes and ears and nose were bringing her, abruptly turning now and then to try to lick the harness off her back. She crept, I now recall with sadness, inexorably away from the house. And once back inside, especially after dark, she would park herself by the screen door, listening into the night. She pawed at the screen and tried to squeeze through where the former owner's dog had torn it. We had to patch the hole with duct tape to keep her in.

I stumble loose from our thicket into the neighbor's trees, and as I turn around our new house startles my eyes. I've been glancing out its windows for ten days but have hardly seen *it* in that time. A plain, brown, slope-roofed oblong box—and it's beautiful. It's almost surrounded in Douglas firs over 100 feet tall. "We live here," I say out loud. Today the carpet, tomorrow our furniture and thousand boxes of things. We're out of the city at last, good city though it was. Maybe, just maybe, we've finally found our place. I'd be wildly happy, I realize, if I hadn't lost our cat.

She could be ten feet away, of course, and I'd never know it. She was relentlessly indifferent to my mother and well capable of the same indifference to me and Marilyn. Many times I've called her from the doorway late at night, wanting to get her in so I could go to bed, only to spy her sitting not twenty feet away, absorbed in the darkness beyond, not only uninterested in my vocalizations but utterly, entirely oblivious to me and to anything human.

Well, to hell with her. I trudge back to the house, scratched and sweaty, itching with nettles, taking no solace from the buttercups I walk through or the tiny pears on the pear tree. There's work to be done if we're going to be ready for the movers tomorrow. I'm hoping hard for the joke to be on me, for Spooky Houdini to have rematerialized by the front door, sleeping or idly licking a paw. But no cat. Inside, the carpet layers are tacking and slicing and gluing away, finishing off our fresh and empty rooms.

In the cool of evening, with Jimmie Dale Gilmore crooning on the boom box, I'm remounting switch plates on creamy fresh-painted walls, enjoying the smell and feel of the new carpet. Its dusty rose color is just right. Even my tilework in the entryways, which in the mortaring and grouting looked like a major disaster, has turned out, with a little cleanup, to be a minor success. Marilyn is on her way from Portland, having watched the furniture into the Bekins truck and said good-bye to our old house. I can't wait for her to get here, to see the work we've done made whole. A fresh start in the country. A creamy white and dusty rose beginning.

I've placed saucers of milk at all the entrances, and occasionally I go out to call—loudly, now that no human being can hear me. All I get in response are frogs chorusing by the stream and the raucous, ratchety cries of guinea hens from across the road.

When I called Marilyn to tell her about the cat, I was surprised to find myself choking up. For a while I could barely speak. I realized after we hung up that I was crying for more than the cat. I thought I was over my mother's death. I thought I had grieved my way through. It's been two years since she broke her hip and went to the hospital and didn't come home. Long enough, my mind declared. She lived eighty-four years, and most of them on her own terms. She lived a full life, a beautiful life.

But I miss her. I miss her very much, I realize, despite my sharp memories of the tensions of those years. As I screw the switch plates to their boxes, sometimes tightening too hard and cracking the plastic, I tell myself that I did all right by my mother in her old age, I did what I could. I tell myself, and I think I believe it. But losing the cat has opened up the emptiness again, renewed the callings of grief. I keep thinking how much she would have liked this place—the birds, the blackberries, the big trees. The garden I'm going to plant.

I drop my screwdriver and turn off Jimmie Dale's infinitely injured voice, his songs that cry so beautifully of loss, and put on Beethoven's *Violin Concerto*—the music whose opening timpani beats will forever wake me into Sunday mornings as a boy, when the hi-fi sometimes issued an ordered serenity into our home. My father, in glasses and bathrobe, would be reading in his rocking chair, my mother on the sofa, the cloth of love they wrung and tore between them momentarily at rest. The music seemed to gather us into its stately wholeness. It was an unspoken communion, a kind of Sabbath we shared.

I open a beer and stretch out on the carpet to listen as Beethoven rises into the authority of his allegro, working up the necessary tensions so that Isaac Stern's fiddle can slip free of them, dancing in a sky where joy and sadness mingle. *My mother and father made a life together,* it keeps coming to me. Despite everything, they made a life, and even after they couldn't live together they made a life for Jim and me. Phrases from my mother's letters pass through me, letters she wrote my father in the 1960s. *They miss you...We're behind on John's orthodonture...Jim is taking courses at the community college...They came from Springfield in fine fettle, as always after visiting you...Thank you for the extra check...Sorry I bawled you out so hard...*His letters to her from that time don't survive, but I know their gist and tone from reading hers.

What is it that so moves me? Their marriage lay in ruins, they each had wounds that wouldn't heal, spites they couldn't control, grievances that could never be redressed—yet this earnestness, this faithfulness, this wealth of caring for my brother and me. As best they could, they kept the broken family whole, so that we might live and grow and go on in the world.

They paid everything their love exacted. They paid willingly and at great cost. I honor them for it. And both of them now gone, and almost all their friends, all my relatives of their generation except for three aunts in their eighties and nineties. All that composed the family cosmos for me as a boy, all the talk and smiles and shouting and tears, all the meals and travels, the touching of hands, all of that gone from the world and yet not gone, all of it as present and vivid as Beethoven's measured exultances, here in the bare rooms of an Oregon house where no mother or father or child of mine will walk through the door. Here in the mystery of memory, the rising of love. I see no end to love. And, forty-six years old, very shaky with a waking joy, I see no end of coming of age.

The slow movement in Beethoven is almost always my favorite, when he wins through his despondencies and turbulent triumphs to the blessed interval, that timeless transitory moment when the soul knows itself and needs no more. Writing scarcely can touch that moment; Beethoven found it many times. I listen outside on the deck, in the company of stars and tall shadowy trees, until something goes wrong in the boom box or the CD. A low, discordant groan crescendoes under the tuneful sweetness of Stern's violin. It takes me several seconds to realize that the sound is coming not from the boom box but from my cat, and that I am looking at her. She's crouched in the spill of light from the kitchen window, her fur puffed up like Halloween, issuing an ominous low yowl to a second cat who has encroached too far into our territory.

I ought to let the drama play out, but I can't stop myself from going to her. The other cat slinks away; my own glances at me with what might be annoyance. She won't be held—too tensed, her awareness too charged—and so I stand nearby until she settles a little and begins to chew a spear of grass. "Spookus, you've been out all day," I inform her, and she lets me carry her into the house. There are burrs and little sticks in her underfur. As I pick them out I remember hidden mushrooms I found while searching the brambles this morning, a blue wildflower I'd never seen before, the sweet and dark and berry-rich smell of the moist ground.

The cat laps up a saucer of milk and pads to the screen door, where she waits to be let out. I tell her I won't have it, and after a while she folds her legs and sinks down on the carpet where she is. She stares out through the screen as my mother used to stare through her sliding glass door, toward things beyond my vision. Beethoven wraps up his sprightly conclusion. The quiet of the night floods in. Soon Marilyn will be here with a few last pieces of our old life. The cat and I will be waiting. We'll let the night breathe in with its quiet stirrings, its stillnesses that verge on speech, its rumors of that deepest wild where my mother and father have gone. We'll breathe the air, we'll keep our eyes open as long as we can, we'll listen for everything the night can tell us of this home where we now live.

Adele Ne Jame

Poems

from *Field Work*

A Blessing (for my daughter)

Silence was Thoreau's proof against cynicism.
William Bronk

Outside your window the morning air is a whirl
of blossoms and rain as if working furiously
toward some gladness—, and you asleep
as I watch, working out some dream
of your life—now where it is all a beginning,
paused like a diver on the high board, balancing
all her weight on her toes, heart like a furnace
that moment before the fall into the unforgettable blue.

And what counter statement can survive
the body's frenetic demands? At your waking
I might say, the moon comes and goes—,
or mention the black angel whose wings are velvet
and always widespread—, or offer instead
the story of my father's sister, eighty years ago
a child herself, who after losing

ten brothers and sisters to the great war,
walked across the blazing desert alone
from Damascus to Beirut. Her whirling robes
like her heart, a weapon against that ruined world.

But on a morning like this when the light
gathers around you with inexpressible
grace and privacy,
the words seem somehow indecorous—,
so I offer instead an unspoken blessing,
the heart's caesura, and yield again
to love's last work, its silent implosion.

Leaving

Two days back from Moorea,
I watch as he leaves for work.
The mitered windows allow a view of the inlet,
the reef beyond, at first light
frigate birds bullet into the sea.

He tosses his briefcase into the back
of the borrowed Italian convertible,
and drives indifferently down the steep incline,
past the bougainvillea we planted together

years ago. The rest of the hillside has gone to seed,
impatiens long ago abandoned.
There is so much to be done.
Forty rose bushes battered by a summer storm.
I prune a few, then start to weed the slope
but no longer have any heart for this work.
I turn to look at the sun rising quickly,
spreading pink and gold over the water,
as it did over Paopao Bay—
and think of the man there who would spend a day diving
again and again, coming up from that sea
offering me simple gifts of iridescent
blue and violet, manageable desires.

Rondeau

The bromeliad by my window
has held its bloom for nearly a year
and without much water. You say
the Mánoa light filtering
through the bamboo shade here in late
afternoon, turns the room sepia,
our bodies golden, figures in a Rossetti painting.
You say we are not like that, really.

                        Tonight I know
you will lie down on a futon with distant
sounds of the city,
the harbor your comfort.
The smell of oriental spice in my hair
won't matter, or the Chinese robes I wear
for you, dragons and cranes
black as this lost night.

First Yellow

The Shower tree, midsummer
in Mánoa or Nu'uanu, petals
drifting toward the ground
in what you might call a dance.
Or the translucent, milky color of
a thousand leaves on a single tree,
once maple, perhaps,
now Japanese yellow, pale, pale
against their own darkening branches.
I saw an old man crying in the streets once,
his mouth was open and silent.
He kept walking, in the music of his weeping,
in the vast, pale morning as if
he had somewhere to go.
This is the field we make
of our bodies: how much healing
there is in repetition and use,
in drinking the other, though
one hand is held open
to the huge and absent sky.
Having nothing, really, and calling it excess.

Father and Son

a conqueror with no luck,
leaving thousands of eyes of blood on the knife point
                                                        Cesar Vallejo

I am cleaning fish at the iron sink.
Thin blood runs over my hands,
over a pile of blue scales.
Across the room the father rubs camphorated oil
into the dark creases of his neck,
over his dark, wide shoulders.

How exactly alike their bodies are—
father and grown son—the tight muscular back, the stance.
The father has pulled on his sweatshirt
and is running in place, laughing,
shouting out his "program": Hakimo Road to Lualualei
and back. Again and again. He boasts of
the victory in advance.

He is sixty, and he does this every day,
training as if he were a prize fighter.
All morning he has cut kiawe in the heat.
He has not stopped even to drink water.
His son still hacks the branches with black thorns
and in the blinding heat quells his anger.

I have cleaned the fish,
dropped them into boiling water
for seven minutes as his father instructed.
The smell is like a bell rung.

The son returns sweating from the field,
spills the kettle water and fish into the sink.

Each noon hour while the father is running,
the son comes to me with determination.
He will have me lie down in the back room,
on the camphoric smelling sheets.
His sex urgent, he lifts my dress.

He no longer notices the small curve of the back
or any detail of the young body his hands own.

Song of a Thousand Empty Hands

I will build you a house of windows to let
the light in, to see the ocean, even the rain
each time you raise your eyes no matter where.
There will be no dry kiawe,
sun-bleached taro, no dark song. The west rooms
will show the Ko'olaus lush from rain,
the nightly rain, common as breathing
and cool verdant air to blanket you.
The wind from the sea on this cliff will take
the dryness from your bones, the dark song
from your heart. You will have only to lift
your eyes to see these succulents, the night-blooming cereus,
and jade, I've planted them all
for you, the deep cup-of-gold along the drive,
hundreds to gather the night rain, not human tears.
I will build you a house of windows to let
the cool light in, the golden morning mist,
the rolling light of verdant hills.
I have a thousand hands for the damp earth, for oleander
and along the ridge, a rush of yellow ginger,
a cathedral of light. You will see
stars, common as breathing, by daylight,
you have only to raise your eyes to see
my body, a tree growing skyward.

About the Men

The white moon, perfect
in the desert sky, in its precisely
dark and moving place.
Making a sound the heart knows:
the violence of beauty we want
to call tenderness, the exquisite moment
of entry, the pleasure of sudden stillness,
that fine body, his arms, thighs. The heat.
Then going past the long dreaming
strewn light,
to the distraction
of dogs barking in the distance
somewhere, the inaccuracy
beginning.

W. S. Merwin

The Winter Palace

from *Orion*

A few yards away, in the tall fir trees beyond a shallow fold that ran up the mountainside, there were thirty-five million butterflies. The dark boughs of the evergreens were bent under the breathing swarms as though weighed down with the black and gold snow that went on blowing in flurries through the trees, glinting in the afternoon sunlight. Pulsing sleeves of butterflies furred the limbs and parts of the trunks. Clusters hung from the drooping ends of branches like nests of orioles. A sound came from them, rising and falling. A breeze echoing. An exhalation without an end.

In our languages the butterflies were the kind that are called monarchs (*Danaus plexippus*), a species familiar to most Americans and many Canadians who have walked in the woods in summer. This was January, in Mexico, in the northeastern part of the state of Michoacan. We were at an altitude of about 10,000 feet in the Transvolcanic Range, on the southwest slope of the Sierra Chincua, part of an area that Mexico's President Salinas, in July 1987, declared a sanctuary because of its importance as one of the ten known overwintering sites in Mexico used annually by the monarch butterflies.

There was a small group of us strung out along the trail. Within

sound of the butterflies no one was chattering. I obtained the estimate of the numbers of that winter colony, with its population
larger than that of many European nations, and much of the rest of
my information about monarchs, later, from Professor Lincoln F.
Brower of the Department of Zoology at the University of Florida.
He is now the preeminent authority in the world on this species, its
behavior, and its imitators. Dr. Brower has been studying the monarchs for over forty years and has been president of the Lepidopterists' Society, vice president of the American Society of Naturalists,
and is the current director of scientific research of the Monarch
Project at the University of Florida. His lectures and papers on his
studies have been supplemented by documentary films and a volume
of essays that he has edited on the subject of mimicry, an integral
theme in his work from the beginning. A few months before our
visit to the monarch sanctuary he had been awarded the Linnaean
Medal in Zoology by the Linnaean Society of London, which can
claim to be the oldest biological society in the world.

Dr. Brower, and the rest of us there on the trail that afternoon in
January, had just spent four days together in Morelia at the invitation
of El Grupo de Los Cien, the Group of A Hundred, an organization
based in Mexico, where it had been conceived and put together
during the '80s by the Mexican poet and novelist Homero Aridjis,
his American wife Betty Ferber, and a number of other writers,
most of them Mexican. The common impulse that brought the original members of the group together was an urge to do something
about the intolerable air pollution of Mexico City, a livid presence
in all their lives which never left them for a minute. As discussion of
the subject progressed among friends, many of whom were writers
and teachers, it was obvious from the start that the foul air they
were breathing was a phenomenon inseparable from the accelerating degradation of the living world everywhere as a result of human
activities. Their subject inevitably embraced what we have come to
refer to with nagging discomfort as the environment. Part of the
unease that the word touches off is a well-learned response to the

facts themselves, the news of which, in our lifetimes, has been consistently and increasingly so ominous that many avoid paying attention to them if they can. But there is also the chronic sense of the word's misleading inadequacy, its suggestion that what we are alluding to all around us, our cause and our effect, is distinct from us. And with that, the realization that we have no other term for it that is not faulty in more or less the same way, and that apparently we did not feel the need of one until recently. It did not take Homero and Betty and the other founders long to recruit a hundred writers and intellectuals throughout Latin America who shared their concerns, and then scientists, writers, and activists from other countries were enlisted as adherents. Funding was acquired from the Rockefeller Foundation among other sources. A manifesto was prepared and the Group took a full page in the *New York Times* to announce the reasons for its existence.

Some of us standing watching the monarchs had been at the Group's first gathering in Morelia, in September 1991, which had proceeded in the glare of television floodlights and had been broadcast live and virtually complete, like a sports event, throughout Mexico and much of Latin America. Many at that meeting felt that it had few precedents if any. There were scientists and writers conversing not with glazed politeness but with obvious and undisguised eagerness to cooperate in the face of a common urgency. Together they prepared and signed the Morelia Declaration, a summary of the world situation with regard to population, consumption, pollution, habitat devastation, loss of species, cultural and social erosion, nuclear radiation, militarization, and then a series of recommendations intended for consideration at the Earth Summit in Rio de Janeiro in June 1992, which "the environmental President," George Bush, and his representatives would manage to jam with double talk and evasion.

The second Morelia symposium had met with the intention of reviewing what had happened and failed to happen in the intervening two years. It had been planned as a smaller, quieter, indeed more intimate occasion, less hung with microphones and the exigencies of the media than the first one had been. And so it was, although cameras and interviewers from the Mexican television system, Televisa, met each of the participants at the Mexico City airport, and all the public meetings and press conferences were televised.

And when Lincoln Brower's turn came to present to the gathering, toward the end, a lecture with slides of the monarchs and their wintering sites, the lights for the cameras made it impossible to darken the auditorium at all, so that what appeared on the screen was a series of gray clouds in which Lincoln kept pointing out ghosts invisible to the rest of us. This must have been what the cameras were recording for the future: Lincoln's voice telling later viewers what they cannot see.

Butterflies, like many other insects, have a limited tolerance to extremes of temperature, but different species respond to the cycle of seasons in different ways. The butterfly known in English as the mourning cloak (*Nymphalis antiopa*), for instance, has evolved hibernating behavior that allows it to spend winters in North America without leaving the zones of hard frost. The monarchs, on the other hand, die if the temperature drops much below freezing, and though they journey far into North America during the spring and summer months they retreat annually before the frost, as many birds do, and despite their fragility they have established migratory flight patterns that the whole species retraces every year. The population of monarchs in the western part of the continent seeks destinations that have been known to scientists, more or less, for 120 years and more. In the autumn they cross the Sierras and spend the winter in tall trees, especially Monterey pines and eucalyptus, at some forty known sites near the Pacific. In March they return to their summer range to lay their eggs in the California milkweeds (*Asclepias crinocarpa*, primarily), and then die.

But the wintering habits of the monarchs from the central and eastern parts of the continent, which constitute the main population, were not known until the 1970s. The butterflies' disappearance from eastern North America in the autumn has been one of the marks of the turning season, like the fall of the leaves, and points on their migrating routes have been noted for a long time, but well past the middle of this century observers in the United States could not say what happened to the monarchs after their itineraries converged in Texas. "They slipped over the border," Lincoln said, "and were lost to us."

The monarchs' travels are remarkable even among the plentiful wonders of migratory behavior. They alone in their subfamily of 157 species have found a way of nourishing themselves on various milkweeds (*Asclepias*)—a plant genus that is widespread in North America, and toxic to most herbivores—while avoiding the North American winter. The achievement is magnified by the fact that a migrant monarch anywhere along the route will be three or more generations removed from its most recent ancestor there. The individual butterfly had never been to the place before and never could have learned the way. It knew it—its knowledge part of a guiding inheritance, along with the aptitude for transforming itself from an egg into a caterpillar, and from a chrysalis into an adult able to fly.

Although individual butterflies do not complete the entire migratory cycle they cover huge distances. From Canada, and the northern United States, some of them, to central Mexico, and then months later, after overwintering, to the southern Gulf states to lay eggs and expire. The evidence of the distance traversed has been found in their tissues in the form of cardenolides, heart poisons derived from the sap of identifiable northern species of milkweed (*Asclepias syriaca*, in particular) occurring neither in the southern states nor in Mexico. The toxins are stored without chemical alteration in the bodies of the monarch caterpillars that hatch on the leaves of the milkweed, and are transferred to the pupae and on to the adult butterflies and retained there—"sequestered" in the language of the professionals—without harming the monarchs at any stage. On the contrary, the sap of the milkweeds has become indispensable to the monarchs not only as food but as protection. For with the heart poisons of the *Asclepias* in their bodies the monarchs in turn become poisonous. Their orange and black pattern proclaims that warning to predators, and the message in their highly visible appearance has been important not only to their evolution but to that of other species, and to the study of them.

Contrasting patterns of orange or yellow or white and black often announce that a species is poisonous. Some that are not toxic have evolved patterns resembling poisonous originals as a protection. How that mimicry comes about sheds light on the general process of evolution, and the monarchs and their imitators have become a classic example.

Brower speaks of some of his predecessors in the study of butterflies with a respect that sounds like affection. A pioneer in the subject was an American lepidopterist, William Henry Edwards, whose account of butterfly discoveries in the Amazon basin during the early years of the nineteenth century prompted the great Victorian naturalists Alfred Russell Wallace and Henry Walter Bates to sail from Brazil and the Rio Negro in 1848. It was an historic journey. Wallace's small, succinct survey of the palms of the region remains a classic, and his deductions from the notes he made at the time—a great part of them lost at sea on his return voyage to England—bore such an affinity to Darwin's theory of natural selection that Wallace has been credited by some with having arrived first at the evolutionary hypothesis. And Bates, who spent eleven years in the Amazon and wrote one of the great narratives of exploration, drew from his monumental records of the insects of the Amazon basin a treatise on mimicry whose importance to the theory of natural selection was immediately apparent when he published it in 1862.

Bates concluded that a chance individual of a nonpoisonous species of butterfly at some point bore a degree of resemblance to a poisonous species and as a result was let alone by predators, so that it and those of its progeny that most resembled it had a better chance of survival than the others with no such protection. The hypothesis left many questions unanswered and in 1879 a German naturalist, Fritz Müller, refined and extended it to cover more intricate relations of mimicry, particularly the imitations of "unpalatable" (toxic) species by butterflies of a different group that are "unpalatable" in their own right. This process turns out to have, for butterflies, the advantage of extending a single warning pattern so that the number of butterflies that are tasted before predators get the picture clear is greatly reduced.

Mimicry, and specifically the imitations of monarchs, had been important in the studies of Brower's Canadian senior colleague, Fred Urquhart and his wife, N. R. Urquhart, who began tracking the southward migrations of the eastern monarchs in 1941. In the '50s, Fred Urquhart questioned some of the conclusions about mimicry and predation that most naturalists by then took for granted as primary illustrations of the workings of evolution. He doubted whether birds really found the toxic butterflies unpalatable in the first place. If they did, he was not convinced that birds could learn by experience to avoid unpalatable models. If they could, he was not sure that they would confuse the mimic with the model. But if, after all, they did, he was uncertain about the point at which the resemblance began to be effective—which is perhaps the most interesting of the questions. Part of Lincoln Brower's and Jane Brower's work in the '50s was directed to finding answers to these challenges.

The research of Jane Brower, in particular, during that decade, established the role of the warning patterns and their imitations more firmly than ever. But the complete migratory path of the main population of the monarchs remained unknown to biologists. It was not until the early '70s that a collaborator of the Urquharts, Ken Brugger, and his wife Cathy, finally discovered a vast colony of monarchs overwintering in the mountains of south-central Mexico. Fred Urquhart published the news of the find in *National Geographic* and the *Journal of the Lepidopterists' Society* without revealing their locations, and he and his team had the place to themselves for a while. But Brower and his students by then had eliminated the mountains of many other possible regions of Mexico, and there were enough clues in the articles to complete what they already knew. One day the following winter several of them found their way to the Transvolcanic Range of western Michoacan, and to one of the sites, and the camp of Dr. Urquhart's surprised researchers.

The people who live in those mountains, not surprisingly, have always known about the butterflies, which had been coming there, as they said, forever. Such pre-Columbian literature as survived the conquest has not, so far, yielded any specific mention of the sites, but the region was border country between the Tarascans and the Aztec Empire, for centuries, and it may have been dangerous and little-known terrain. In the language of the Mazahua Indians, however, in the village of Santiago in the state of Mexico, there is a word that means "the butterfly that passes in October and November," and the Mazahuas, according to tradition, have eaten monarchs for a long time, stripping off the wings and frying the thoraxes on flat *comales*, and they still do it, though nowadays mostly as a show for tourists. I have not heard how they deal with the taste, and the nausea-producing cardenolide toxins. Jane Brower, in the course of her researches, tasted the milky sap of the *Asclepias humistrata*, one of the milkweeds frequented by monarchs and a source of their toxin, and she vouched for its bitterness and for its causing a rush of salivation, and nausea. It is hard to believe that monarchs ever occupied much more than a ceremonial place in the Mazahuas' diet but the presence of the monarchs has been part of the local lore for a long time. There is a recurrent belief in the region that they are the souls of the dead returning, which may be related to the fact that their arrival begins some time near November 2, the Day of the Dead in the Christian calendar. Homero Aridjis, who grew up in the state of Michoacan, not far from the sites, learned as a child of the winter butterflies filling the trees in the mountains. (Many of those trees, as he has written, are gone now.)

At the other end of their cycle, Brower, as a child in New Jersey growing up near a kettlehole pond in the woods, saw the summer monarchs come and go with their season, and loved butterflies, he says, by the time he was five. He talked about them on the bus cross-ing Michoacan, heading northwest toward the wintering sites. Lin-coln is an amiable, gentle, slightly rotund figure who carries his weight of knowledge lightly. He was wearing a dark tweed suit, in the mountains of Mexico. In a youthful, rather reedy voice he imparts information as a matter of common interest, without push-ing it. Something about him of the grown cherub, clear and benign, kindles his general conversation and shines in his unabashed fond-ness for his German shepherds Rosie and her son Uhlrich, whose pictures he carries with him.

As we moved away from urban areas, the family resemblance that runs through the mountains of central and southern Mexico became more apparent. The ridges of western Michoacan rise in shapes and contours and qualities of light reminiscent of the highlands of Chia-pas, where organized rebellion had begun two weeks before, on New Year's Day. Talk on the bus kept reverting from monarchs to the events in the south—what was known of them. Homero was in daily contact with friends in the Mexican government. One of the participants at the Morelia symposium, Jeffrey Wilkerson, is an anthropologist who has directed the Institute for Cultural Ecology in the Tropics since 1977. His main office was in the country outside Vera Cruz and he had led research expeditions into the Lacandon forest of lowland Chiapas. At Morelia he kept telephoning friends and colleagues in the region, or trying to, and occasionally return-ing with bulletins.

And in the early '70s I had lived in Chiapas myself, in San Cristóbal de las Casas, one of the principal centers of the Zapatista forces and of the government's buildup in response to them. I had visited that beautiful region within the past few years, and have old friends there. The colonial town set high in its ring of mountains had changed relatively little. The streets were still alive with Indians. Their faces were familiar, and their garments that told what village they were from, what language they spoke, sometimes even who their parents and grandparents were. I heard the sound of their feet

half running on the flat stones like a voice I recognized, heard once
more the muffled clicks of the Mayan words, the clanging of the thin
bells in the towers, the popping of rockets (handmade in Indian villages as a cottage industry) at all hours of the day and night, cele-
brating that very moment.

I knew the cold of the nights and the sere colors of the winter
cornfields on the shoulders of the mountains, and the abiding anxiety about the circumstances of the highland Maya people, their
poverty, the way they were treated by officials and townspeople, and
the inexorable and accelerating deforestation of the mountains, the
awareness of which was like knowledge of a malignancy. Laws
against cutting trees seemed to amount to nothing but an occasional
pretext for taking something else away from an Indian, since it was
the Maya villagers who cut and hauled wood in places where there
were no log roads. On winter mornings I would wake at first light
to the sound of heavy wood being dragged over cobbles out in the
narrow street where the fog still hid the tiled tops of the whitewashed walls, and would listen to the clop of a small horse pulling
two raw pine beams, their top ends lashed to the packsaddle, one on
either side, and the lower ends trailing behind. If I opened the low
door in the garden wall I would see them pass in the cold cloud, following an Indian in a straw hat and a long woolen *chamarra* who was
hurrying ahead. Later in the morning Indian men would weave
along the street balancing on their heads tables and rough chairs of
raw pine wood still oozing amber pitch, made of trees cut illegally
with axes and machetes and shaped into boards with the same tools.
They had carried the furniture for hours, in the dark, over the
mountain trails, to sell in town. The prices were very low because
the furniture was badly made, because the wood was illegal, and
because they were Indians.

The old buildings in the lovely town had been made of adobe—
mud mixed with pine needles and certain half-magic bodily ingre-
dients such as horse manure, milk, and urine. But the new construction had armatures of iron rebar and cement, and the walls

were of bricks made out on the flats in the no man's land where the dirt streets splayed out. The brick kilns were fired with large quantities of contraband wood brought down from the dwindling forest.

In April the clear air of the mountains began to fill with smoke as the Indians' cornfields were burned over and patches that had been felled to make new fields on the slopes high above the valleys were set alight. Outside the town we could see the thinned and flayed areas spreading upward along the mountains, month by month, season by season. The slash-and-burn agriculture whose damages had been less apparent and more gradual in the level lowlands, with small populations, had brought obvious devastation to the mountains, and as the population grew the wreckage was spreading like a fire. When the trees were felled on the steep gradients the winter rains eroded the topsoil, starting at once, and after a few years when the fields were abandoned the forest could not grow back. Up until then most of the cutting had been done by Indians using only axes and machetes, but huge log trucks also went hurtling along the narrow, twisting cliffside roads. And one spring morning in the early '70s I saw a crowd of Indian men in the broad hats, fringes, and ribbons of Zinacantan and Tenejapa, their machetes on their shoulders, gazing with fascination into the display window of a hardware store, at the center of which, like the infant in a crèche, lay a yellow McCullough chain saw.

Many of my friends there at the time were anthropologists, biologists, ethnobotanists, and after each trip down into the lowlands they came back with woeful news of the Lacandon villages and the rainforest. The first road into that region, built in the early '70s, became at once an avenue for ruthless logging and for nefarious traffic of every kind, and rapidly widening areas of an ecosystem that had evolved over many millennia were wiped out for quick-fix agricultural projects that could not possibly be maintained for more than a few years. The pollution of most of the watercourses was an immediate result, and the plan—which became a perennial growth —to dam the Usumacinta River and flood huge sections of the lowland forest, including major archaeological sites, was under consideration even then. Impoverished and discontented highland Maya from communities near San Cristóbal were transplanted into the lowland rainforest and "given" land to slash and burn and starve on. Such laws as existed relating to indigenous peoples and conservation were ignored, and it was generally taken for granted that the Federal police and of course the army were incompetent, corrupt, and distinguished by nothing but their arrogance and brutality. All of that had been in place in Chiapas in the '70s and had been gathering for at least a generation before that, and as we traveled toward the monarch sites we kept trying to guess why it had happened when it did, and not at almost any point during the past few decades.

The deforested ridges of Michoacan were a continuing reminder of the flaying of the mountains of Chiapas, and it was a surprise to find ourselves suddenly passing through the cool shade of a remnant of old fir woods under trees of indeterminate age. Then these vestiges of the life that had covered the slopes there for so long ended abruptly to disclose an ideal image of the magnificent geography of that region. We were high on one side of an enormous valley hazed with distance, whose breadth and depth appeared to be on a scale that one could not grasp even if one knew the numbers, and around it in the colors of smoke rose the shadow of a vast flower of some other time, a ring of sharp summits broken, jagged, receding behind each other as far as we could see. It is not surprising that the place has been called the Valley of the Thousand Peaks.

We had reached the Sierra Transvolcanica, the Transvolcanic Range of western Michoacan, which includes all the mountains to which the major part of the eastern population of monarchs travels so far every autumn without calling them, as we do, Pelon, Acuña, Chivati, Picacho, Campanario, and Chincua. The Sierra Transvolcanica represents a relatively small area of the continent, and it is possible to do no more than deduce from what is known of the monarchs something of how they came to evolve a migratory pattern fixed upon this particular region.

The monarchs belong to a subfamily of butterflies, the Danainae, found in the Americas and the eastern hemisphere. They are tropical creatures and because of their inability to survive freezing temperatures at any stage of their life cycle, as egg, caterpillar, chrysalid, or adult, few of the Danainae besides the monarchs have been able to extend their range into the temperate zone. Only two other species of Danainae are to be found north of Mexico, and they do not go much beyond the southernmost parts of the States. The floral sustenance of the Danainae, the milkweeds (*Asclepias*) are also predominantly tropical, but during the last few million years some species of *Asclepias* have adapted to the cold and have spread north, developing 108 new species in North America. In northern and eastern Mexico the months from November to May are dry, and the milkweeds, along with many other plants, die back during that season. In the areas where this deprivation occurs, the monarchs, in response to it, evolved a kind of hormonal suppression cycle. In the autumn they produced a generation of butterflies that remained in a state of reproductive dormancy, did not hunt for milkweeds, and aged relatively slowly. It is thought that once they had achieved this method of waiting out the famine they began to extend their range northward each spring to take advantage of the new growth of milkweeds. But as days shortened and temperatures fell with the return of autumn they retreated southward again. The northern and southern movements of the monarchs came to coincide with the autumn and spring equinoxes and apparently the length of days is an important signal for the beginning of their journeys.

The requisites of survival that led the monarchs to overwinter in the western mountains of Mexico include, of course, the improbability of freezing weather. Places that are too hot are not congenial to them at that season either, because high temperatures encourage activity which would exhaust their stored food supply in a season when it is hard for them to replenish it. They need constant access to water, which must not be too far away, for the same reason. And they need shelter from winter storms. The fir forests (the tree is the

Abies religiosa, called *oyamel* in the region) of certain slopes above 10,000 feet, near the summits of the Transvolcanic Range, provide all these. The sites are not unvarying. Wandering bands of monarchs have been found overwintering elsewhere in Mexico, sometimes even to the east of Mexico City, but they have been relatively small assemblies and the sites have not been used regularly.

Large parts of the autumn routes of the eastern monarchs are now known. They narrow into a current crossing the Rio Grande into Mexico, travel south to the Sierra Madre Oriental and then west across the mountains to the Thousand Peaks. The summits of the eastern part of the range average 7,000 feet, with some rising to almost 11,000 feet. The generation that left in the spring will have multiplied into a large summer population that coalesces into bands of increasing size on the way south. The monarchs fly by day and congregate in trees at nightfall. As they travel they drink the nectar of the autumn composite flowers, asters and goldenrods. In spells of warm weather, if the flowers are abundant, they linger, and when the days turn cloudy, cold, or windy, they move on. The bodily fats that they are building up to see them through the winter are known as lipids, and the nectar sources are important to their survival, for the winter flora in the mountains is sparse and unreliable. In early November the first groups of migrants begin to arrive in the oyamel forests on the peaks. Butterflies that have flown from Maine will have traveled 2,500 miles at least. Most of those that have been examined were not, as would have been expected, tattered and exhausted, but appeared to be in perfect condition, as though they had just left the chrysalis. The egg from which each of them had grown had been laid singly on a milkweed leaf, and the caterpillar that emerged had immediately explored the rest of the leaf looking for other monarch eggs there, to eat them in order to make sure that there would be enough food for one caterpillar, at least. But as adults, and great travelers, there are advantages to being part of a large assembly, and the first groups that settle into the oyamel firs obviously welcome still larger congregations: they have been seen above their trees in spiraling columns 1,000 feet high, signaling to other groups, "Here is the place."

Our own approach, some two months later in the season, was directed toward the Sierra Chincua, the most accessible of the sites to human visitors. Part of the peak is designated as a monarch butterfly sanctuary named El Campanario, the only such reservation that is open to the public. The site itself has been intensively studied by Lincoln and his colleagues.

The road descended along the side of a valley through a scattering of firs standing near the road like people waiting on a station platform. The oyamels bear a resemblance to other *Abies* occurring in the ranges of the western part of the continent. Superficially, the *religiosa* looks like a smaller version of it. The trees we passed through were a park at the outskirts of the town of Angangueo. Houses at the edge of the municipality appeared in pistachio greens, cranberry pinks, and butcher blues. The bus nosed around corners under balconies overflowing with potted petunias and geraniums, ferns and aloes, daisies and roses. There was an Alpine aspect to some of the buildings in the pitch of the roof, the eaves and balconies and windows. Some of the roses in tubs and some that were tumbling from untended hedges looked like varieties from the last century or earlier, and I was reminded of the old French roses with trunks like trees, in gardens in San Cristóbal in Chiapas, which must have been taken there by Napoleon's representatives during the administration of the hapless Maximilian. The bus stopped under a balcony from which an Alaskan husky barked at us through a row of flower pots. The road beyond Angangueo is too steep, rough, and mean spirited for a self-respecting bus, and we climbed out and into the backs of small rugged open trucks that would shake us and jolt us to the end of the line, at the monarch sanctuary. The trucks represented one form of human employment that the butterflies have recently brought to the region.

Across the street on the hillside was a complex of mine buildings —scaffolds, conveyors, trestles, metal towers, all painted yellow and all silent, climbing the slope like the escarpments of a tin castle. The glimpse of prosperity, current or remembered, in what we saw of Angangueo, is a legacy of what has been one of the major silver mines in Mexico. The mine had finally closed, very recently. The shafts had been dug back into the mountain for a considerable distance, but eventually the lode was worked to the point at which the ore no longer repaid the cost of extracting it. As the trucks spun their wheels and wound up the dirt road that climbed out of the end of the street, we passed the piled guts of the mountain: long, vast yellow mounds layered like pyramids, cracking and eroding along the side of the road until the road wrenched away from them at a hairpin turn. A man and a dog walked slowly and without evident purpose along one ridge of tailings over whose parched contours the first sparse grasses and scrub were struggling to start from scratch. The story of the mine—the discovery of the lode, the displacement of the indigenous inhabitants, the excavation and development, the wealth, generosity, and injustice of the owners, the legends and accidents—were the local lore and identity of the town for generations. Foreign investments were important in the mine's history, and silver out of that mountain had become part of the fortune that endowed the Guggenheim Foundation. Through the whole age of the mine the butterflies had come every autumn to the forest on the summit. In the history of the monarchs and their migration the anecdote of the mine amounts to only a page, though it may prove to be one of the last.

The mine had increased the population around Angangueo, and its closing inevitably reduced the opportunities for making a living in the region. We saw log trucks parked in the back lanes and beside the mounds of mine tailings. As the trucks rocked and reared over the ridges we could see that the slopes had been denuded far up toward the summits and in some places all the way to the top. Homero told us, and we heard from other sources, that in Michoacan, as in Chiapas, the logging continues with little or no regard for legality, and such ordinances as may exist are not enforced. Illegal sawmills operate openly, and in great numbers, and officials tolerate them for reasons not hard to guess. An oyamel fir tree can fetch $500 on the black market, and some of the small communities run their own lumber mills. We passed small cornfields, with the dry winter stalks standing in them, hens scratching in the roadside bushes, slat and adobe houses scattered on the mountainside. No bustling activity. Homero said that when he had asked people living out near the mountain what they lived on they had said without exception or hesitation, "the forest." Most of the households have many children—ten, fifteen, even twenty—and take it for granted that they will have many more. "What will they all live on?" he had asked, and again they had said at once, "the forest." At the foot of the mountain a nursery under the auspices of the government employs a sizeable work force growing seedlings to put back into the forest. Near it another sawmill is cutting up trees that have been growing for the better part of a century, at least. The arguments in favor of logging are the usual ones based on the assumption that of all the species on earth only one has a right to exist.

The forest that remained reached to the top of the ridge and to the peak ahead of us, and a sweep of bared valley fell away to our right. Lincoln raised a hand and said, "There they are." The truck stopped to let us look where he was pointing, at several big trees near the top, whose color, instead of being the dark green shadowed with black of the rest of the forest, was dimmed with a suggestion of old gilding. The trucks lurched on to where the road narrowed, and stopped. A series of stands like oversized packing crates, made of very recently sawn rough boards, lined the downhill side of the road, nothing on their shelves but a few bottles of soft drinks. Down across the shallow upland hollow with its rustling cornfields a line of slate roofs, like a stopped freight train, covered benches and tables, and charcoal stoves for feeding the visitors who come now during the winter months, mostly on weekends, to visit the sanctuary and see the monarchs. We were there on a weekday when no one was expected. Several small boys appeared from between the stands to beg in a halfhearted way. The meandering settlement is called El Rosario.

From there on we walked. The ruts curved between cornfields and dusty bushes. Schoolgirls appeared in twos and threes with articles to sell—glass lapel pins in the shape of butterflies, resting in plastic foam inside elaborate clear plastic cases, all turned out in some factory far away. One child had diminutive napkins, not entirely clean, each of them embroidered with a small orange and black butterfly in cross-stitch. She told me she made them herself when she got home from school. How many did she make in a day? "Maybe one," she said. She asked less than a dollar apiece for them.

A trickle of water crossed the path and I looked down to see a cluster of monarchs trembling on the damp earth beside it. I could see that some of them seemed to be sipping at the water's edge, but others, perhaps because the day was cool, had been too weak to keep from falling in and drowning. The small watercourse was no broader than a hand, and the sticks and dead leaves along it were adorned for several yards with the orange and black wings of dead monarchs.

The path came to an intersection and a few more stalls offering cross-stitched embroidery and T-shirts hanging on clotheslines, and a sign announced the sanctuary of El Campanario. A number of men, none of whom looked unquestionably official, materialized to make sure we paid to enter the preserve. The transaction was carried out in a dark building like a trading post, according to an apparently impromptu procedure. A dusty footpath led up from the building along a section of chain-link fence that appeared to be more symbolic than effective. From there on up the mountain we were accompanied at every step by an assorted contingent of men whose job it was, they said, to keep an eye on us, to make sure we did not leave the path and stray into the forest. Some of these escorts came and went, some hung around in groups talking, at bends in the trail.

From a distance, and from below, the forest on the upper slopes and the summit looked dark and dense, broken here and there by

openings that looked like part of the natural order. The steep, pow-
dery path above the fence led up into what was indeed a forest, but
a much disturbed and damaged one. The scuffed track across worn
roots told of the passage of many feet. The trees had obviously been
thinned. Clearings showed up as we climbed, and there were few
young firs in the open spaces. Trunks had been cut and, for some
reason, left where they had fallen. If one stepped a few feet from the
path one found stumps in the undergrowth, which had grown dense
in the sunlight. Placards commanded pedestrians to stay on the path
and urged them not to step on butterflies. As we walked the wings
were everywhere in the dust, and under the bushes to either side.
Some of the wings were fluttering feebly, some were still, some
flew up and floated away. The butterflies' energy depends partly
upon temperature, and those that fly out of their trees after basking
in the sunlight, and glide down to water, may be caught in tree shadows, cloud shadows, or cold drafts, and not have the strength to get
back before they die on the way.

I was wondering about the understory flora of the forest that I
could see along the path: various labiates, senecios, and geraniums,
many of them no doubt endemic, some looking like widespread
introductions. I asked one of our escorts what he called one small
flowering bush. "Maria Antonia," he said. My luck was different with
another of the men and another flower. "I call that a green plant," he
said. But several of the men turned out to be biology students from
Mexican universities, who were interested in these nectar sources.
Studies have identified many of the flowers—*Alchemilla procumbens,
Senecio anguilifolius, Eupatorium mairetianum,* and a number of *Salvias*
prominent among them.

To our left, as we went up, was a shallow side valley, sunk into the
mountainside. We turned a corner of the path and looked across the
long hollow, and a clearing, to the tall trees. Again Lincoln pointed,
and we stopped to watch the nearest of the oyamel firs dripping
with butterflies, the flurries of sparks swirling in the sunbeams, and

up over the forest, down toward the main valley, and back up toward us.

As we watched them a cloud passed overhead. We saw its shadow cover the trees, and felt the warmth drop out of the air, and as it did a great cloud of butterflies rose out of the firs and spiraled high above them, circling around and around. Lincoln told us that a sudden chill was a danger signal to them, a warning that they must not remain away from the colony, weakened by cold. If the air temperature drops below a measurable "flight threshold" the butterflies cannot take off at all. They respond to a cloud shadow by flying up to hurry home—even if they are home already. The apparently inappropriate maneuver allows the butterflies to resettle into the trees in groups arranged not for exposure to sunlight but for insulation.

We were not yet close enough to hear them, and as we stood there watching them return to the trees Lincoln told us something about their poison. Many butterfly species have evolved ways of using plants that are toxic to most herbivorous forms in order to nourish and protect themselves. There are species that feed and lay eggs on various kinds of Solanaceae fatally poisonous to almost all herbivores that might make the mistake of ingesting them, and the South American Heliconiinae butterflies feed on *Passiflora* species, the leaves of which release hydrogen cyanide when digested. The monarchs' tolerance of milkweed poisons allows them to use the sap for nourishment and to sequester the plants' defensive toxins. The toxic plants' evolution of their own defenses, in the first place, is an earlier chapter in the story. Those butterflies that have managed to incorporate the plants' defenses need to signal to predators that it would be unwise to taste them, and the bright colors and contrasting patterns perform that warning. The easily recognizable appearance reduces the risk of being eaten, but does not eliminate it, for the birds' knowledge of such matters is not instinctive but learned, and a bird may taste a bright butterfly, or more than one, before being certain that it is not a good idea. The distinctive appearances of many poisonous species of butterflies which have led, in turn, to imitations by butterflies without such defenses, have also produced complicated variations. A primary example in research into butterfly mimicry is the viceroy butterfly, *Limenitis archippus*, which has developed a close resemblance to the monarch where their ranges overlap. But in southern Florida where monarchs are rare most of the year the viceroys have come to resemble a different member of the Danainae, the Florida queen, *Danaus gilippus berenice*, which is not orange but a dark-shaded walnut color with white spots. And in southern Texas, where the prevailing member of the Danainae is the paler birch-hued *Danaus gilippus striposa*, the viceroy becomes as pale as its model while retaining the black wing-veining reminiscent of the monarch. But only in the adults does mimicry appear. Whereas the caterpillars of the poisonous species are banded in bright colors and unmistakable, the earlier phases of the mimic species are camouflaged to disappear into the bark and foliage around them. Some of the mimic species, including viceroys, appear to be developing toxic arguments of their own. And the actual toxicity of the poisonous species varies depending upon the time of year, the region in which the butterflies have hatched and grown, the members of the milkweed family on which they have been nourished, and the age of individuals. Alfonso Alonso, one of Lincoln's students, has discovered that monarchs lose their stored cardiac glycoside toxins as they grow older, so that if a bird were to fail to recognize their warning appearance after a certain age they would turn out to be digestible after all.

The delicate temperature balance that the monarchs need to survive the winter and set out on their spring migration has been provided with some certainty by the forests near the summits—though a sudden exceptionally cold spell in the winter of 1991–92 destroyed more than half of the butterflies at some sites. But another evolutionary development in the history of their poison and its uses has overtaken them at the winter sites. Two kinds of birds that prey upon butterflies have found ways of dealing with the monarch's toxic defenses. It is something that may have happened fairly recently, as agricultural practices in the monarchs' northern range, in the U.S. and Canada, have led to the proliferation of milkweed species with low toxicities, on which the butterflies feed in the early stages of their lives.

It was afternoon when we stood watching the outskirts of the colony at El Campanario. At sunrise, Lincoln said, when it is too cool for the monarchs to fly, flocks of black-backed orioles (*Icterus abeillei*) and black-headed grosbeaks (*Pheucticus melanocephalus*) arrive from the valley and fall upon the immobilized butterflies clustered densely in the trees. They tear into the monarchs, devouring them into a storm of wings, killing some fifteen thousand a day in one colony. In a single winter, Lincoln said, they may destroy close to a million butterflies. By the late 1970s they were known to be wiping out over half the population in some places. Bird predation upon monarchs on such a scale has never been observed anywhere except in Mexico. Monarchs in Massachusetts, at the other end of their cycle, averaged a very much higher level of toxicity than was found in those in Mexico.

The grosbeaks, furthermore, have developed a tolerance of the milkweed-derived poisons that amounts to effective immunity. The orioles have learned to determine by taste which of the butterflies are less poisonous than others. And besides tearing off the wings, they strip out the thoracic muscle and the abdominal contents where the stored poisons are concentrated, and eat only the internal tissues. As the monarchs' bodily poisons diminish in the course of the winter the predation increases. Some research suggests that the butterflies have begun to evolve a different kind of poison, or several kinds of poison such as pyrrolizidine alkaloids, but so far the evidence is not consistent or substantial.

In contrast, the western population of monarchs which overwinters in California feeds at all stages on milkweed species with a dependably high cardenolide content. Some butterflies average more than four times the toxicity of the ones overwintering in Mexico, and the birds know it and let them alone.

Besides the dwindling effectiveness of their toxic defenses, the monarchs at the wintering grounds in Mexico are threatened by the steady depletion and destruction of the oyamel forests which provide the very conditions for which they have evolved their migratory cycle. The mitigating effects of the forests on extremes of heat and cold have been studied in detail, and so have the consequences of thinning and clear cutting. If the reduction of the forest continues the larger eastern population of the monarch species, at the end of its vast migrations, will be edged out of existence.

Up until now the Mexican government's administrative flourishes establishing sanctuaries and preserves and regulations of the overwintering area have amounted to little more than environmental rhetoric to convey the illusion that something has been done, while allowing business to proceed as usual, a phenomenon that has become familiar on both sides of the border.

Brower is convinced that the principal danger to the survival of the eastern monarchs is not bird predation nor climatic uncertainties but the destruction of the sites by human population pressures and the logging industry whose appetites and mores are everywhere the same. He has argued for preservation of the forests at the monarchs' wintering sites not only in order to save the eastern monarchs themselves but in order to allow the migratory phenomenon that they have evolved, this extraordinary natural achievement with a value beyond our estimation, to survive. He and others see a possible approach in the outright acquisition of the wintering sites and their administration along the lines of national—or international—parks. Mexican officials invoke laws that would make such ideas difficult or impossible, and they claim to be legally and financially helpless.

"What good are butterflies?" ask those inhabitants of the region who are impatient to cut the trees until none are left. Certainly alternate employment must be found for the local people, some-thing besides whatever they can take out of the forest, and means must be found to limit the geometrical multiplication of their numbers.

The monarchs' cycle is not confined to Mexico, and perhaps the other two nations through which it passes without regard for human boundaries can provide the Mexican government with help and influence to safeguard the treasure they do not own but share. A conservation group in Mexico, Monarca A.C., under the leadership of Rodolfo Ogarrio, is working with governmental departments to try to save the sites. The World Wildlife Fund has been supporting conservation efforts connected with them. Before the second More-lia conference was over writers and scientists from the three coun-tries the monarchs pass through formed the Monarch Alliance, ded-icated to trying to elicit international support for the butterflies.

We stood in the afternoon sunlight in the sound of them, a sound of words before words, a whisper of one syllable older than lan-guage, continuing like a pulse. In the updraft from the valley the monarchs fluttered toward us, lighted on us. At one moment there were fifteen of them on me, trembling on their way. The fragility was not only theirs.

Louise Wagenknecht

White Poplar

First publication

There is a valley south of Mount Ashland, where the sharp timber-clad peaks of the Siskiyous become rounded brown hills, capped by remnants of ancient seabeds. On them grow oaks and junipers and sagebrush. Here the large mule deer of the high deserts to the east meet the small Pacific blacktails, and the hybrid bucks grow great antlers. Here ranching, mining, and logging met on Cottonwood Creek, and a company lumber town called Hilt grew near a railroad when the century was young.

We of Hilt, about 400 of us, lived within a circle of peaks, as fixed as the stars. Around the compass we named them: Mount Ashland, Pilot Rock, Skunk's Peak, Sheldon Butte, Black Mountain, Mount Shasta, Bailey Hill, Cottonwood Peak, Bullion Mountain, Shaft Rock, the long rolling gap into Beaver Creek, then Hungry Creek Lookout with the lone fir close beside it on the skyline, and Mount Ashland again. Mount Ashland was in Oregon, Hilt just barely in California; but the line was a fancy. The mountains were real.

Within the mountain circle were nearer landmarks: Watertank Hill, Adobe Street, Little Italy on the rise across the railroad tracks, and the little juniper-topped ridge behind the old ballpark, where yellowbells bloomed before the dry season.

Closest of all were the neatly fenced yards, bordered with iris and Shasta daisies, little islands of green in the four-month summer drought that seared the old hills.

Down the middle of every front yard ran a board sidewalk. A gate led to a wider boardwalk, running beside the dirt street. Every unpainted frame house had a front porch. Ours was draped with Virginia creeper, cool and private in summer. And in front of the porch of that house, where my mother brought us to live with her parents in 1951, was an enormous white poplar tree.

Three feet across at the base, with craggy wrinkled gray bark, its lower branches were as thick as a pony's barrel and almost as low to the ground. My sister and I could dig our toes into crevices in the bark and scramble astride. Above our heads, the corrugated skin of the old tree became white and smooth. The leaves, bright green on the upper side, fuzzy white beneath, shook and whispered in the wind that spilled down Bear Canyon on hot summer afternoons.

The poplar cast deep, dark shade, sheltering hundreds of sprouts springing from its knobby ankles. White poplars are a cloning species, so although Grandfather mowed the tree's children down with the grass, they always grew again.

In spring, long tendrils of catkins, oozing white cotton, dropped from the tree, falling in a litter, blowing into fence corners. In autumn, layers of leaves fell, six inches deep, until my aunt led us in raking them into huge crackling piles of brown and white, scooping them onto tarps, and dragging them across the road to be burned to white ash, below the smoke drifting from the sawmill's tepee burner.

There were many white poplars in Hilt. We called them cottonwoods. Squat, weedy, wide-branching, virtually unkillable, they came to the dry western lands as unconsenting pioneers, to remain in small towns and old homesteads, surviving drought, cold, and more fashionable landscaping.

Utterly useless for fenceposts or lumber, barely adequate as firewood, they are solely and staunchly shade trees. I think that women spread them, giving to friends and relatives little sprouts in cans of mud. Perhaps all white poplars are related, lost members of a single tribe, scattered, like those who planted them.

Around the base of the tree was a ring of smooth pale rocks, filled with soil. The rocks came from a bar on the Klamath River, fifteen miles away. Intended for growing flowers, the bed was too shady, and we played there too much for plants to survive. It became our sandbox, and the tree above it our stoic nanny. We hid from passersby behind its trunk, lay on our backs beneath it in the summer heat, ants crawling under our shirts as we watched the sky behind the nervous leaves.

The tree was the oldest living thing I knew, and so I believed, in those days, that it was more preoccupied by the past than aware of us. It seemed to me, when the thunderheads turned to fire in the sunset and the nighthawks flew before them, that the old tree saw not those birds, but other creatures, gone beyond reach toward a lost western sea.

Perhaps twice a year I have a dream, in which I find myself set down at night, alone, at the end of Front Street in Hilt, where our house stood. But the row of houses that once faced the railroad tracks is dark. There are no stars out, and when I run to our house, the big front-room window is black and dead. The tree, my tree, thrashes in a chilly wind, the pale undersides of the leaves leprous. It hides in a cold, clutching shadow, no longer like a living thing.

I run through town, past many houses, but find them all locked and dark. I turn back toward home, and find it suddenly lit, alone of all the others, and the big front door standing open. I can see the white wainscoting and the flowered wallpaper, and Grandmother entering from the kitchen, her light hair in coils on top of her head, her voice calm and unsurprised, twenty-five years after her burial.

She walks to the front door, and I follow her onto the porch, now warm with sunshine. The tree is calm and alive, its shade friendly in the lambent light of a June morning. And I awake, with Grandmother's voice and the rustle of soft leaves in my ears and in my mind.

Two years after Grandmother died, words were spoken around a boardroom table in Los Angeles, and when the men who spoke them stood up, the houses and the sawmill and the people of Hilt were gone. The poplar tree, its top dying, was sliced to the ground. But whenever the dream comes, for a few days afterward I wonder if a sprout from that tree remains, pushing up through the packed soil of a deserted street. I wonder if it sees the nighthawks silhouetted against a falling sun. I wonder if it remembers.

Homer Kizer

At Abby Creek

First publication

Breeze rustled chittams, foxglove white
pink purple, fireweed, thistles, roses
along the tracks, meadowlarks & sparrows,
yellow tansy heads, fleece from the curly
ram caught on berry thorns, a kite
tangled in power lines, an Okie Drifter
cast into an alder—a Brown Leghorn rooster,
wings spread, neck stretched, bled

from his beak as he hung beside Mrs. Parks' night
gown. In Elk City, they said Vern January
died as had Vern Young, names that carry
memories of Abby Creek and things right
with us, that era before you shut
our life. We're still married, but

2.

split like the maple that shaded our spring,
you remember the one there at Abby Creek,
the one that hid the magnolia (a good stick,
the maple was planked for gun stock blanks),

yes, that one you could see when walking
the railroad tracks, that one where Kathy
found the medicine bottle, now empty—
that bottle & a picture of her grandpa are all

she has of Oregon. You kept everything
else that belonged to us as a family, awards,
slides, photos, even my fishing records.
Kathy says they're in your shed, molding,
stored next to the stock blanks I couldn't fit
in (for keeping them, thanks) on my last visit.

3.

Through the park there at Elk City,
down, across the concrete and mud, I slid
my Zodiac into the Yaquina, warm & stained red
(the pulp mill at Toledo had another spill;
remember how lucky G.P. used to be,
their settling pond only overflowing
on the rising tide). The Big Elk, clearing
after last night's rain, slipped past

the stinking water, stayed against the shady
bank, not mixing with the tide in the middle.
I saw on the surface, under that broadleafed maple
with initials carved in hearts (where we
used to park by the bridge), my reflection lying
across the joined waters, still and shimmering.

4.

On a landing across the Yaquina, a yarder
tooted; its mainline snapped taut, snapped
the stick up. Like a man hung, the chokered
log dangled on the rigging, dropped, swinging

past the shovel. The green steel tower,
a gypo's Skagit with six guys, stood
erect like a bully's middle finger, stood
overlooking Abby Creek and the tansy

filled pasture where, long ago, fallen timber
fed a whining headrig. The mill once employed
fifty men. Their sons & grandsons have moved
to Toledo, drive Hondas & Toyotas, drink beer
brewed in Milwaukee, and watch *America's Team*
on cable. I drive a Ford with a bent I-beam.

5.
A beaver with a willow branch between its curved
orange teeth saw me, slapped the river—
the cut willow, floating on the bruised water,
rocked in my wake as I sped past stakes
marking lot lines on the subdivided
south bank. Remember that corner of blackberries
& cattails between the Grange and Vern January's
fenced garden—log trucks and garden

tractors were parked on new lawns, limed
with mud from G.P.'s causticizers, sprouting
satellite dishes and skirted mobile homes.

My wake washed the sand bank and muddied
the creek coming from the bog where, trapping
muskrat, I caught mink in pushup domes.

6.
War in Israel made me a trapper…
hunting season over, I had muzzleloaders
to build, but the gas shortage left customers

sitting in two-hour lines, two
and a half hours away. I had to catch fur
if we were to stay off welfare, traded
deer antlers (trophies I'd mounted,
had bragged about) for traps. Hippies made

pipes from the antlers, sold them mailorder.
Too far out of town, we agreed it was time
to move (now we can't agree on what a dime
is worth). I asked who owned the house there
at Abby Creek, the one I passed when I ran
my traps. No one would say but Don.

7.

Publishers Paper owned the house and didn't
want to rent to hippies—afraid of fire—
(*returning to the land* for so many kids our
age—yes, we were still kids ourselves—
meant living with wood stoves they couldn't
bank). Don said to call Publishers, but
nine hundred acres? when we couldn't
afford the one-forty we rented at Logsdon.

I don't remember their forester's name.
He looked at my hair—it was on my ears;
I needed a trim...his apples & mossy pears
needed pruning. His fruitless cherries were the same
variety, and I would've left right
then, but his wife invited us in for a bite.

8.

You never knew how we got the house there
at Abby Creek. Publishers' forester served
chocolate cake and coffee, and said,

"Wayne let that fucking fence down again
last night." His bull was in Wayne's pasture,
siring blooded calves in scruffy heifers.
I asked if his red hogs were 'shires.
"Only the near ones." Then as if a foregone

conclusion, he asked if three-fifty
would be too much—Dick Parks was already
leasing the river pastures. I wanted
the place, but not that bad.
He said that'd be thirty a month, twenty
in December, as if he owed an apology.

9.
Two bedrooms and a bath upstairs,
a flagstone fireplace in the living
room, a second flue and a stove facing
the kitchen, cork tile floors, full-length
utility room: a house for growing daughters.
You hung clothes on lines strung
between the house & the woodshed, strung
chicken wire down to the creek, up & back,

and laughed when Wayne Hodges sawed the flat
roof off the chickenhouse I'd built
at Logsdon—it was too tall to fit
through the covered bridge. The roar of that
chainsaw woke up Elk City and started
roosters crowing. Even Flip barked.

10.
Flip, muzzle white, stiff and blind,
was asleep on the store's porch. I guess
the new owners adopted him. Yes,

he's fifteen or more & not the Labrador
that fought Paul Newman's dog on the inclined
ramp to the boat landing or the dog that swiped
potato salad & pickles from three hundred
picnic lunches one summer. He was a better

thief than any goose in the park. He stole
the left boot of Willie Brown's new
corks—Willie saw him & called the store.

Flip lugged it a mile to that hollow willow
by the bridge. Luckily, Frankie saw him through
the chittams he was peeling across the river.

11.

Remember the chittams, peeled trunks, drying
and dried bark, broken and sacked, sold
to the store there at Elk City—and the ferns rolled
in bundles of fifty. I don't think Vern made money
handling either. It was beer that kept him going,
nine thousand in profits that summer they filmed
Sometimes a Great Notion. Storekeeping overwhelmed
him (everyone knew it would). An old gypo who grew

up logging, the last with a whistle punk signalling
the yarder, the last to use butt rigging, Vern
hated change: soap & salad wasn't how a man should earn
his living. He sold me that True Temper casting
reel, the knucklebuster like I had as a kid,
charged four dollars for it, two onions & a fid.

12.

The tide swung my Zodiac upstream across
the mouth of Abby Creek, and covered the gravel

bar where with worms & patience Kathy & Kristel
caught that cutthroat too heavy for them to tote
up the bank. It wiggled free, flopped across moss
and berry cuttings, leaving a trail of silver
scales & slime on Kathy's shirt & sweater.
Trout & daughter, remember, dived for the water.

She couldn't hold on & Kristel was no
help. They were five & three, then, and we
were proud, humbly proud. A skinned knee,
dirty faces, cold tears, a scratched ego—
you baked them cookies, said they could go, yes,
the next tide change. But what changed was us.

13.

Frankie Hunt and I used the fid to splice eyes
in buoy lines for his crab rings. He stretched
a spool of line between the apple and the shed
where that doe hung I shot in our garden,
the one under the tarp when, wanting to socialize,
Vern Young hailed us from the boat landing
there by the bridge, offered a beer, not realizing
we couldn't stop, not with a cop

on the river checking for life jackets & fire
extinguishers. Frankie kept in the middle,
engine idling. Vern asked, "What's under the bundle?
Been fishing sidehill salmon?" A liar
with a sunburned face, I said, feeling like a louse,
"No!" I sat on the chopping block by the chickenhouse.

14.

Frankie came back from Vietnam…strange,
remember? him walking the tracks on dark nights

with a seven-cell and twenty-two. By rights,
the cops should've nailed him; they could've
if they wanted, but they knew his range,
that he kept on his side of the river,
that he shot at eyes, blue ones (there
were always a few deer among the ewes)

usually. I went with him (he wore black
jeans and blackened his face) before dawn
the time he found Old Man Abby's sheep on
the tracks. Fence down—he sent me back
for staples while he herded them through
the break…his eyes shined pale blue.

15.
There by Abby Creek hidden by berries,
that rick of alder you wanted still rambled
along the edge of our garden. I pulled
the cane back: quartered blocks, black
with orange splotches of faery jelly, with bees,
winged termites, red ants & fat white borers,
lay soggy like local news in old newspapers.
Eleven winters of drizzle, eleven summers

of crawling bugs left us and our memories—
clearing blackberries, you laughing,
stacking blocks, sitting on the rick, dressing
clothespin dolls with wild morning glories
and blouses of foxglove (Kathy, Kris & Kori
loved them)—like the alder, split & punky.

16.
Fifty-three posts: I still remember
how many I set for the chicken yard.

Saplings & salvaged plywood—I tarred
the roof I put on the chickenhouse, but
before being fenced in, they plucked bare
the hill in front of the covered porch, laid
eggs under the house, and tripped my mouse

traps…Remember the mice, how bold
they were, running across the living room—
and the mouse that hobbled from the bathroom
with a trap on its hind leg. You told
me it was time to get a cat. Wayne offered
a couple bobtailed kittens his Manx had sired.

17.
Saw a hunting cat in the river pasture,
there, then gone, a blue Manx,
one of Elmer's…heard that Toledo's banks
got his homestead after he died.
Maybe, but his road wasn't any smoother
& his chickens still roosted in the walnut tree.
(Remember him with his 30–30,
hunting roosters for Sunday dinners,

a shot each. He popped heads slicker
offhand than Don or I could punch
paper targets, same distance, from a bench.)

I'd walked in, feeling like a trespasser.
His house, boarded shut, sagged more,
and his garden had gone to weeds & borage—

18.
bees worked the small blue flowers.
I caught one by its wings, a Caucasian

like I kept before I knew how to requeen.
I let it free and watched it fly wobbly
toward the two hives of unpainted supers
stacked six high behind the barn.
A dark kitten the size of a peach can
pounced on it, yowled, batted at it,

then disappeared under a beam, bristling, ears
back. I remembered Elmer's barrel of kittens—
the barrel was still there full with kittens.
I shoved my arm in: clinging like cockleburs,
three hissing toms, each blue
Manx, growled like long-tails never do.

19.
I pulled the kittens loose from my sleeve,
got scratched but knew I would…
the smallest two, not weaned, purred
when I stroked their ears. They yawned,
blinked barely opened eyes (I believe)
satisfied I meant no harm,
& with tongues like sandpaper, nuzzled my arm,
but the big one hissed when I stroked his chest.

He reminded me of you…Even Wayne's Manx
came from Elmer though Wayne always said, "I wouldn't
have one of his queer son-of-a-bitches." And he wouldn't
ask Elmer for another kitten when his hounds yanked
the head off his…The kitten wet in my hand;
I was going to keep him until then.

20.
Wayne brought the kittens on his second trip
(remember how his Cornbinder would wallow

through mud that stuck my Bronco;
its diesel engine, taken from a combine,
would idle down until its tall mudtread gripped
the slick clay beneath that snot that slides
into creekbottoms). Both kittens had round eyes,
ear tufts and claws hidden in fluff;

they chased buttons and mice. I had to kill
what they caught: ringworm was the toughest.
I buried both bobtailed kittens there next
to the creek, and Kori smelled of Desenex until
her birthday…The Cornbinder broke a ring,
had to be resleeved—took only a week to get it going.

21.
That Merino ram of Dick Parks, the one
he put in the lower pasture with those
seven ewes & lambs, remember? Coyotes
killed a lamb that first night, chased the ram
all the way to Mill Creek—he bred that dun
Suffolk of the people who kept Dobermans,
ran their dogs downriver to Ken Wildman's
there in Toledo, four miles or so;

Dick laughed even though he had to run
to town to get him. Well, that old ram
(he must be twenty) was causing bedlam
in the second, low pasture between the river
and the tracks; he was mounting a blind ewe
in belly-deep buttercups & she didn't know what to do.

22.
Remember the tracks, steps out of synch,
and Kori, naked & wet, waving to the train.

She had a baby's pot belly and that pain-
ful (she still remembers being held still)
blood boil, her leg with that deadly pink
line swollen hard. You lanced it…you
miss her, I know you do—and it troubles you
that she chose to live with me.

We don't have to end like this. Blink!
See if those irritating grains of sand
haven't washed away. If you've the mind,
the patience of God, perhaps you'll wink
at my ignorance, the injustices I did
you. You've repaid them a thousandfold.

23.
The otter slide upriver of the trestle
over Abby Creek had fresh tracks
to its head: raccoon & mink tracks,
single sets, both probably by boars—
the coon left freshwater mussel
shells piled in sedges above the high
tideline; the mink had pissed by
each pile…I could smell

what he'd done…I still wrestle
with whether I ought to trap, my instincts
a traffic signal light. Trapping links
my past with the mountain men who rustled
the West from Indians. It keeps me
outdoors where I want to be;

24.
it's something I know…
Don Lynch told a story about a logger

who trapped the Big Elk after
fall rains shut down his Cat show.

Depression. Money was scarce. Fur high.
He caught eight mink one winter,
enough for a used Model A, and flour
& beans to hold his family until July.

Cops thought he used venison for bait—
one cop was determined to trap him,
checked his sets, spied on him
& turned up missing after a bit. The State

never found the cop's body, nor
his pickup though they sniffed around like predators.

Jan Grover

Becoming Native

from *North Enough: AIDS and Other Clearcuts*

As anyone attentive to the outdoors up here will tell you, Minnesota is not the "land of 10,000 lakes"—it is the land of over 15,000 of them. Like pride in winter's cold and duration, natives take pleasure in the state's almost outlandish extent of waters. Each spring the public is greeted with the news that one in every five Minnesotans has a cabin somewhere, and most of those can be described as being "up at the lake." These lakes are very fishy, as are a great many of the streams. In 1994, the last year for which records are complete, the state Department of Natural Resources (DNR) sold fishing licenses to 19.3 percent of the men, women, and children in Minnesota (931,086 of its residents) as well as to 201,533 nonresidents. The DNR has also somehow figured out that nearly 25 percent of Minnesotans' recreational hours are spent on the water, most of those fishing.

And yes, it is just as big a deal as these numbers suggest. Each May on the morning of the lake fishing opener, I have stood on an overpass of I-35 in south Minneapolis's predawn murk to watch— the first year in awe and disbelief, in successive years with considerable tenderness—as the northbound lanes clog with sports-uts and pickups hauling aluminum fishing boats, all patiently headed out of town, bumper to bumper, for the land o' lakes' opener up north.

The opener for me is a month earlier because I confine my fishing to trout streams, most of which open on April 15. A few streams have a winter season as well, a precious guarantor of solitude and, usually, extremity-numbing cold. I have never fished an opening day; I am still very much a tyro and painfully aware that fly fishing remains a pursuit in which my lack of svelte technique earns unasked-for disruptions of my solitude.

"Here, can I show you something?" asks a good-intentioned angler. "May I?" (Minnesota nice.)

I hand over my rod silently.

He hefts and flexes it. "Mmmm. Do you think you really want to be fishing that midge? Your leader's too short for that sorta delivery, anyway."

I flush, filled with my guilty secret: I have no intention of catching a fish at all. Whether I fish a midge or a trico is more a matter of aesthetics than tactics. The dirty truth is that I enjoy casting, I like what fishing teaches me about the life of streams, and I enjoy what Robert Traver described, in his *Anatomy of a Fisherman*, as "the environs where trout are found, which are invariably beautiful," but I do not give a hoot in hell for hooking and releasing trout. I employ flies (surgically altered by a pair of wirecutters) only because I think they are beautiful and for form's sake on busy streams. When I am absolutely sure that I am fishing alone, I usually tie a yarn ball onto the end of my tippet and cast without any pretense to a fly at all.

Early last spring, even before the male red-winged blackbirds had returned to their marshes, I traveled down to the valley of the Whitewater River in southeastern Minnesota to stand in the waters and cast my way through an afternoon. The valley is one of a number ruined in less than half a century by imprudent farming. Its steep limestone hills were shorn of their trees and prairie cover in the 1850s–70s and planted to row crops, but by the turn of the century, the soils, freed of the network of roots that had bound them to the hillsides, poured down into the valley each spring, silting the river and its tributaries, killing the fish, burying the floodplain beneath feet of sand and clay. At least two townsites were engulfed in mud and afterward abandoned. By the start of the Dirty Thirties, the farms of the Whitewater had been mostly abandoned and the land had reverted to the counties through tax default, much as it did in the cutover farther north. Today, the valley of the Whitewater is part of the Richard J. Dorer Memorial Hardwood State Forest and is coming back from a near-century of misuse. Its restoration is the handiwork of Richard J. Dorer, who joined the Minnesota Department of Conservation in 1938 and oversaw the replanting of the Whitewater's hills to native shrubs, trees, and grasses, the elimination of grazing on its mucky bottomlands, and the filling of erosion gullies. The valley still floods some years—you can see the waterlines etched into the bark of its trees—but even this is turned to good use in the impoundments that create habitat for thousands of geese and ducks each spring.

In *Round River*, a posthumously published collection of his journal entries, Aldo Leopold lamented, "One of the penalties of an ecological education is that one lives alone in a world of wounds." The damage done to land, he said, was often unnoticed by laypeople. If my account here sounds like a threnody for the abused northern places of Minnesota and Wisconsin, it is because of this fact: a discerning eye can see how unstewarded most of this land has been. The charm lies in finding ways to live with such loss and pull from it what beauties remain. Leopold believed

> ...an ecologist must either harden his shell and make believe that the consequences of science are none of his business, or he must be the doctor who sees the marks of death in a community that believes itself well and does not want to be told otherwise.

The Whitewater is not yet well; that is why I write of it. But I write not only to point out the continued agricultural overloading of the river's north branch but the extraordinary resilience of a system that had been reduced, by the time Dorer began his humble, long-term restorations, to something approaching biological death. Dorer did not live to see the fulfillment of his vision of a restored valley: Humantime is very brief compared to the life of a complex system like a valley. But he chose to doctor rather than numb himself. I am trying to grow into such feeling and action too.

After several hours on the water of the middle branch, I saw that I should be heading back to the Cities, so I crawled up the muddy banks and across the rotten snow to the shoulder of the road and then back to my truck. I clambered in and was sitting there, thinking, when a heavy-duty half-ton American pickup heading south veered across the road and headed onto the shoulder facing me, gunning at top speed, as if the driver feared I might get away. He jounced to a stop, radiator to radiator with my truck.

I promptly elbowed down the lock button on my door. After all, thought this still-too-much Californian, suffused with tales of mayhem in state parks, this could be some mad angler, some nothing-to-lose wanderer—who knows?

But it was merely a conservation officer, and he was here to tell me that I was on Forbidden Waters: the special area for winter fly-fishing started about a mile farther north above the next bridge.

"I saw you stumbling around in the creek," he said, "so I went back to get you this map." He presented a poorly reproduced map, the winter special area highlighted in day-glo yellow.

I fished around on the front seat for Humphrey and Shogren's *Wisconsin and Minnesota Trout Streams: A Fly-Angler's Guide*, in which I had found the map I followed to get to what appeared the proper special-regulation stretch of river. But I could not find it. Wanting to establish that I had tried to match my place to their map, I dug frantically. I might as well have been trying to dig a hole to China.

"Well, I'll let you go this time. But you need to stay inside the area of the special regulations. They're posted."

"I'm sorry I misread my map," I said. "But if it will make you feel any better, I'm not using a fly." There: it was out.

"Not using a fly," he said curiously.

"No. I love trout streams, I love to be where fish are, I love to cast, but I don't want to play fish for my pleasure. So I don't use a hook."

"You don't use a hook." He looked at me as if I had asked him for a pair of his wife's dirty underwear. *Now I've heard everything.*

"No," I said happily, relieved that at long last I had revealed my dirty secret to someone, and a conservation officer at that.

"So how do you cast?"

I pulled out my reel, the billowy dust bunny still attached to it. It dripped, so I held it out, dangling between my fingers, and shook until it fluffed up. "I tie a piece of day-glo acrylic yarn to my tippet to weigh in a little."

He shot me a bemused look. Was it *Women!* or *Wait'll I tell the guys back at the office about this one!?*

"Anyway," I went on, "I've never had a chance to ask a DNR person this question, but since I don't use a fly with a hook on it, I can cast wherever I want, in season or out, can't I?"

"Hey," he said, spreading his hands wide, "for you, the sky's the limit."

My angling began as a literary passion. I admired the precision and thoughtfulness of W. D. Wetherell's stream accounts in *Vermont River* (1984) and *Upland Streams: Notes on the Fishing Passion* (1991) and John Gierach's sweet, funny essays about fly fishing in the Rocky Mountain West (books too numberless to mention individually). It seemed to me that both writers managed to avoid what Kim Stafford terms "first-person euphoric," that effusiveness that a great many writers fall into when recounting their experiences in the woods. Possibly the fact that fishing has a certain instrumentality— one learns to read the water, the hatches, the geology, after all, with the aim of using this knowledge to hook up with fish—saves angling writers from the gooey prose that defines less focused explorations of nature. Or maybe not: fishing also evokes plenty of hairy campfire prose and perfunctory "then-I-tied-my-Wendell's-Brainless-onto-a-0-1x-3x-4x-5x-12-foot-Rat's-Nest-tippet..." Wetherell and Gierach, however, were onto something I did not want to ignore once I was living in the land of 15,000-plus lakes. Fishing proved to be my way into thinking about what it means to be native to a place—and not just a native human but a native fish. In this sense, fishing became an epistemological tool, an object-to-think-with.

Like humans, fish are animals that can easily move or be moved from one place to another. They are the only vertebrates whose deliberate introduction into nonnative habitats these days has the active support of federal and state agencies. Birds and mammals are increasingly "*re*introduced," which is to say returned to ecosystems in which they formerly played parts, even when those systems have become so altered that they apparently can no longer support them —witness the reintroduction of the California condor into Southern California desert highlands, where habitat has been changed so drastically that successful reintegration of the birds is unlikely—but importations of new vertebrates are commonly frowned upon in these days of ecosystem-based management.

The U.S. Fish and Wildlife Service (USFWS) and state DNR, however, historically have had few qualms about introducing wholly foreign populations of fish into new waters—indeed, the DNR is still hard at it in northern Minnesota and Wisconsin, as they have been for over a century. (This may soon be changing.)

Robert Barnwell Roosevelt, a New York angler and conservationist who fished Lake Superior and its tributaries during the Civil War, before nonnative introductions began, described the native brook trout ("speckled trout," *Salvelinus fontinalis*) along Superior's shore in his book *Superior Fishing: Or, the Striped Bass, Trout, and Black*

Bass of the Northern States, published in 1865. Near the Bois Brulé's mouth in northern Wisconsin, Roosevelt encountered

> ...the best of fishing, united with good hotel life. In the neighborhood of [Bayfield] two hundred and fifty pounds weight of speckled trout have been killed in one day by one good fisherman and one poor one; fish of two and three pounds are common, and in the sheltered channels, between the Apostle Islands, the namaegoose [lake trout, *Salvelinus namaycush*] are taken in unlimited quantities. The Brulé River, and the many streams that empty into the lake in the neighborhood, although often choked with drift, are filled with fine trout.

On the North Shore, Roosevelt declared, brook trout weighing six pounds were not uncommon.

But already the habitat for native trout was changing drastically. The "many streams...often choked with drift" that Roosevelt described were silting up and growing warmer as loggers cleared the north woods, sending slash and sandy soil rushing down the streams.

Brook trout, the only extant native stream salmonid in the eastern half of North America, are generally small, quicksilver creatures, rather chunky and deep bodied, their backs a deep, inky green-black with a scatter of paler, green-yellow vermiculations—wormlike markings that from above resemble sunlight breaking on green stream water. Below their reticulated saddles, the trouts' sides become brighter and, to my human eye, even more whimsical: red bull's-eyes surrounded by rings of forget-me-not blue and blotches of cadmium yellow. Their bellies are white or orange, their fins an appropriately salmony red, and their tail fins squared like a sturdy rudder. Staring down on resting brook trout is like looking into the stream itself; the fish are one with their waters, and only the waving white edges of their pectoral, pelvic, and anal fins betray their hold near the streambed. This is useful cryptic coloration, for the brook trouts' most indefatigable natural predators are birds.

Though not as flashy as the golden trout of the West or as imposing in size as the introduced rainbow and brown, brook trout have a
supple, shape-shifting *rightness* in the dark waters of their home
streams. The fact that they seldom exceed six to eight inches in the
headwaters they are now consigned to bothers me not at all; Minnesota and Wisconsin are ancient country, their mountains become
flat and distillate through time. That their native stream trout are
also small and diamondlike makes a kind of poetic sense.

Sea-run brook trout (salters) and Lake Superior brook trout
(coasters) can grow imposingly large, matching their waters, but
average stream brookies can only be described as diminutive. They
are feisty fish for their size compared to the immigrants who have
displaced them, and preeminently fish of fast northern and mountain streams. Brookies cannot tolerate high temperatures; they prefer to congregate in waters whose temperature ranges between
57.2°C and 60.8°C, do not spawn at all in water warmer than
66.2°C, and can seldom be found where the temperature exceeds
68°C. The muddy runoff from late nineteenth-century logging,
coursing down escarpments to Lake Superior, became too warm for
brook trout and smothered their gravel spawning redds.

This is a story that had repeated itself east to west across the eastern half of North America. Brook trout had been almost eliminated
in New York and New England in much the same way fifty years
before. Logging and mill ponds had warmed stream water beyond
the trouts' tolerance, and overfishing nearly finished the job. Private
hatcheries in the East had been established to raise and release brook
trout obtained from tributaries of Lake Superior since the 1850s. By
1870, the New England states, as well as New York, New Jersey,
Pennsylvania, Maryland, Virginia, Alabama, and California had
established fish commissions to study the decline of native fish. Two
years later, the U.S. Fish Commission was established to deal with
falling populations in federal waters. The answer, each of these commissions concluded, was to establish government hatcheries.

So quickly did the hatchery movement become popular that by

1881, the Reverend Myron H. Reed, a New England minister, wrote sadly:

> This is probably the last generation of Trout fishers. The children will not be able to find any. Already there are well-trodden paths by every stream in Maine, New York and Michigan. I know of but one river in North America by the side of which you can find no paper collar or other evidence of civilization; it is the Nameless River.
>
> Not that Trout will cease to be. They will be hatched by machinery, and raised in ponds, and fattened on chopped liver, and grow flabby and lose their spots. The Trout of the restaurant will not cease to be. He is no more like the Trout of the wild river than the fat and songless reedbird is like the bobolink. Gross feeding and easy pondlife enervate and deprave him.
>
> The Trout that the children will know only by legend is the gold-sprinkled, living arrow of the Whitewater—able to zig-zag up the cataract, able to loiter in the rapids—whose dainty meat is the glancing butterfly.

In 1883, private hatcheries began importing European brown trout (*Salmo trutta*). Brown trout first appeared in the north woods in 1884 at a hatchery on Michigan's Upper Peninsula. Wisconsin raised one thousand imported brown trout eggs at a state hatchery in Bayfield in 1887 and released them into Superior and the Bois Brulé River. Minnesota followed suit in 1888. By 1900, brown trout had been introduced into the waters of thirty-seven states. The same scenario spread rainbow trout, which are native to the northern Pacific coast and the Cascades, throughout the country.

Browns and rainbows tolerate higher temperatures than brook trout. Because of their greater size as adults, they are favored by most trout anglers over the smaller brookies. As conditions favoring the imports increased, native trout were crowded further and further toward their headwaters, which are colder but also poorer in nutrients. Predictably, populations of brook trout declined as the browns and rainbows took over the richer and warmer feeding grounds downstream. Before the introduction of West Coast salmonids to Minnesota's North Shore, brook trout had inhabited the streams and rivers that emptied into Superior below the falls and cliffs. They were not native to the headwaters, which suggests that they arrived in the region less than 8,000 years ago, when the banks of Lake Superior rebounded from the crushing weight of retreating glacial ice and formed the ramparts of the North Shore, thus separating the streams west of the headlands from those below and east of them. Brook trout were crowded out of their native streams and rivers below the headlands by rainbow trout (*Onchorhynchus mykiss*), a much larger Pacific coast salmonid, after the province of Ontario introduced it in 1883. Today the only redoubts of brook trout in northern Minnesota are above the waterfalls and promontories on small feeder streams to which they have been introduced by humans. Most of these streams depend on precipitation rather than springs for their flow, so their brook trout populations are not stable: during spring runoff, fry are swept down the flood along with the invertebrates they feed on. In summer, streams often dry to trickles. The Precambrian bedrock over which the waters flow is not mineral rich, so few plants and invertebrates flourish there to provide shelter and food for the trout; such waters are only ten percent as productive as those to the south. In the Arrowhead, a ten-inch brook trout is a leviathan. Most of them are six, seven inches— stunted through lack of suitable food. Starved, diminished, and displaced.

W. D. Wetherell lamented similar losses to the brook trout in his adopted Vermont river:

> Brook trout are the natives here, of course, but in this part of the river there is a rootlessness about them that makes them seem like interlopers. I catch them in...spots that are probably their second or third choice after the rainbow- and brown-usurped pools. It's a pathetic story, this—a hundred years ago, the river was entirely theirs. The human analogy would be the sons of farmers you see milling about the bars in New England towns, perpetual renters, their fathers' land gone to condominiums and malls.

The human analogy in northern Wisconsin and Minnesota is its native Ojibway people. They too have been pushed into fewer, smaller, and less desirable habitats. We justify their removal, like the brook trout's, on economic grounds: the land/water has more profitable uses.

It is economic sense that has dictated the diminishment of native trout habitat. Trout restoration projects are computed on the basis of cost/benefit analyses, which weigh the likelihood of additional angler days on a stream at x dollars per angler pumped into the local economy *vs.* restoration costs.

Anglers want Big Fish. The summum bonum of stream trout fishing in the north woods is the steelhead—a lake-dwelling rainbow that pounds up Superior's lower tributaries each spring to spawn. But problems come with introductions. Salmonids are territorial, although that is probably not quite the right word for water dwellers. At any rate, they defend their lies and feeding grounds. Trout who have grown up together in a stream, like dogs in a household and children on a playground, quickly establish hierarchies. The largest and most aggressive usually win the spots they want, and the others assume the remaining positions based on their place in the hierarchy. This is why, once an angler has learned the lie of a particular fish, she can return years later and, if the fish has not died and the stream has not appreciably altered, still find him beneath that same undercut or below that same graywacke boulder in midstream.

But introduce hatchery-raised fish who have not learned the ways of wild trout, who instead have spent their youth swimming without surcease down the crowded concrete lanes of a hatchery run, and that stream's delicate system of social observances is disrupted. Hatchery fish do not understand the natives' hierarchies. They are like footballers at a tea dance or clubmen at a slam: they haven't a clue to the rules, and they cost the native fish otherwise-needed energy simply to drive them away. If the interlopers happen to be much larger than the natives, they may succeed in running off the latter because the natives equate largeness and rogue behavior with aggression.

If this sounds like a victory for the introduced hatchery fish, it is usually a Pyrrhic one: They are not as cagey as wild trout, and studies of their survival suggest that less than half of them make it through their first season. They are winterkilled or caught by human anglers, rising trustingly to bait and flies, or they are killed by other predators. Their formative months in the hatchery did not, after all, include lessons in seeking cover or avoiding enemies. In Minnesota, their chief wild predator is the loon, but as a DNR management brochure ruefully admits:

> …limitation of the predators is the obvious, but often not feasible, remedy…most of the bird predators are protected by state or federal law which precludes shooting or harassment. In Minnesota the loon also enjoys added status as the state bird.

Too bad. M. R. Montgomery, an ardent advocate of native trout in native streams, remarks that a friend of his who works in a state fishery calls stocked fish "point-of-purchase merchandising."

"Put-and-take" is the official designation at the DNR, which bases its stocking practices on the assumption that planted fish are likely to be "taken" almost as soon as they are "put." For this reason, although the surroundings on a stocked stream or lake are vastly pleasanter, their put-and-take fishing is not so very different from the trout experience offered at the spring sports fair each year in Minneapolis. There, the trout pond is a coffin-shaped fiberglass trough about four feet deep and thirty feet long, filled with small scared hatchery trout who herd aimlessly under the bright lights as boys and squealing women lunge at them with fiberglass rods. There, a kid always falls in while trying to grab a fish bare-handed, and by close each night several fish float belly up, to be discreetly skimmed off as soon as the crowds leave.

Northern Minnesota is the site of over 150 "rehabilitated" lakes. In DNR-ese, this means that their native fish have been poisoned out with rotenone or Antimycin-A and then replaced with hatchery trout or salmon. This program began in 1954 to increase sport fishing for anglers. In it, we can see the tensions between majority human intentions toward ecosystems and whatever claims those systems' native creatures and their human supporters have on their habitats.

Management of Lakes for Stream Trout and Salmon, a DNR publication from the Division of Fish and Wildlife, lays out the rationale and techniques for altering lakes for put-and-take fishing. Its vocabulary is revealing: a lake is first *treated*, the *crop* is then *stocked*, and later it is *harvested*. (Death waits only in the wings in this discourse.) Nonnative rainbow trout are the principal *crop*: they grow larger, are easier to catch, and adapt to a wider range of water conditions than brook trout. Browns are less desirable than rainbows because they are difficult to catch after their first season and because old ones become piscivorous—if they survive their first seasons, they may soon turn to *harvesting* newly stocked fingerlings and yearlings faster than humans and birds can.

The lakes selected for this practice are ones that in the DNR's opinion harbor fish that do not interest (human) anglers. They must meet other criteria as well: because stocking is an expensive process requiring continual "planting"—stream trout do not reproduce in lakes—the selected lakes must lack outlets in order to prevent the return or arrival of undesirable fish species and to prevent the planted salmonids from escaping in quest of streambeds in which to spawn. Such lakes are not hard to come by in northern Minnesota, however, since by definition any small landlocked lake does not already possess a stream-spawning fish population.

Small populations of the luckless "undesirable" fish are first captured and placed in twenty-gallon plastic bags, garbage cans, and other containers. These are then immersed in lake water that has been treated with the toxicant. The lowest concentration of poison that kills all the fish in the container within twenty-four hours (in warm water) or forty-eight hours (in cold water) constitutes the minimum lethal dose (MLD). The DNR recommends that concentrations slightly higher than the MLD be used to ensure a complete kill: "Fish can detect rotenone and will attempt to avoid it. A pocket of untreated water will provide a refuge for fish and some will probably survive."

What species of fish are designated to undergo this death by suffocation in order to produce fisheries worthy of human anglers? The list is long: gar, bowfin, northern pike, muskie, pickerel and chain pickerel, carp; longnose, white, and northern hog suckers; buffalo, redhorse, bullhead, burbot, white bass, rock bass, sunfish; smallmouth bass, largemouth bass, white and black crappie, perch, sauger, and walleye. Some of these species are favored game fish in their own right, of course, and waters they inhabit are unlikely to be poisoned to support salmonids. I reproduce the entire list because the creatures on it suggest the range of habitats that managers envision altering, ranging from warm, shallow, alkaline lakes to cold, deep, relatively acidic ones. Each of those habitats is also the source of food and shelter for birds, mammals, other fish, invertebrates, and plants too numerous to mention. Each of those habitats' other creatures is also susceptible to the effects of "rehabilitation"—for example, rotenone is highly toxic to crustaceans. What are the effects of eliminating these other creatures' natural prey species or symbionts?

Humans do not know.

How does the biological impoverishment of "rehabilitated" lakes —by definition home to only two species of fish after "rehabilitation," the introduced salmonids and minnows—affect the network of creatures that depend on these lakes' former balance of life forms?

Humans do not know.

Paul Schullery, a wise veteran of park service in Yellowstone and an angling historian, cautions:

> Our [human] goal is stabilization; Nature's goal is a complex suite of
> processes that constantly reshape the landscape while they test its

inhabitants. We introduce non-native sport fish, and we remove "undesirable" native fish that don't suit our purposes. We do all these things, and then we celebrate the resulting stream for the quality of its "wild trout fishing."

I do not believe that being native to a place gives any creature unqualified claims or advantages over those of a nonnative; to believe so is to deny the importance of adaptation, of history. Once the place in which a population has had its being becomes radically altered, its exquisite former evolutionary adaptations may no longer be assets—in fact, they often become liabilities. Witness the brook trout and the caribou: logging warmed the trout's waters and destroyed the caribou's ancient forest browse. Newer arrivals were arguably better suited to survive than the creatures who had adapted to these particular niches over thousands of years. As Schullery reminds us, "We tend to see trout as finished products—as if somehow, around 1800 or so, Evolution dropped them off at our door and said, 'Have a nice time.'"

So it is not through assertion of a transcendent suitability that a native claims its right to a place. Nor can the simple claim of prior possession suffice, for *first* is invariably a recursive concept; there is always someone more firstly than the claimant. On what grounds, then, has a native a right to continued occupation? How—and how long—must someone inhabit a place to plausibly claim it as native ground, as a place she has a right to?

These are no idle questions for me, a writer who has chosen in middle age to move alone to a new place, expecting to remain here for the rest of my life. What claims have I on this place? How, in any terms less venal than those of a real estate contract, can I justify my occupation of this place when other and prior claims exist? And why do these questions matter? In the name of what cause should native species be preserved, should native peoples retain their choice of lands and ways of life, should I be allowed to naturalize in some poor place I choose?

It is in the name of a radiant diversity that I claim room and right for us, and this does not always shake out in favor of the preferences of the purist or the displaced. Introduced populations of brown and rainbow trout may have made some streams more, not less, diverse, now that the waters run warmer. There they presently belong. Where streams continue to run icy and to support brook trout, there the imports do not belong. Subdivisions make country places less diverse, not more; they eliminate native or come-lately species' habitats for a monoculture of bluegrasses, high water consumption, and pavement. Condo developments on the North Shore drive out small innkeepers, storekeepers, mushers, cottagers, and fishing operations in favor of clones of city neighborhoods. Put-and-take wilderness, you might call it.

This argument acknowledges the violence that we humans, as well as other sources of natural perturbations (a retrovirus, a bark beetle, a forest fire), can and have done, the shifts in damage and adjustment that occur as one population declines and opens opportunities for others. It assumes that pain and displacement are also engines of change, of new designs.

But beware of argument by analogy, I tell myself. Am I not myself an introduced species, a Western trout out of place here? My answer is no, because I come as a nonreproducing individual (like a single ant, caribou, or merganser), not as an entire population, though arguably all of us—the insect, rodent, bird, and I—are less than whole, mere pieces of a larger entity that is waiting somewhere in the wings to complete us: the colony, the herd, the flock, the family. I am not forcing another population toward extinction unless I multiply, unless I alter its habitat. My choice has been to find the poorest, most obscure spots—pine barrens, miry streams—from which to ask my questions alone. To embrace the fate of the declining brook trout.

Let me tell you about one of my favorite fishing spots, a place-to-think-with. It has a particularly soft spot in my heart because it was the first place I fished alone. It is so far downstream from the haunts of most trout in the upper Nemadji basin that the occasional lunker who surfaces there in the spring has the shock value of Nixon rising from the riffles. Mostly, though, it succors suckers, this opaque, muddy run of tannic waters trickling boggily down a syncline to the southwest shore of Superior. In its clearer-running headwaters, the Blackhoof is home to brook trout, but I am content to witness and celebrate whatever surfaces downstream to sip from the murk. Besides, if I have learned anything of value from fishing, it is this: the appearance of a body of water does not necessarily tell me if it is healthy or not. This turgid red water supports a healthy and varied population of creatures, more so than the clear picture-book streams farther north or the topologically perfect *ur*-trout streams of the acidified Northeast and Smoky Mountains.

But the first time I waded the Blackhoof, I found myself hoping that around the next bend I might find a north-woods equivalent of Beaver Creek, a small, exquisite, and very *productive* (as the DNR folks would say) trout stream in southeastern Minnesota—a microcosm of all that is rapture-producing in trout habitats: tropic-green pools, margins crowded with pubic mounds of watercress, long, clear, unbroken runs beneath which trout shapes shoaled and swiveled, all of this shaded by a pleached corridor of trees. But wanting y to be x is futile as well as a disservice to whatever y has to offer. So I trudged up the Blackhoof, trying instead to think positively about its murky red waters, which ten pairs of polarizing glasses could not have penetrated, its eroded slopes and wound-deep gullies, its downed firs and alder-choked banks.

Just upstream of a crude footbridge, a rat's nest of downed trees dammed the river. Below lay a deep pool. I fished that for a while, practicing my sidearm cast, but I might as well have been casting into the great cloud of unknowing—the water was that opaque. Still: the sun was on my back, warblers were in the woods, and I fell into that soothing rhythm, emptied of thought, which casting produces. My right arm rose, a dreamtime lurch like a body starting in earliest sleep. At the top of the stroke, my line streamed out in slo-mo behind me, lazy as words from a slack mouth. I watched my arm drift back down, stop. The line shot out in a radiant arc and landed before me quietly on the red water.

I did this again and again. Around me spring gathered: A thrush, surprisingly plump for a small spring migrant, watched this Worm of All Worms as it flicked, rose, straightened, shot forward, and fell again to the water. A pair of crows mobbed a small pale hawk, and in nature's orgy of seasonal overkill, geese oared down the high wind.

This dense weave of beauties found its focus in my arm's metronomic rise and fall, the faint stir of my line as it cut through the fabric of raw spring air. Over and over I did it, and each cast rent the dream, and through the tear I saw first the river bounded by alders, and then the tunnel through spruce, and a stone-laddered riffle. The line flicked, and mild skies rose hazily above the sheeted waters.

The trail back to the road wound along the top of a moraine. A ten-minute hike brought me to a crude bench apparently built for a giant—even with my 33-inch inseam, I swung free of the ground when I sat down. The bench faced south, overlooking ridge after ridge of the old shorelines of glacial lakes Nemadji and Duluth. These ancient basins accounted for the clay that covered everything below with a red slip. In effect, the Nemadji's one-hundred- to five-hundred-foot depositions were the dirty rings around the bathtub left when glacial meltwaters receded, terrace by terrace, toward the present shore of Lake Superior.

Directly south of my aerie, an entire ridge had been clearcut. Beyond it, other east-west ridges still lay dark and forested to the horizon. This serpentine moraine, the Nickerson, promised an enormously satisfying *lebensraum* to all us creatures. I sat amid that bright expanse and watched the light mute from pale and spring-bright to moody gray. A sharp breeze came up and rain began to fall.

I finished my walk reluctantly. As I came within sight of my truck, a battered old station wagon pulled up behind it. Three doors opened, and two doughy teenage girls in windbreakers, tennis shoes, and stretch pants tumbled out of the back seat and began unloading coolers and folding chairs and spinning rods. They were joined by a short lifelong smoker in work jacket and boots, cigarette dangling like a growth from the corner of his mouth. He watched me pick my way across the drainage ditch on the west side of the road and scramble across the highway.

"Fishing good?" he called, finally.

"Too silty," I answered.

He smiled, perhaps a bit pityingly, then picked up his rod and tackle box. His girls were already winding their way down to the river, headed into the Nemadji's murk with their liter bottles of Mountain Dew.

"See if we can find us some suckers," he said, then turned and followed them.

I drove past Deer Creek, Rock Creek, Mud Creek, and Clear Creek, the last a clear misnomer, since it ran as red as the Nemadji. But as far as that goes, *ran* is inaccurate, too: the creeks' gradient was so slight that they *stood* pooled and listless, more like drainage ditches than free-flowing streams.

I was looking now for the upper stretch of the Blackhoof. There the river ran shallower and faster, and the water that flowed past me was the clear deep amber of old varnish. I saw no fish, though I peered long and deep into the water pooled below boulders. But I didn't particularly care. Here in the highland it was still sunny, and the breeze cast bright spinners of light above the stream. I sat in the pale winter grass watching the water, and the air near the ground rose resinous and soft. The river made its appearance upstream from the west, curving around a bend overhung with spruce, white cedar, and fir. I watched as a bubbleline hooked away from the far bank and straightened into a clean narrow incision that ran down the center of the stream. Something immense and profoundly peaceful settled over me, and I understood for the first time why many anglers view time off the water as something not quite real, something to be endured—a lesser order than their dreamtime on streams.

The Nemadji basin attracts backcountry bushwhackers and a strange breed of traditionalists who seek out fish in improbable and marginal habitats. I am among these, and I have continually to ask myself why. The lower Blackhoof is a melancholy- and pleasure-making place, for everywhere human influence of the direst sort is distressingly evident. Yet everywhere a powerful beauty remains. Like a recent cutover, the river stirs up a thick stew of conflicting feelings in me—horror, sadness, wonder, gratitude—that reconcile themselves into what I call, for lack of a more precise word, *savor*: a state deeply familiar and grace-charged, a complex reaction to careless human use and the land's slow, mute resiliency. It is like looking at a festering lesion and noting the beauty of its smooth margins or marveling that cells still divide and defend the crumbling body they also built. Their life is too short to change their ways: this is their only place, the only way they know.

David Rains Wallace

The Bumpy Bridge

from *The Monkey's Bridge*

In a way, it's not surprising that Spain conquered half of Central America in a few decades. From Tehuantepec to Darién, it is not much bigger than Texas. Yet two-dimensional size can be misleading. Central America is a diverse place as well as a small one, and in many ways is more like a continent than a state. It has continental features—two very long and involved coastlines, wide lowlands, a "continental divide." The weather has a continental scale and complexity, with a very wet, hot Caribbean coast, a comparatively dry and hot Pacific one, and inland climates ranging from semi-arid to temperate to semi-alpine.

On "real" continents, such features cover huge areas, simplifying the describer's task. But Central America has the exacting intricacy of miniaturization. "I regret that I cannot communicate to the reader," wrote John Lloyd Stephens, "the highest pleasure of my journey in Central America, that derived from the extraordinary beauty of scenery, constantly changing."

Stephens didn't even see it all, traveling overland by horseback, and such a trip from Tehuantepec to Darién would not be easy today. The term "land bridge" implies smoothness and simplicity, qualities that rarely confront the Central American traveler. To the conquistadors, it must have seemed a fortress moated with reefs and swamps, walled with mountains, even defended with artillery of a sort as earthquakes shook their houses and volcanoes rained fire and brimstone on their heads. Perhaps that's why they called *it* the mainland, *tierra firma*, as much as the bigger but flatter continental coasts to the north and south.

Columbus was lucky that he bumped into Central America where he did, in the Gulf of Honduras. It's one of the less tortuous stretches on the Caribbean coast. If he'd hit farther north, at Belize, he'd have run into a maze of mangrove-covered coral reefs from which he might never have emerged if bad weather had caught him. Hurricanes roar out of the central Caribbean with the climatic equivalent of earthquakes. They leveled Belize City so often that in 1961 the government moved the capital 50 kilometers inland to Belmopan. Winter northeasters can be almost as violent. Such a storm on the Honduran Bay island of Utila woke me with a start when it hit at midnight, and detained me on the island a couple of days. An old resident said islanders almost starved when northeasters lasted weeks, because no boats could reach them.

There are coral reefs along the Caribbean south of Belize, but they are more scattered and farther offshore. Much of the coast Columbus explored consists of long barrier beaches fronting lagoons that can have a lakelike placidity, although the Caribbean's shallow waters are also lakelike in the speed with which bad weather can arouse them. I experienced this during a sudden thunderstorm while crossing Ibans Lagoon on the way to my Plátano River trip. It was in one of the motorized dugouts called "*tuk-tuks,*" and the waves were higher than the boat within minutes. As we bounced along, the bottom felt palpably close, but not close enough to be of much use if the boat swamped.

Columbus also may have been lucky he *didn't* find a strait into the Pacific, which is much deeper and rougher than the Caribbean, as Dávila learned when he tried to launch his homemade ships. Columbus's leaky tubs might have fared as badly. Along the southern

Pacific coast, at least, he would have found shelter. Large peninsulas such as the Azuero and Nicoya form over a dozen bays and gulfs, some of them sizeable like the Golfo Dulce inside Costa Rica's Osa Peninsula, which biologist William Beebe compared to the lower Amazon. On the other hand, the Pacific north of Costa Rica has few bays and only one large one, the Gulf of Fonseca. Most of the Guatemalan, Salvadoran, and Nicaraguan west coasts are straight beaches backed by coastal plains or volcanic uplands, and interrupted only by swampy estuaries. The long Pacific swells hit them hard.

"Guatemala's coast seemed too smooth and even, on the chart, to suggest good shelter," wrote Beebe on a marine collecting expedition from Mexico to Panama in the 1930s. He sailed past it without landing, as had many earlier mariners. Even pirates had trouble on windblown Pacific strands. One of them, William Dampier, sailed along the whole coast north from Nicaragua without a single chance to be piratical. Off El Salvador and Guatemala, his fleet "met with very bad weather, seldom a day went past but we had one or two violent tornadoes, and with them very frightful flashes of lightning and claps of thunder." Off Tehuantepec, "the waves all along this coast run high, and beat against the shore very boisterously, making the land wholly unapproachable against boats and canoes." When a party tried to go ashore to attack the town, their canoes overturned in the surf, and they got lost in mangrove swamps.

Lowlands and Rivers

If adventurers found Central America's coasts forbidding, they found its coastal plains more so. The biggest is the rolling limestone one that covers Yucatán and much of Belize as well as northern Guatemala's Petén. I had never encountered anything like it when I looped across in 1971. At first a pleasant change from the lowering highlands, its flatness became oppressive as it continued day after day. The only change from the Caribbean at Puerto Barrios to the

Gulf of Mexico at Mérida was that the vegetation turned shorter and drier, from evergreen forest to brushland. I could walk for hours and never see a stream, because surface water quickly sinks into the porous limestone. Formed in shallow seas a hundred million years ago, then uplifted to its present few hundred meters above sea level, the limestone didn't seem quite land as I understood it. The elements were there—rocks, soil, plants—but arranged in too rudimentary a combination. Maya homesteads seemed more campsites than settlements.

The Petén does have large rivers like the Usumacinta on its north side, and a huge "everglades" of sawgrass and hammocks, the Laguna del Tigre. I don't understand why a region largely without streams should have a "river of grass" at one edge, but limestone terrain has its own mysterious ways. Arthur Morelet, a French explorer who in 1847 was one of the first non-Spanish Europeans to traverse the Petén, wrote, "Nothing can be more complicated than the hydrography of this little corner of the globe, where the capricious waters percolate slowly from lagoon to lagoon, and seem to run athwart of each other in their devious courses."

Northern Central America's other big lowland is the Mosquitia in southeast Honduras and northeast Nicaragua. Once a mountainous land mass, it sank beneath the Caribbean about thirty million years ago, then emerged as a low plain twenty million years later and has accumulated some 4,500 meters of sediments since. Being an alluvial lowland instead of a limestone one, the Mosquitia is laced with rivers like the Plátano, and these make it a less bizarre landscape than the Petén. They haven't made it more amenable to human settlement, however; in fact it is less so. The rivers spread out to form almost impenetrable wetlands which look from the air like vast algal blooms, and some are so impregnated with minerals from the ancient seabed that plants become coated with black calcium in a kind of living petrification. Uplands are mainly sterile white sand.

Except for the Plátano's mysterious ruins, the Mosquitia seems never to have been occupied by more than shifting agriculture. Early adventurers hurried past, and it remained largely unknown in the 1850s when E. G. Squiers, U.S. Chargé d'Affaires to Nicaragua, published accounts of his explorations there. They sound like my Plátano trip. "Throughout it wore the same flat, monotonous appearance," he wrote, "a narrow strip of sand in front of a low, impenetrable forest, in which the fierce northeaster had left no tree standing." In one book, Squiers described a failed German colony's relics—a graveyard, rusting farm gear, a few dazed survivors—and concluded, "The folly of attempting to plant an agricultural colony on a lone, murky tropical shore is inconceivable."

Beside these huge plains, many depressions or "grabens" slice across northern Central America, formed by land subsidence along faults. The Motagua Valley where cactuses surprised me in 1971 is one, not so much a valley as a trough beneath the almost perpendicular Sierra de las Minas, which soars from near sea level to over 2,500 meters and cuts off damp Caribbean air. Fault depressions tend to be more habitable than coastal lowlands—fertile, healthful, and protected from hurricanes. Stephens was rhapsodic about Guatemala's Río Dulce, part of the Motagua fault zone. "On each side, rising perpendicularly from three to four hundred feet was a wall of living green," he wrote. "For nine miles the passage continued thus one scene of unvarying beauty, when suddenly the narrow river expanded into a large lake, encompassed by mountains and studded with islands, which the setting sun illuminated with gorgeous splendor." Lakes are typical of large grabens, as land subsidence turns floodplains into pools. Central America's biggest are in the Nicaraguan Depression, "Mahomet's Paradise," which runs 500 kilometers long and 50 kilometers wide from the Gulf of Fonseca to the Bay of San Juan. It is half-covered by water, mainly Lake Nicaragua, the greatest freshwater expanse between Superior and Titicaca.

Yet the habitability of grabens has been a mixed blessing because of the earthquakes which have toppled Central American cities since they were first built. The biggest recent one was a 1976 *terremoto* along the Motagua Fault which nearly razed Guatemala City and killed over 20,000 people. In the Nicaraguan Depression, quakes are particularly destructive because the floor is composed either of unstable lake sediments or of recent volcanic deposits which Nicaraguan naturalist Jaime Incer has described as "layer upon layer of old volcanic mud flows, ash, cinders, and pumice—which is really just hardened volcanic foam." Managua is a monument to this instability, its downtown leveled in a 1972 quake and still unrestored.

The Nicaraguan Depression demarcates northern Central America, which has been land since the dinosaur age, from southern, most of which has arisen from the ocean within the past 50 million years. There is less of this new land. Costa Rica's only really large lowland is its swampy northeast, which is really just the southeast end of the Nicaraguan Depression, although it is still impressive, particularly in the Tortuguero area where the forest remains uncut. I've never felt more strongly the sense of invincible wildness a tropical lowland can evoke as when I stood on the tiny volcanic cone of Cerro Tortuguero and looking northeast across an unbroken expanse of treetops to hazy mountains.

Costa Rica and western Panama have coastal plains and fault zone depressions, but they are smaller than the north's. Even in the largest depressions, like Costa Rica's Valle Central, the mountains never seem far away, and calling a basin at 1,500 meters a lowland is stretching a point anyway. For every flat expanse in the Valle Central there seems to be a corresponding steep gorge, in one of which I almost got trapped during a rainy season afternoon. I'd climbed to the stream at the bottom to look at fish, and it was so narrow I'd easily jumped it. When the daily storm came, as though somebody had turned on celestial firehoses, I took shelter under a rock overhang. An hour later, I had to wade up to my waist to cross water roaring and red with silt from coffee plantations above.

Central American rivers in general have this unpredictable mixture of insignificance and intransigence. Even the biggest ones like the San Juan, Coco, or Usumacinta aren't on the scale of an Amazon or Orinoco. They simply don't drain enough territory. Yet the combination of gravity and rain can give them a force out of proportion to size. When I rafted down Costa Rica's Pacuare River in April 1990, the late dry season, the river's ponded stretches were swimmable in a few strokes, but rapids still had enough strength to bounce several rafters into the water. Where the river entered the coastal plain was an unforgettable display of its downcutting power. At a place called Dos Montañas it sliced through sheer cliffs of volcanic stone so high I barely could see the twilight between their tops.

Darién and the Chocó Basin, where Panama and Colombia ambiguously meet, do rival the northern Central American lowlands, and in a sense surpass them, since they are the newest substantial dry land on earth and never have been anything *but* lowlands. They are not an eroded mountain range like the Mosquitia or even a mildly elevated bit of shallow seabottom like the Petén, but basaltic deep ocean floor thrust into the daylight. Flying over southern Darién, it's not always clear where the Gulf of Panama ends and the land begins. Richard Weyl, a German geologist who studied Central America from the 1950s to the 1980s, observed of central Darién, "The valley floor divide between the river systems of the Río Bayano and Río Chucunaque is so flat that it cannot be seen from the air, and the inhabitants of the country cross it in their boats."

Plateaus and Sierras

Central America's highlands are safer than its lowlands, free of hurricanes and malaria. Their subtropical climate is as close to perfect as anywhere on earth. Yet they're mostly too steep and rugged for more than marginal occupation. It took the conquistadors a long time to reach them, and they remained difficult of access. "For five long hours," Stephens wrote of just the beginning of his 1839 ascent from Caribbean coast to Guatemalan Plateau, "we were dragged through mudholes, squeezed in gullies, knocked against trees, and tumbled over roots; every step required care and great physical exertion."

Modern transportation masks this ruggedness somewhat. The Chiapas plateau's limestone strata accumulated over 400 million years, most of the Paleozoic and Mesozoic eras, but the steepness of its slopes seemed unreal from a bus in 1971, and when I reached the relatively level top, I forgot how high I was. I retained no memory at all of Central America's highest plateau, the Altos Cuchumatanes, which I skirted after leaving Chiapas for Guatemala. When I returned in 1995, it seemed incredible that I'd forgotten that rock wall looming overhead. It is a cliché to liken mountains to walls, but the Cuchumatanes really do look like one. Their escarpment is straight, almost perpendicular, with jagged peaks on the tops like the broken bottles that line the walls of Huehuetenango, the city at their foot. "We must imagine the Cuchumatanes as a gigantic, up-lifted block," wrote Richard Weyl, and it takes little imagination to do so.

The Cuchumatanes' top is a huge tableland whose Mam Maya inhabitants are little more influenced from outside than when an Englishman named Thomas Gage crossed in the 1600s, staying at villages and finding "the poor Indians willing to give me whatsoever I demanded." It seems as close to a lost world as exists today, and I had a craving to see it, like Stephens with his Maya city. Even in 1995 there were no towns on the plateau, however, and the only bus service was to the valleys on the other side. A theater of the 1980s guerrilla war, it still wasn't a good place to wander alone, but I was lucky. When I went to the office of a rural development organization, Proyecto Cuchumatanes, and expressed my interest, Director Pedro Guzmán Mérida invited me on his next trip to the top.

Dr. Guzmán's four-wheel-drive took an hour to switchback up the dirt road from Huehuetenango's 1,700 meters to the plateau's 3,500. First we passed through a brush-covered belt of red and green serpentine rocks, the source of pre-Columbian jade as well as the gold and silver the Spanish coveted. Such riches are long gone, but little mines opened beside the road, dug to quarry gravel from limestone strata above the serpentine, the bed of a 200-million-year-old sea. Guzmán, who had a veterinary degree from U.C. Davis but was interested in everything, said he'd found coral fossils in the greenish-white stone. The limestone is fertile, and the steep roadside was solidly planted with maize, although the air grew chill as we got higher. "The people here have varieties of maize for every microclimate, over a hundred of them," Guzmán said. "It grows right to the top of the plateau, then it stops. They can't grow anything on the top except crops like potatoes."

We crested the rim, and entered a grassy valley lined with gentle limestone hills. It did seem a lost world, the air and light somehow older, mellower than below. A dense scrub of agaves, junipers, and cypresses covered the hills, reminiscent of northwest Mexico 1,000 kilometers away. We drove past tile-roofed cottages and potato patches, then entered a winding rocky defile where Mam Maya shepherdesses in black and red tended little black and white flocks or reclined on the greensward as in a Claude Lorraine alpine pastorale. An old man, also handsomely dressed in red and black, led two small and bony but pretty horses beside the road. He waved and came to the window.

"Give me a quetzal, *Tat*," he said. (The quetzal is the Guatemalan currency unit.) I gave him the coins I had in my pocket, and he looked at them disapprovingly as Dr. Guzmán drove on.

"What does '*Tat*' mean?"

"It's a Mam term of respect. It means 'father' literally."

Above the defile we entered an even older world, where the lower valleys' tile roofs and plastic trash disappeared and Mam homesteads were built of rough-hewn planks. Women sat outside some, weaving on hand looms. Others looked deserted, and Guzmán said the owners were away in the Pacific lowlands, doing seasonal work on export farms. "The people here may have lived a migratory life even before the Spanish came," he said, "going back and forth between the mountains and the coast." He showed me where the Guatemalan army had cut roadside woodland to stop guerrillas from ambushing convoys. The trees were growing back vigorously, forming a thick scrub. We passed a concrete foundation, all that remained of a North American missionary's house burned in the eighties. Near it, an old Mam man appeared who might have been the brother of the one who'd asked for a quetzal. This man, who carried an axe and wore a tweed jacket over his red and black tribal costume, was friendlier than the first and didn't ask for money. He shook hands ceremoniously and questioned us diplomatically as to what we were doing there. He didn't call us "*Tat.*"

A jeep trail led to a craggy ridge which Guzmán said was the highest point in the Cuchumatanes, about 3,700 meters. From it, an endless tangle of blue mountains extended to the eastern and southern horizons. Kestrels and red-tailed hawks swooped past, but to see the black vultures that always seem overhead in Central America, I had to look far down into the Huehuetenango Valley.

Some of the mountains I saw from that vantage were jagged sawtooth ridgelines, bedrock thrust up endwise by fault-line pressures instead of plateau walls. The Sierra de las Minas above the Motagua Valley is a classic example (*sierra* means "saw"). It is largely marble, limestone hardened by heat and pressure, and such metamorphic rocks predominate south of central Guatemala. With greater resistance to tropical rains than sedimentary ones, they can have extraordinary peaks. Honduras's north coast has some of the most spectacular summits I've seen, particularly where Pico Bonito rises to 2,435 meters. Forested to the top, it seldom has been climbed because the only trails on most of it are those made by tapirs. From the Bonito River below it, waterfalls many meters high appear silver threads, and the landscape is an archetype of tropical splendor. The river boulders are the deep red color of which only metamorphic rocks seem capable, and they glow under the blue peak. When I was there, in February, the gallery forest was rose and gold with new growth, parakeet flocks flashed iridescent emerald in shafts of sunlight, and a rainbow hovered against bruise-colored clouds.

Similar ranges run southward through Honduras to the Sierra Isabellia of northern Nicaragua, where 1,990-meter Cerro Saslaya is that country's highest peak. Because of heavy forest cover and almost continuous guerrilla warfare since the Spanish chased the Matagalpa tribe into them after the Conquest, Nicaragua's cordilleras are probably the least explored in Central America. Nobody I talked to had set foot in their remoter parts when I was there in 1993. "I've flown over" was the refrain. They're not that high as mountains go, however, and they vanish into the Nicaraguan Depression.

One might expect southern Central America's mountains to be like Nicaragua's—impressive enough for their jungled wildness, but not as dizzying as Guatemala's continental massifs. A land under the ocean until recent geological times would logically have a certain inconsequence. Yet a wall as impressive as Guatemala's ancient plateaus rises at the south end of Costa Rica's Valle Central—the Talamancas, a granitic mass which has attained its present elevation within the past three million years. A conquistador named Perferan de Rivera who crossed it in 1572 is said to have done so on the backs of Indian porters, too cold and exhausted to move. His expedition returned to civilization presenting what Benzoni called "a sad but curious spectacle...for their clothes had rotted on their bodies."

The Talamancas' highest peaks lie around 3,819-meter Cerro Chirripó east of the town of San Isidro El General. Rimmed by foothills, Chirripó lacks the overbearing immediacy of the Cuchumatanes or Pico Bonito, but its distant, rectangular summits seem mystically remote from San Isidro, jungle fantasy mountains. It takes an afternoon on narrow dirt roads to drive to their base, and a day to climb to the alpine zone on a trail that ascends over 2,000 meters in fourteen kilometers. I heeded Rivera's plight when I was there in 1995 and hired a local man named Cristóbal to carry my backpack as far as the National Park Service shelter at 3,500 meters. It seemed a good way to celebrate my fiftieth birthday. The men of San Gerardo de Rivas at the mountain's foot don't only work as porters, they race up for fun. Cristóbal got me up at 4:00 A.M. to start the climb and gave me a glass of sweet tea at his house. The lower part of the trail is called *el gymnasio*, and although it was still dark, my glasses fogged so in the humid air that I might have been climbing in a shower room.

"*Es duro*," Cristóbal said encouragingly. I stopped trying to keep up with him and his teenage son and met them coming down when I got near the shelter around 11:00. A chill, driving rain was falling by then, and I was glad I'd been self-indulgent. A young couple equipped with streamlined new backpacks and Spandex clothes reached the shelter two hours later, when it was raining even harder. They crawled into their fiberfill sleeping bags, muttering about hypothermia, and the next morning they turned around and climbed right back down.

Southern Central America's surprising heights dwindle as suddenly as they appear, however. Granite peaks continue along the Talamanca crest as far as the Panamanian border, but elevation drops to about 2,000 meters in the western Panama cordillera. Impressive heights remain visible west of Panama City, but east of the canal the sense of mountains piled on mountains that prevails in most of the land bridge ends. Darién has only narrow *serranias* along the Caribbean and the Gulf of Panama. On the Colombian border, the Tacarcuna and Pire highlands rise to around 1,000 meters, but on the other side the swampy Chocó Basin extends to the Andes' northern foothills.

Caves

The land bridge's complications aren't only above ground. In one of the Altos Cuchumatanes' little valleys, Dr. Guzmán showed me an opening among some boulders at the roadside. It didn't look like much, a grassy pit, but when I dropped a stone we could hear it echoing down a long way. Caves open throughout "karst" landscapes like the Cuchumatanes, carved by groundwater dissolving the soft limestone. Subterranean rivers flow through them, rising to the surface in places, then descending again. As far as I know, the Cuchumatanes' caves are unexplored.

The largest known Central American caves are in Belize's Maya Mountains, which I first glimpsed in 1971, when a blue escarpment loomed south of the jaguar-haunted savanna which the Guatemalan students who gave me a ride from Tikal found so exciting. This also excited them. "The Maya Mountains!" they cried. "Nobody knows what lives up there!" A mass of granitic rock which has thrust 1,000 meters above southwestern Belize, the mountains may be a continuation of the highlands farther west, although their geology is not well understood. As they rose above the plain, they lifted limestone strata into which groundwater carved spectacular passages. The Chiquibul Plateau just west of the mountains conceals a vast underground system that includes the largest known cavern chamber in the Western Hemisphere, but cave formations are common almost everywhere around them.

Typical of these is a place called Blue Hole at the east edge of the Mayas, where a cave river rises in a cliff-ringed pool, runs above ground for a few meters, then dives back into a low limestone portal. When I was there in 1994, cichlids swam in the sunny shallows, and big mountain mullet lurked in the depths. The fish struck at thrown fruit, but fled into the darkness when I approached the water. A park ranger told me the river surfaced again downstream in a much bigger hole frequented by tarpon and snappers that swim up from offshore springs where it flows into the Caribbean.

A half mile from Blue Hole, the same river is accessible by a cave which yawns on the side of a forested hill, Herman's Cave. Big tooth-and-claw-shaped stalactites hang from its portal, and rough-winged swallows and large bats fluttered among these as I entered. Their twittering combined with the drone of cicadas in huge overhanging trees to sepulchral effect, as though I was at the mouth of Xibalba, the Maya underworld. In fact, the Classic Maya had cut steps down into its mouth. They led me past slippery boulders, then became a faint, sandy trail into utter darkness from which came the sound of running water. By the time I reached the river, the last faint light from the entrance had disappeared, and I could hear only water. Nothing moved as I shined my flashlight along the bank and in the water. When I turned it on the distant ceiling, I saw what looked like thousands of tiny eyes, but they were only reflecting water droplets. The cave seemed lifeless, and when I turned off the light, I began to wonder if *I* was alive.

Stories of bizarre cave fish, salamanders, and insects always have attracted me, and I was disappointed at the relative lifelessness inside Herman's Cave. Yet I did find a cave that crawled with life. Limestone caves aren't confined to northern plateaus—the scraped-up sea floor of southern Central America has them too, mainly in coastal lowlands and offshore islands. This cave, known simply as La Gruta, is a tunnel a few hundred meters long in the coral rock of Panama's Isla Colón, where a stream has cut through a hillock. A Panamanian I met there named Appolonio told me it is a religious site for local people, who had planted flowers and placed statues of the Virgin Mary at the downstream entrance. When a first statue was erected, Appolonio said, the real Virgin had made an appearance, so a second one commemorated that event.

La Gruta's entrance yawns jaggedly like Herman's Cave's, but seems gentler. Ferns grow around it instead of giant tree roots, and the stalactites on the upper portal look more like elongated breasts than teeth and claws. Inside, translucent, ivory-colored stalactites and stalagmites form vaulted chambers above the streambed. Other Central American caves had grown quieter as I entered, but this one got noisier. Energetic "*treet, treet, treet*" calls filled the darkness, made by big, spindly beige crickets which occupied every square meter of the pockmarked ceiling. They waved their antennae and sang by rubbing tiny vestigial wings together. One was eating a moth. Scattered among them were whipscorpions, large arachnids that resemble a cross between a scorpion and a tarantula, and big black millipedes. All this creeping and crawling might have been unnerving, but the crickets' songs gave the cave an incongruous cheeriness, like a shady woods on a summer's day.

A muffled roar came from a dark corner, and I turned my flashlight to where the ceiling rose in a conical chimney. Dozens of bats flew around in this: the roar was the reverberation of their wingbeats from stalactites so thin as to ring when struck. Most of the bats were so small that they looked mothlike in my flashlight beam, but a few were much larger—vampires, Appolonio said. Perturbed squeaking came from the circling throng, so I turned the light away, and they settled back into their roost. Farther in, the cave took a bend. As the light from the downstream entrance disappeared, a dim glow from the upstream one touched the walls. Small reddish-brown bats with the long snouts and large eyes of nectar feeders seemed unbothered by my flashlight, peering down at me from the ceiling and, occasionally, yawning. The chamber turned again, and the upstream entrance came into sight. Another vampire colony fluttered and squeaked there, and the volume of cricket song, which had dwindled in the darkness of the interior, increased again.

It seemed strange that this little cave had so much more life than the big Belizean one. Even the entrance of Herman's Cave had fewer bats, and I'd seen no crickets or whipscorpions. Air currents moving between the two entrances of La Gruta probably carry a more reliable supply of cricket and whipscorpion food than at the larger cave's single entrance. Yet the crickets at La Gruta seemed specialized for cave life, pale and flightless, and I wondered how they'd colonized such a small, apparently isolated one. There may have been other caves nearby, but I didn't hear of any. Similarities between cave organisms in widely separated places have led biologists to suspect that cave networks may extend surprisingly far through limestone terrain. Perhaps the La Gruta crickets arrived through such an underground pathway.

Volcanoes

Volcanoes ultimately express the ambiguities that bless and curse the land bridge: rich coasts and hurricanes, sheltered valleys and earth-quakes. Except for the earthquakes, they make its biggest surprises. Huge cinder cones accumulate in a few generations or blast into nothingness too quickly for flight, and ash deposits from such explosions blanket about 400,000 square kilometers, reaching far out into the Pacific. Fertile with erupted minerals, volcanic soils have supported rich civilizations for over three millennia, but cones provoke an endemic anxiety which seventeenth-century Englishman Thomas Gage expressed in describing two of them, Agua and Fuego: "That of water hanging on the south side, almost perpendicularly over the city; the other of fire standing lower.…That of water…yields a goodly prospect to the sight, being almost all the year green…but the other…is unpleasing and more dreadful to behold.…Thus is Guatemala seated in the midst of a paradise on one side and a hell on the other."

Central America's highest mountain, the 4,220-meter Tajumulco volcano, looms directly east of the high Cuchumatanes, and the two awesome heights form a kind of demon portal for the Pan American Highway. I passed through this obliviously in 1971 but encountered the active volcanic zone a little farther south, at Lake Atitlán, where an ancient cone has collapsed to form a caldera ringed with basalt cliffs and younger cones. One of my hitchhiking rides called it "the most beautiful place in the world," and it was certainly spectacular, but the thing that struck me about Atitlán was an apparent discrepancy of scale. To my unaccustomed eye, its cones looked more like the rear-projected backgrounds of movies than real mountains. They seemed too high to believe.

Volcanic disasters have been horribly real, however. One of Atitlán's cones exploded ten times in the nineteenth century, and "unpleasing" Volcán Fuego has erupted fifty times since 1524. Girolamo Benzoni described how a landslide and flood from Volcán Agua, the *less* threatening cone Thomas Gage mentioned, destroyed

Guatemala's first capital in 1541. "Soon after midnight there began to arise from that mountain so great and so terrible a quantity of water, and with such an impetus and fury, as to precipitate rocks of incredible size, carrying along and destroying whatever it met within its course; and there were heard in the air cries and lamentations and frightful noises." A dose of riding rickety, overcrowded buses around the highlands, and the sense of ever-impending disaster that conveyed, cured my initial incredulity about Guatemalan volcanoes. Perhaps because the country around them is so high and steep, they never seemed safely distant as they might have, however deceptively, on a lowland plain. It seemed they might slide downhill anytime, as they have in the past.

Guatemala's volcanoes are the highest in Central America because they stand on a twenty-million-year-old plateau accumulated as eruptions spewed lava and ash 2,000 meters deep over 10,000 square kilometers. The plateau also covers western Honduras and eastern El Salvador, and I got a sense of its massiveness where it looms above the breezy Salvadoran town of Matapán. Because it isn't near an active fault, Matapán gets fewer earthquakes than most Central American towns, so it has some of the oldest churches. This makes it seem anachronistic, which is typical of the volcanic plateau, a region that remains remote although the Spanish settled it in the early 1500s. With black vultures on its slaughterhouse roof and bats emerging from downtown eaves at dusk, Matapán probably was much the same in 1993 as in 1893.

The peak that marks the plateau's south edge, 2,418-meter Montecristo, has some of El Salvador's last virgin forest and was one of its two functioning national parks when I was there, but getting up it wasn't easy. First I had to walk five kilometers from town to the park entrance because there was no other transportation. Even walking wasn't encouraged since it had been a guerrilla zone during the recent civil war. When I got to the entrance, I found another reason why walking *to* the park wasn't encouraged. My permit had a provision I'd overlooked: "*No se permiten caminatas dentro del parque*" —no walking *in* the park. I had to wait until a vehicle would pick me up. Luckily, some meteorologists soon came along on their way to examine a weather station abandoned since the war's beginning, and I got a spine-jarring ride in the back of their pickup with the ranger assigned to accompany them. He had worked in the park before the guerrillas took it over, then had returned but wasn't happy about the situation. Poaching was common because the staff didn't have the equipment to stop it. The local police poached. When I asked why I couldn't walk in the park, he said it was because of the danger of assault.

As the truck banged up increasingly steep switchbacks of red and white volcanic dust and mud, I was glad I hadn't walked. I'd never have made it in a day. The trees at the top had seemed close from Metapán, but Metapán didn't look at all close from the plateau slopes; in fact, it soon disappeared. Above about 2,000 meters, we were climbing in the clouds. Four kilometers from the station the road got too muddy even for four-wheel-drive, and we walked the rest of the way through huge, epiphyte-covered trees. Birds I'd never seen before flew among them, bushy-crested jays, dark blue like North American Steller's jays, but bigger, with yellow eyes. They made squeaky, murmuring sounds, stealthily feeding on grubs in the branches. The station was in a steep pasture, but the clouds obscured everything more than a few meters away, so I didn't see the plateau top at all on that trip.

In the rest of northern Central America, volcanoes rise above lower lands, like central El Salvador's Valle de las Hammacas. One cinder cone there, 1,870-meter Izalco, has grown from a cornfield in the last two centuries. A local clergyman told John Lloyd Stephens it had been "a small orifice...puffing out...pebbles" in 1798. By 1840, it was so high that the fires of its eruptions were visible from far out to sea, a growth that excited Stephens to a semi-erotic enthusiasm. "The sight was fearfully grand," he wrote. "The crater had three orifices...and after a report, deep in the huge throat of the third appeared a light blue vapor and then a mass of thick black smoke, whirling and struggling out in enormous wreaths, and rising in a dark, majestic column, lighted for a moment by a sheet of flame." Izalco kept this up almost continuously until 1957, when entrepreneurs who shared Stephens's enthusiasm built a hotel with bedrooms overlooking it. Then it stopped, although when I saw it in 1993 it remained bare of trees, a gargantuan slag heap above the fields.

Salvador's volcanic past has been even more active. Like Guatemala's Atitlán, its Lake Ilopango is an ancient caldera whose explosion about 1,800 years ago destroyed an area 3,000 kilometers square and expelled the region's population for centuries. Thick layers of pumice called *"tierra blanca"* cover ruins from that period. A later explosion created a mini-Pompeii at a place called Ceren, entombing a clay-walled farmstead which yielded traces of a flock of domestic ducks and a Maya book. Ilopango remains active, periodically extruding domes that could explode, and more Cerens undoubtedly lie in El Salvador's future. Surrounded by live volcanoes and built on volcanic calderas, its towns made me feel not just under volcanoes, as in Guatemala, but *in* them.

The active zone changes in Nicaragua. Volcanoes there rise from the Depression's level floor and thus seem preternaturally high. When I drove north from Managua one morning in 1993 with Jacinto Cedeño of the Nicaraguan National Park Service, I had to crane my neck to see their tops through his pickup's windshield. Each cone or cluster of cones stood isolated, gargantuan, like a receding file of Goya colossi. One would loom over the horizon, stand obdurately for awhile, then be gone, replaced by another.

Cedeño had invited me along while he did some park business near Cosigüina, the northernmost Nicaraguan volcano, which is also its first nature reserve, established by the Somoza government in the 1950s. Cosigüina is unimpressive now, low and tree covered, only 870 meters high. In 1836, it stood at almost 3,000 meters when it exploded with the biggest bang in Central American history, which, John Lloyd Stephens wrote, "startled the people of Guatemala 400 miles off." Just hearing about the explosion excited Stephens to an apocalyptic vision: "The cone of the volcano was gone," he wrote, "a mountain and field of lava ran down to the sea; a forest as old as creation had entirely disappeared, and two islands were formed in the sea; shoals were discovered in one of which a large tree was fixed upside down; one river was completely choked up, and another formed, running in an opposite direction…wild beasts, howling, left their caves in the mountains, and ounces, leopards, and snakes fled for shelter to the abodes of men."

The country around Cosigüina still looked disaster stricken. The only modern homesteads were big export *fincas*, apparently abandoned, their fields overgrown with orange sunflowers. Everybody else seemed to live in palm-thatched huts dotted about the savanna. Cedeño, a portly, patient man, said it was "*tierra maliosa.*" The people were withdrawn, distrustful. He'd come to dispute with a *finca* heir who'd returned from living in England during the Contra War and wanted some forest land from the government. They argued a long time, standing outside a tumbledown worker's barracks, while orange-chinned parakeets and ladder-backed woodpeckers squabbled in the trees above them.

"*La lucha para la tierra,*" Cedeño sighed, getting back in the truck. The struggle for the land. We drove south again to the beachfront resort of Jiquilillo. I was scouting locations for an ecotourism guidebook, but a *maremoto*, a tsunami, had swept through the resort the year before, and it looked like it. The wave had buried the asphalt beachfront road in a sandbar and stranded houses out in the surf. "This used to be a very popular place," Cedeño said. "Lots of people came out from Managua for the weekend." Smoke billowed from Volcán San Cristóbal, the next peak south of Cosigüina, as we continued south toward Managua. A perfect 1,780-meter cone, Cristóbal is Nicaragua's highest, and its cap had shone white as snow when we'd driven past it in the morning, but that had been only the mist and smoke that usually hangs there. It glowed red in the twilight. When we stopped for gas in León, the station attendant told us there'd been an earthquake about an hour earlier, just about when we were driving along the devastated Jiquilillo beach. It had been a deep one out at sea, probably the kind that had caused the previous year's tsunami, but we hadn't felt a thing.

Perhaps the most awesome Nicaraguan volcano is the twin one of Concepción Maderas in Lake Nicaragua. The lake can be as rough and dark as the sea, and the two cones, Maderas black with forest, Concepción gray with cinders, appear fantastically high from its surface. Their scale seems incongruous with the historical world of towns and ferryboats, as though the backdrop for a Jurassic diorama of plesiosaurs and ichthyosaurs has fallen over the horizon by mistake. All I saw in the way of dinosaur relatives while crossing to Omotepe was a flock of cormorants, but they looked antediluvian enough beneath the cones. "The lake is too large to be called beautiful," wrote Thomas Belt, "and its large extent and the mere glimpses of its limits and cloud-capped peaks appeal to the imagination rather than to the eye."

Concepción and Maderas are visible from far to the south in Costa Rica, where their starkness looks even stranger. Southern Central America's volcanic zone, where new oceanic land replaces old continental land, is very different from the north's. Indeed, volcanoes change so quickly below the Costa Rican border that they seem to have a kind of national identity. Compared to Guatemala's lowering cones and Nicaragua's looming ones, Costa Rica's seem amorphous, almost understated, although there is one remarkable exception to this. The huge cone of Arenal in north central Costa Rica exploded so violently in 1968 that cannonading boulders covered 12 square kilometers with impact craters and glowing clouds filled the sky. The eruption killed 78 people, and lesser eruptions continued through the early 1970s. When I was in the adjacent Cordillera de Tilaran in the late 1980s, Arenal's occasional rumbles shook the ground like sonic booms.

More typically Costa Rica is Volcán Rincón de la Vieja northwest of Arenal. It looks impressively volcanic from the Guanacaste coastal plain and has ejected lots of ash as recently as the 1950s and -60s. When I camped at Rincón's foot in 1990, however, the cone seemed to fade into the dense forest that covered its lower slopes and trees even obscured the fumaroles and other infernal devices that welled up at the base. Living gumbo limbos grew over mudpots that periodically flung boiling glop four meters in the air, and strangler figs enclosed fissures that steamed sulfur like a mineral bath.

The big volcanoes of Costa Rica's Cordillera Central—Poás, Irazu, Turrialba—seem even more cryptic, clumped together in cordilleras so massive that the active craters are obscured. It's not that they aren't dangerous. Volcán Poás near San José expelled an 8,000-meter smoke plume which blanketed most of the Valle Central with ash in 1910 and did similar things in 1952, 1974, and 1978. When I was there in 1990, the farms around it had been declared a disaster area because of poisonous fumes and acid rain. Poás has the potential to become as explosive as Cosigüina. Yet my first sight of its active crater was anticlimactic. One moment, I was walking through a gently sloping meadow of ragwort and blueberry bushes, the next standing before what might have been an open pit sulfur mine dug out of the forested ridge. There were great heaps of yellow ash and steaming green lakes, but less sense that this was an opening to internal fires than in Nicaragua.

Inactive craters seem mere lakes buried in elfin forest, and their cones may be hard to recognize as volcanoes, they are so heavily covered with clouds and plants. At an extinct cone called Volcán Cacao in northwest Costa Rica, I embarrassed myself by referring to some "sandstone" outcrops when talking to a geologist. The brown, granular stone of the outcrops was volcanic ash, of course, not sedimentary sandstone, but in the damp forest it was hard to remember that the mountain had once been smoking and barren. Much of Cacao never has been mapped because continual cloud cover prevents aerial photographs.

I'm not the only one who's been fooled by Costa Rican volcanism. Early geologist Miguel Obregon thought he'd found an active volcano at a hill called Barra Honda on the Pacific coast's Nicoya Peninsula because vertical holes on the top issued sulfurous fumes and rumblings. In 1937, ornithologist Alexander Skutch recognized the holes as "sinkholes, such as one finds in many calcareous formations, rather than volcanic vents" but also described inexplicable volcanolike features. "From this cavern issued a gas with an unpleasant odor, which was neither that of hydrogen sulphide nor that of sulphur dioxide. From the depths of the cavity came a continuous fine, shrill whistle, as of gas escaping under pressure from a narrow orifice." Skutch's guide told him that the gas came out of one vent "with sufficient volume and force to sway the boughs of trees." Skutch speculated that roosting bats in the limestone caves might be causing the noises and smells but couldn't think of any reason why "so much gas issued from them." A cave explorer told me that the gases might in fact have come from thermal vents under the limestone, but when I visited Barra Honda in 1990, I found neither smells, noises, gas, or bats, only a juvenile mottled owl teetering on a branch above one cave's mouth.

The final surprise of Central America's active volcanoes is that they suddenly stop. No active volcanoes occur south of Volcán Irazu in central Costa Rica, and even inactive ones disappear from the Talamanca mountains. There are volcanoes in western Panama, but they are inactive. The southernmost, El Valle, last erupted about 40,000 years ago. The most impressive is Volcán Barú, a peak which, although quiescent, seems a kind of sum of Central American volcanoes. Like Guatemalan and Salvadoran volcanoes, Barú looms over a plateau broken by deep gorges—the gorge of the Río Caldera just east of it is one of the most dizzying I've seen. Like Nicaraguan volcanoes, Barú is isolated and brooding, its summit often capped by cloud. Like Costa Rican ones, it lacks a classic cone shape and might seem nonvolcanic if it didn't have seven craters at its top and hot springs at its bottom.

Like all the others, Barú has attracted a large human population with its fertile ash. I met a Guaymi man in the Caldera Gorge who was staring up at the cliffs, which are fluted with basalt blocks so regularly shaped they might have been handcarved. When asked why, he said he was thinking how to grow vegetables up there.

Penny Harter

Poems

from *Turtle Blessing*

Buffalo

Heavy as petrified wood,
you stare from the rock face,
slow body aging in the moonlight,
feet lost in crevices.

You sniff the air.
It is not the same wind
you remember.
Your mouth is as cold
as the sky.

Dusk at White Rock Overlook

Cumulus rise from the ridges.
The river glints brown in the gorge.
Thunderheads deepen the mountains.
Soon it will be evening.

Two ravens float from the cliff edge.
Their shadows follow the current.
Long ripples drift in the canyon
Carrying darkness to shore.

This is the clock of the shadow.
This is the gong of the skin.
Rock walls spill down to the water
Taking what's left of the sun.

Solar Eclipse, New Mexico

The great rim of the sun
grazes on red cliffs
as it rises to meet
this day's shadow.

Under the ring of fire
a child remembers flashlight games—
rosy palm and fingers
against the light,
blood flowing in the webs.

Everything is distance and perspective,
cat and mouse, an apple's orbit
on a string above your mouth.

Turtle Blessing

After the boy threw the pregnant turtle
hard against the brick wall
of the courtyard, screaming
"What are you, some kind of
fucking humanitarian?"
to the girl who called him crazy,
the creature bounced off,
crawled a few feet, blood
seeping into the weeds
from her cracked shell,
and stopped.

She died last night,
was buried, her eggs gone
with her into the earth.

This morning in the mist
by Seeley's Pond, an ancient turtle,
huge and black on the wet grass,
turns its blunt head this way, that,
as it crawls up the slope
toward the road, and I bless it
against the crunch of its dark shell,
against the driver who will not swerve.

In Deer Country

Part leaf, part shade,
they stand beside the road,
and we are foreign. Out there
at the edge of the clearing,
some drift into the sun,
faces lowered to crop clover,
backs flecked with light.

In deer country, they live
in their own time; even running,
their limbs flow softly into grass,
their bodies weave like water.
They are the old way
of moving on the earth.

How Can We Not

How can we not be lonely,
one species among the many,
having lost the mother tongue,
forgotten how to speak in the old way,
throats open, teeth shining
as the word slides over them,
growling, warbling, hissing
our breath?

Feather, fin, and fur
are no longer of our flesh
except for the dark fuzz in our armpits,
the springing hair of our heads,
the wiry tangle where we generate
others of ourselves.

How can we not be lonely?
Listen to the wind tonight,
how it teaches the trees
to know themselves;
how it carries the cries
of the neighbor's dog
to others of his kin;
how it wants us to join in.

Willow

The green window of the willow deep in the woods,
shining from among the still bare trees,
opens into the first sunlight
so pure its branches singe the air,
so bright that I remember living there.

Tulip

I watched its first green push
through bare dirt, where the builders
had dropped boards, shingles, plaster—
killing everything.
I could not recall what grew there,
what returned each spring,
but the leaves looked tulip,
and one morning it arrived,
a scarlet slash against the aluminum siding.

Mornings, on the way to my car,
I bow to the still bell
of its closed petals; evenings,
it greets me, light ringing
at the end of my driveway.

Sometimes I kneel
to stare into the yellow throat,
count the black tongues,
stroke the firm red mouth.
It opens and closes my days.
It has made me weak with love,
this god I didn't know I needed.

Dusk

I lower my ear
to the purple grass,
a murmuring that runs to the horizon
pearled with the dampness of dusk,
and all the shining sheep
like laughter scattered
here and there across a life
lie down where they are in the fields,
filling the dark spaces
between the spokes of some great wheel
before it creaks and rolls
into the sky.

In the Rain

In the rain, the earth shines;
leaves hold their sheen to the sky,
and I remember the weight of my hand
on your forehead, your taut skin
pale in the dark, my fingers curving
to fit your skull, the way water fits
everything it finds, its tributaries running
between black branches, green leaves
all the way to the ground.

Reading the Tea Leaves

After winter rain
dead leaves have steeped
in the gutter.

Easter eggs dipped in this tea
would darken
to barnyard brown.

On the neighbor's lawn an inflated swan
adrift on a stake like a weather vane
wheels slowly to face us.

I bend over the puddle,
stir with one finger
the cold silt at bottom,

watching the shredded leaves rise,
swirl and settle, as if I were
shaking them in a tiny globe.

Night Watch

All night I watch for
the movement of snow
toward water.

Waking again and again,
I check the window
looking for a thaw
under the streetlight,
a white withdrawal
at the edge of the lawn.

Across the planet, missiles
discover one another,
kin embracing kin
in the night sky.

How briefly each one lives
above or in the dirt
that cannot refuse it.

Asleep You Are a River

Asleep, you are a river
        face rippling over stones
                legs drifting like branches
                        torso heaving currents.

When you stretch your arms upward
        you call tributaries home,
                breed clouds from your fingertips.

Even your breathing
        is a long journey
                to the sea.

Sister Death

My death grazes just out of sight
over my right shoulder.
I hear the whisper of green
between her lips.
I imagine her as mare
heavy with foal,
tail swishing flies from her strong back,
eyes brown as a farm pond.

Each day I toss a lump of sugar
back into that unseen pasture,
murmur soothing words under my breath.

Wherever I go she migrates with me.
Even in winter
when fodder is scarce,
I feel her warm breath on my neck
and dream of bundled hay in a heated stall.

One day in some field
neither of us has visited
I will forget to toss the sugar
or to dream of hay,
and my death will canter closer
whinnying softly
until her nose finds my palm.

The Llano

Stark as piñon
cows graze the horizon,
adrift in a field of light.

Around them, mountains
hold sky on dark flanks,
ancient muscles rippling
under the sun.

Above the cows a storm gathers,
herding lightning around the pasture
purple as twilight.

As the Earth tilts toward night,
the hills turn to blood,
and we come home,
kicking the dust of the road
into starlight.

Chip Rawlins

Head of Murphy Creek

from *Broken Country*

July 30

I built a fire and started coffee and wrangled the horses in before
the alarm sounded. Mitch seemed subdued, while Roger talked as
if all things were the same, and for him perhaps they were. I took
refuge in silence. I licked the cut on my hand. My dreams and a corresponding lack of sleep had filled me with dread: by killing the
bear we had upset things, and they would rebound. We would get
hurt.

But the day dawned clear and calm, without apparent blemish.
We packed the camp and lashed it to the backs of the horses, and
they cooperated, even Elhon. As Mitchell and Roger started the
sheep with shouts, I got underway with the pack string. The sheep
moved in clots and clabbers through the morning shadow that lay in
the bowl under the pass.

Etched into the mountainside, the trail was steep and narrow,
lacking a solid edge. I rode Tubby, slow and surefooted but fat. I
heard shouts and the frenzied yips of the dogs as Roger and Mitch
came behind, awash in the herd, holding them tight and shoving

them up. The sheep overflowed the trail, dodging and blatting, loose rocks clattering from under the hooves of one to roll under the hooves of the next. The clamor rose almost visibly, disarranging the morning air.

I wasn't used to sitting so far off the ground, above such a drop. My boot stuck out at a sharp angle into space, the oiled leather brick red, the laces yellow, and the sole a creamy white. When my eyes shifted from the toe of my boot to the distant floor of the cirque, the leap in focus made me feel faintly sick.

So I stopped looking down. Enough of perspective, irony, all that. I was closer to the ridge now and I could see the big snowdrift, light blue in shadow with a dark blue edge that seemed to vibrate against the rising sun. I stopped to let the horses blow, hearing the air catch and grate in their throats, the grind of iron shoes against rock as they adjusted the weight of their loads.

At last I led them onto the pass. It was a bare swoop not much wider than the horses themselves, and I got off to breathe and gaze, glad to have my feet out of the air. The snowdrift, which lapped over the bare rock and dirt of the ridge, was frozen hard. I could see the sets of tracks where Mitch and Roger had scouted, postholed into the snow in the day's heat. I stepped on the margin of it, and it crunched as my boots sank two inches. There were veins of dirt and broad reddish stains, like dried blood, which I knew to be algae. The drift curved out of sight to the east, and I could see the horse tracks disappearing. Following them to the lip, I looked into the cirque below.

The high basin was a long oval hemmed to the south by fractured walls and shaky towers, which threw long shadows toward the pass. To the north, the ridge was a bright golden curve, snowless and browed with Neanderthal outcrops. A black cave-mouth yawned under a castellated point, and remnant snow slanted down on all flanks. From the snow emerged streams of loose rock, flowing east through reefs of stunted conifer: no apparent place to camp.

The air was cold, but the sun touched my face with a quick heat.

I stomped out a path through the drift to where the muddy trail emerged, once, twice, three times. I could smell the snow, a dusty, moist scent, and the air of the uninhabited canyon below. Pookie followed me dutifully, then stopped to roll in the snow and snap at the morning air.

The horses watched. On the pass there wasn't much to eat, but they nosed at patches of tough grass and jerked a few stems out. I noticed a faint trail along the ridge, leading north to the ramp of Prater Mountain. A fringe of pines seemed to hold it in place. To the south, the ridge curved up into a pine-shagged height that broke off into rubbly cliffs.

Leaving the drift, I walked back, four long steps to the western rim. The herd was struggling up. As they saw me, the lead ewes stopped and blatted over their shoulders. I had to get off the pass or the herd might turn back.

I mounted and drew a long breath. The packhorses balked at the snowdrift, and the rope snapped taut. Fat Tubby danced. I could feel her front feet breaking through the crust and her back feet sliding into the holes. I yanked Red's lead, and he jumped into the drift, dragging the others off balance. They collided and Red almost went down. Tubby floundered out of the snowdrift and slipped in the mud below—followed by all that struggling bulk—then clawed her way to dry ground. I yelled and pounded her ribs with my heels, and we dragged the others out of the snow and across the slick mud, to the security of the trail.

But the trail wasn't secure. In the angled plunge of rock and mud and ball-bearing pebbles into the bowl, it was barely present, a foot-wide scrape. I had a precise vision of how we would look, falling, a tangle of packs and rope and thrashing hooves, an avalanche of live things. Time was suspended in a great, fearful ball, spinning above the head of the cirque. "Don't get off once you start," Mitch had warned. "You'll knock your horse off balance. Don't look back, just go."

The first switchback was so abrupt that Tubby had to lift both front feet and wheel, grunting with the shock as her hooves struck down. Her back feet slid, and I yelped, but we made it. I passed the lead behind my back, looking at Elhon's big hooves level with my head, almost in reach. Tubby coughed and the bit rattled against her teeth. *Go.* One by one the packhorses lunged and recovered.

The second switchback looked worse, a shingly about-face on the spine above a tusky pinnacle. "If your horse slips," Mitch had said, "toss the rope down the hill and jump up. Then dig in, or you'll slide under the hooves."

I looked down the ridge. It was like looking down the bar of a chain saw. The old mare hesitated. I shut my eyes for an instant as she spun and opened them looking south at the cliffs. Her back feet skated, and then she had them under her and I could feel her ribs heave as her breath puffed out in a big *whoosh*. I had to blink as each packhorse repeated the dance-step. But the horses handled themselves with care. At the tail of the string, Elhon lunged too far and her back hooves skidded off the trail, but she dug in and held.

Dizzy—I realized I'd been holding my breath. The next switchback was easier: Tubby didn't even grunt, and the rest of the string stepped through. Below, the trail was carved into the slope instead of sketched across it. I lined the horses out and then stopped. "Whoa up. Let's rest. Whoa up." My voice shook.

On the slope above, at eye level, there were tiny flowers bedded in the gravel, forcing their way up between rocks. In the morning light I recognized buttercups, yellow as tiny suns, and spring beauties, white with flashes of pink, seven-pointed stars rising from the earth. The air was alive and sweet. The sky, framed in the rocky cirque, was blue as an upside-down ocean.

At the first fringe of grass I dismounted and untied their lead ropes. They dropped their heads to graze, nodding, their colors brilliant: oiled rust, coffee, and ripe wheat.

On the pass I saw two wobbling white heads, then six, then a jostling mob. It took an hour to get them all down the slope. Mitch and Roger rode down the switchbacks, letting the dogs push the sheep. It seemed at any moment that the whole mass would come unstuck and tumble, as one, down the shingly slope, but only one lamb slipped. It rolled twice before gaining its feet, but that was all.

As the herd spread out in the basin, and Roger and Mitch rode through, I caught the packhorses and tied them together. Roger looked sideways at me. "Not too bad. The drift was smaller than last year."

"We made it," I said, and looked at him. "But it's bad. We ought to dig the trail out."

Mitch laughed. "We like it that way. Keeps the *turistas* out."

"Pretty early up here. We should get them down to some feed," Roger said. "I guess a guy could set up camp. Just follow this on down. There's a trail coming across. Make a right, up around the corner of the mountain. On top's a level spot under some pines, with stakes and stove rocks. That's camp. We'll get a scatter on the sheep. Then I have to ride out."

I was glad to go. I was still uneasy with Roger, and the high bowl wasn't a welcoming place, under its unsteady cliffs, blue-gray and ghost gray, streaked with mustard and white. The trail wound through heaps of stone, neither following the bony crests nor falling into the dips where snow held late. Between was a band of soil hedged by low, shaggy conifers, and the trail followed it down the pitch of the basin, curving with the contours, east.

Riding, I tracked the water's course, saw the snowmelt singing in rivulets then carving gullies above which scraggly firs tipped. Dead fir trunks, none larger than a wrist, were jackstrawed in the chill cascades. Leaving the water we passed through fir thickets, twenty hooves muffled by dirt, then knocking on rock.

The trail dropped off the end of a moraine and out of the high basin. We sidehilled from one knuckled glen to the next, through lush pockets and big trees. From the lip of the bowl, the canyon's west face opened in softer curves and then dropped off again. Two headlands thrust out, draped with green and crowned with pines. Separating them was a narrow tributary hidden by its angle of descent. I could hear the roar of water, but the stream was out of sight.

The opposite wall of the canyon seemed too close. The snow on it had melted, and it was gray, not green, mostly talus or cliff. Conifers formed narrow ranks along each folded ridge, acutely angled from right to left, separated by landslips and gulleys. I looked for a trail but there was none. It was all ragged, all steep.

I wanted to be someplace where I couldn't fall off the edge. The bear's death, followed by the crossing of the pass, had left me with a hollow foreboding. And there was something else uncertain, unexpected, something I had missed. It was visible, not a scent or an emotion, something I had seen but not grasped. The thought was uneasy, so I tried to let it go.

After dipping low to a junction, the trail climbed south through pockets of green, loomed over by old firs, huge after the stunted growth of the cirque. There were berms of papery-scaled fir cones across the trail, dry enough that they crackled when the horses stepped on them. Knotted limber pines claimed the ridgetops and rock ledges as the trail roved south, up through eroding draws and cupped meadows, and then reached a narrow divide. I looked off: a headwater creek thundered down in a loose flume, then disappeared between cliffs. I waited until the horses stopped puffing and began to graze, and then rode along the ridge to the east.

It wasn't hard to find the camp: it was the only level spot. Tubby jigged her head and nickered, as if to say *This is the place*. We pulled up by a bleached stack of poles, and stove rocks like squat monuments. I untied the lash ropes, heaved the heavy packs down, and dragged them into the shade. Elhon had broken her britchen strap, and one end hung loose. The leather was rotten. Two more strings had broken in her front cinch. I'd have to ask Mitch how to fix it. I turned the horses out to graze, and they found a wallow of loose dirt and took turns rolling, then ambled off, tails flashing in the sun.

I got the camp up, and Mitch rode in and we ate. He opened the kitchen box and examined what was left of the food. "That damn *Rogelio* eats better up here than at home."

"Is he coming back soon?"

"Probably not. This part's steep, but the herding's not hard to figure out."

I built a fire and we made coffee and toasted bread on the stovetop, smearing it with peanut butter and raspberry jam. We sat outside and ate, scanning the country. Above the gorge, the head of Murphy Creek formed an amphitheater, curved walls without a floor. It was all either up or down; wild, crumbling slants, and creeks brawling white through boulders and deadfall.

"We'll work the *borregas* up and around the head of Murphy," Mitch said. "Wild and lonesome. I like this camp."

July 31

To keep meat in a mountain camp, you hang it in the night air, where it cools and acquires a dry surface film. At sunrise you roll it up in canvas and put it in the shade. If nights are cold, it keeps for days, even weeks: that seemed like primitive magic.

At midmorning I dug a pit with our sawed-off shovel and built a fire in it, under the wide, bright sky, then gathered more wood, carrying it up armful by armful. I unrolled a front quarter of mutton and cut chunks for stew. Then I rolled the quarter back up and stowed it in the shade. It struck me that there were varieties of knowledge that went with certain places and situations. Someone had found this way of keeping meat fresh, just as someone had thought up the sawbuck packsaddles, and the trick of making rope.

I cut onions, potatoes, and carrots, the knife making a solid *chunk*. I set the Dutch oven on the fire. When it was hot, I browned the meat, then tumbled in the vegetables: rudimentary and grand. I added salt and pepper and chili. The lid fit on with a satisfying *clink* and I felt gifted, suddenly, with this practical heritage, with these things that were simple and worked so well.

Beyond this work, there was space and light for me here. And I liked being unobserved. I made a gargoyle face at a limber pine. Hah! Nothing I could say would make the tree mad. That was a positive sensation.

I scooped hot coals out of the pit, set the oven in, and shoveled the coals on top. Then I buried it with ashes and dirt. Wonderful. I could leave and it would still cook.

At midday, Mitch was napping in the tent. I went to check the horses and found them in a green swale. A low burst of thunder crossed the stainless blue, followed by echoes traveling the ground like invisible trains. Then the first cloud exploded over the ridge, lifting to reveal a gray belly filled with turbulent darkness. As I hastened toward camp, cloud after cloud rose up, diminishing the light. The whole landscape shifted from the colors of hawk to the colors of dove.

A shadow raced down the talus, over me and into the firs, falling into the gorge and then climbing faster than any animal, up the east wall and over the Star Peaks. And the cloud trailed a sudden coolness, prickling the hair on my arms.

Then came more thunder, closer and higher in pitch: I could hear it burst in one part of the sky and then cross to another. As I reached the camp a bolt tickled the rimrock, burning a blue hole in my sight. Then a hard gust flattened the pocket meadow, and the leaves of the sunflowers flashed their silver undersides up to the racing sky.

I hear wind purring in the conifers, nudging dry cones into a stumble, and then I see the leading edge of the rain, the border of blurred silver, see the raw contrasts soften, hear the wind's brush and snare, see flowers dip and bow, and then: the air is rain, your skin is rain, your clothes, your breath, your heart, all rain.

I lowered my arms. Mitch watched me from the tent, nodding to himself: *Not enough sense to come in out of the rain.* He was starting a fire in the box stove. I stepped in and looked out through the door flap. The canyon was lidded. Clouds lapped over the high ridge to the east. I went out and brought wood in. The ground was wet, but there was a dry circle where I'd buried the Dutch oven. "What about the stew?" I asked.

"The heat'll keep the rain out. It'll cook," he said. He started a pot of coffee. I dug out my classics text and opened to the chapter on the Chinese. "Do nothing and all things will be done," said Lao-Tzu. Check. I'd try that on Mitchell, next time he asked where the horses were. After scouting Lao-Tzu, I read an excerpt from the *Analects* by Confucius:

> Humility is near to moral discipline (*li*); simplicity of character is near to true manhood; and loyalty is near to sincerity of heart....For with humility, a man seldom commits errors; with sincerity of heart, he is reliable; and with simple character, he is generous.

The rain ceased. I studied the sky. The clouds opened but then closed softly over us again, and rained again, gently. Mitch poured some coffee, and steam curled under the brim of his hat.

I asked him about the bullet hole in the ceiling above the big table in the Preston ranch house. "That was Ray," he said, and shook his head. "He's one wild bastard." A tale was about to commence. "Married a thirteen-year-old girl." I looked up.

"But this isn't about that," he said. "Anyhow, during lambing season, Preston hired Ray to feed. Roger and I were doing shifts: I had the days and *Rogelio* took nights."

Another livestock memoir; I sighed.

"Anyhow, I was checking the ewes in the pasture north of the house and Ray was feeding from that little bobsled I showed you: the one-horse job."

"About the size of a VW bug."

"Right. Well, Ray'd been out on an expedition the night before. After leaving Dad's Bar, they got his six-cylinder Olds Ninety-eight upside down in an irrigation ditch during a little snow flurry. Took most of the night to get it out."

"It's a lie!" I burst out. "A *six-cylinder* Olds Ninety-eight?"

"*Potentially* it was a V-eight, but at that point it was, practically speaking, a V-six, or maybe even a V-five. Your average Star Valley native is tough on machinery."

"First threats," I said, "then the ball-peen hammer, with new spark plugs as a last resort. So, had he been partaking of spiritous liquors? Ol' *Ramón*."

"Mmmmmm, not *Ramón*...he's Ray. These Star Valley guys don't like to be called by Mexican names, especially if they hire out as ranch hands. Good way to get your nuts kicked off."

I looked over my shoulder and hissed, "He's hiding behind that pine."

"Do you wanna jerk my cinch or hear the story?"

"Story. *Por favor.*"

"So Ray does everything (really fast.) He drinks a pot of coffee before he even gets his boots on and another with breakfast. And he eats so fast that it looks like somebody is vacuuming the food up—I don't think he chews. And when he goes to work it's like one of those old movies where it looks speeded up and jerky."

"So that's why he makes love to thirteen-year-olds?"

He ignored it. "So anyway, we're lambing and for April there's a lot of snow. Ray's feeding the ewes with the little bobsled, and he's whipping the horse up and making these wild strafing runs. You can see daylight under the runners. The horse is snorting and steaming, and Ray's face is red, like a balloon. And he's cussing a blue streak and flailing with the pitchfork, scattering a bale, maybe a bale and a half each time across the pasture. So the hay is spread pretty thin. The ewes aren't getting much to eat in any one place, so they're charging after the sled, trying to find a pile of hay bigger than a...a..."

"Hamster."

"No. A..."

"Dictionary."

"More than two or three damn bites! So anyhow Ray is flying low, and the hungry ewes are charging after him, and there's this other bunch of sheep in a pen by the shed..."

"What pen?"

"We stuck some steel fenceposts into the snow and ran sheep wire around, to hold the ewes we wanted to take into the shed. About ten or so. So Ray goes cussing and tearing between the shed and the pen, a hundred and fifty miles per hour, and almost runs into the shed, and reins the horse hard right, and the right front runner catches the sheep wire, and *bing!*"

"Bing?"

"The wire. The pen goes right along with the sled, and the posts pop out of the snow: *bing, bing, bing.*" He takes a deep breath. "And those poor ewes are bagged up like fish in a net. By the time he gets the horse stopped he's dragged 'em halfway across the pasture, and they're squalling and kicking their pointy feet out through the holes in the wire, hell on earth!"

I laugh. "Yeah?"

"So he looks at the sheep all tangled up. His mouth's so wide open he can't even cuss. I'm standing by the shed and I start to laugh. I can't stop. And he looks at me, and at the sheep, and back at me, and I see little Zippo-lighter sparks in his eyeballs, and then he grabs that pitchfork and chucks it like a...a..."

"Spear. Harpoon. Lightning bolt."

"Like a damn bolt of lightning. And it comes whooshing through the air right at my face and I can feel the cold breeze on my cheek and *SPANG!*"

"He kills you," I said.

"No, dammit. It sticks in the shed, right into the planks, and the handle is right next to my head, *k-doing, k-doing, k-doing,* just like a great big...tuning fork."

I nod, impressed.

"And Rays says, real slow: 'Laugh at me again, you're dead.' Like that."

Mitch's eyes are wide. "And it takes both me and Roger to pull the damn pitchfork out."

I wait a bit, to show my appreciation. But I'm still wondering about the bullet holes and the thirteen-year-old bride. "Sooo, did they have a Mormon wedding?"

"Mmmmmm. Rain quit. We'd better go out and herd sheep."

They were scattered in the bowls between the lip of the cirque basin and the camp, feeding contentedly. "Not much herding to do," Mitch said, taking out his pipe. "We'd better enjoy it while it lasts." He leaned back against a boulder.

I felt like exploring. I headed west and climbed into the huge bowl below the pass, over the piles and humps of loose rock. The more stable heaps of rock were capped by jungles of stunted fir and separated by scarce and verdant little pockets, with buttercups and spring beauties and nameless little purple devils starting up from the mud between the rocks.

Farther up, the north-facing slope was striped by slide paths and herringboned with dead fir trunks. The surviving firs were spiky with broken limbs, and their bark was peeled and scoured on the uphill side where they were ridden down each winter by the snow. These beat-up trees, I realized, lived more of their lives under snow than in the open air.

Above the trees, old avalanche tongues overlapped, like dinosaurs buried in the run-out. I sat on a big boulder around which the snow current split, thinking of how snow moves after reaching the ground: either a creep or an avalanche, slower than water or faster. There were veins of dust on the snow, and dead flies and leaves embedded.

Pikas buzzed over the hollow expanse, and a raven circled high under a cloud. Walking on hard snow in the center of the bowl, I found the corpse of a weasel in full winter white, curled on its side in a melted-out cup. Its fur was soaked and transparent, and the brown skin showed through. The quick black eye was sunken and shut. The elongated form of the skull showed through the wet fur, a searcher's head. It was killed, I thought, in an avalanche, buried by more, and harder, snow than it could dig out through.

Why live in such a place? The conifers grew in little huddled villages, and the snow flowed in great cold waves around them or over them, crushing and breaking, as random and predictable as war. It seemed like a place where live things would always suffer. Yet the trees lived because it was their nature, as much as it was the snow's to layer and fracture and fall. And the weasel's to run, with black sparks for eyes, and to seek. There was no logic in it, only rhythm.

A shadow enveloped the bowl and clouds deepened. I hiked down again through krummholz and mats of snow-pressed willows, just melted out. A few large spruces grew on the south-facing slope, but what I noticed was the ragged skyline, the raw scarp faces, cracked and jointed cliffs, great spills of frost-split stone, and debris heaped in sizes from bricks to pea gravel.

Everywhere I looked there was breakage. Exposed to the weather, the bedrock separated along its layers: thin layers formed plates and shingles, while thicker ones split into angular blocks, sharp on every edge. Broken pines lay strewn on the avalanche runouts, gray twigs tangled and moldered, and brown needles were matted and sodden underfoot. I walked through the wreckage, following the milky stream that appeared from under the snow. The water was turbulent, flowing over spalled rock, fractured wood, and cosmic trash. Jointed by rivulets, it braided and twined, and took on a faint roar.

I hiked out of the basin and down toward the joining of the trails. I didn't know what it was I'd missed the first time, but I felt it again —an absence, or a strange withholding. I looked around at the clouds, the cliffs, the rock, the stunted fir, the stream.

But there was no stream. That was it: I'd started down with the stream on my right. Leaving the basin, I'd turned right and then climbed, without ever crossing it. That contradicted the laws of the landscape, as I knew them. What I felt was the stream's disappearance.

I hiked back and found the stream above and followed it through the stunted, springy fir jungles. At the basin's lip it roared into a bowl floored with coarse rocks, then sank out of sight, gone into the dark, its green and liquid line broken off like the fir twigs under my feet.

August 1

We shared the light of one candle, set in a jar lid on the kitchen box. Waiting for the coffee I read more of Li Po:

> Journeying is hard.
> There are many turnings—
> Which am I to follow?...
> I will mount a long wind someday and break the heavy waves
> And set my cloudy sail straight and bridge the deep, deep sea.

I read it again, aloud. Mitch was listening. "That's good," he said. "Who?"

"Li Po. Wild old drunken Chinese sheepherder-saint. Here's another one:

> 'Addressed Humorously to Tu Fu
>
> 'Here! Is this you, on the top of Fan-ko Mountain,
> Wearing a huge hat in the noonday sun?
> How thin, how wretchedly thin you've grown!
> You must have been suffering from poetry again.'"

"Hah! Suffering is right. I'll stick to Joe Back." Mitch had adopted my packer's bible and was studying it. In my classics book, Tu Fu was next. "Certainly he is finest in the classical tradition," I read, "though foreign readers and the commoners of China have preferred Li Po, his close friend." I was prepared to hate Tu Fu. But my cup was empty and it was time to go.

The plan was to move the herd slowly around the head of Murphy Creek. The sheep would naturally go to the best forage, so we had two tasks. The first was to keep them moving slowly around the headwater slopes. The second was to keep small bands from straying over the top.

Morning light showed the bony contour of the place. West was a steep climb to a hanging valley, backed by the spine of the Salt River Range, impassable except on foot. South was a complex set of curves where the creek began in small, snowy basins that gave into steep gullies. Due south, a divide ridge was sparsely furnished with limber pine and fire. On the other side was Cedar Creek. If the sheep went down there, we'd have a hard time getting them back.

Mitch rode the red gelding back to the pass to hunt strays. Feeling both foreign and common, I clambered over the rocks and down steep dirt, herding as the day warmed.

The sheep moved slowly, nibbling and calling. I led Pronto, the young mare, and she jerked at the reins to gather clumps of grass. I could hear the wet crunch of it between her teeth. The colt played among the sheep, then charged Pookie. The dog dropped her tail and ran to me, and I laughed as the colt whirled away.

I liked it here. I felt free. And I felt a kind of peace, but when I looked hard at the place, I wondered why: there was no permanence, nothing static. In the steepest country, things move fast. Streams have the power of their high angle, and every loose slope speaks of movement. The peaks and ridges crest like slow waves. Limber pines come flexing and spiraling up from cracks in limestone, to cast cones and die and fall, to be caught in the gray torrent of scree, lost in the gravitational rain of all things.

I dozed off with Pookie at my side. From above, sitting on a cloud, the herd must have looked like a white amoeba, extending pseudopods between outcrops and pines. Loose herding—the idea of it—was to let wooly pseudopods extend and circulate without allowing them to break off and squirm away. When an amoeba grows too large, it yearns to divide, to become two, four, eight, or ten. And constantly, small bands of sheep struck out, each with its stubborn matriarch.

A fly bit me and I woke up. I stood up. The sheep had scattered all over the place. I spent a hot and itchy hour finding surly ewes and rogue lambs, dogging them out of the fir jungles and chasing them toward the main bunch. Naturally, it occurred to me that I was harassing the poor, stupid animals because they wanted precisely what I did: to distance themselves from that critical mass of idiocy, the herd. But so what?

Mitch said I would learn to like sheep, but I hadn't. I hoped to discover at least a tolerant interest in them, but my hopes were confounded by the sheep themselves. They had a pissy, bad-cheese stink that clung to leaves and soaked into the soil. Their swarming numbers, the multiplicity of dumb looks, and the swath of broken stems and harrowed earth they left behind all aroused not simply dislike but a hot and active loathing. Sometimes the ewes would set their back feet and piss great yellow gouts, looking back, eyes witless and jaws quivering as they bawled sheepish curses. I had to restrain myself from picking up rocks and taking aim at their wobbly heads, as I longed for a machine gun.

Mitch said it wasn't their fault: they were bred to be stupid, wooly, and fat. The fact that generations of men had carefully debased generations of sheep to their present loathsomeness aroused in me, if anything, only a deeper loathing. And anyhow, who loves the whole of creation? A fool with a sandwich. Junkies, after a fix. Lobotomized nuns. So I hated sheep. It was okay.

The process of herding, quoth Mitch, required skill and patience, which I lacked. I tried to make up for it with verbal mayhem, wild downhill slides and uphill scrambles, and a wealth of extravagant gesture. But my bravura technique would excite the dogs to the point that they would chase strays away from the herd rather than back to it. Then my curses on the sheep were interspersed with death threats hurled at the dogs, who seemed to relish the barbarism and disorder. Yipping like coyotes, they acted proportionally worse.

I wasn't a good herder and would never be one. I simply hated sheep too much.

But I liked the swearing. My father had a gorgeous fluency when a tire sank in the mud or a horse stepped on the toe of his boot. I thought of it as a rich folk tradition, one to be cultivated. But if you spend hours yelling at sheep you become rather hoarse. Thus I found that Spanish, rolling off the lips and tongue, was better for cursing sheep than English. So I called them *borregas*—woolies—and also *putas, moscas, cresas, cabroncitos,* and *chingaderos*, none of which mattered in the least: animals care only about your tone of voice. Pookie, for example, would waltz up, tail a-flag, at being called a brainless, stinking, hairy sack of porcupine guts, as long as it was sweetly spoken. To dogs, and also *borregas, cabroncitos,* and *moscas*, Form equals Content.

With these weighty issues in mind, I bedded the sheep. (So as not to inflame the suspicions of the nonherding audience, I hasten to say *bedded* means that I stopped plaguing them until they dozed off.) Then I whispered a few parting threats and rode back to cook.

In the midst of my culinary operations, Mitch returned. "Beautiful morning. No strays," he said. The beans boiled merrily on the stove, still hard as stream pebbles. He tested them. "High altitude," he said. "Low boiling point." I'd been wondering why they wouldn't cook.

"We'll eat the beans tomorrow," he said. "Let me show you how to make tortillas."

There were two classes: flour and corn. Flour tortillas were quicker, so we'd start with the corn. Since the Mormon-owned market didn't stock *masa*, the ground hominy that went into real corn tortillas, we would use Christian Maid Bright Yellow Corn-meal, the best the Prestons could offer. It was somewhat coarse, so we would boil it to render it pliable. So said Mitch.

"Mush! I can do that," I replied. I set a pot of water next to the stovepipe. "Now," said Mitch, "we're gonna make beautiful flour tortillas." He took a bowl and mixed flour, water, salt, and a glop of lard. "Knead it like bread, but not as long." He pinched off a walnut-sized lump of dough, and sprinkled flour on the little kitchen-box counter. "Observe."

He groped in the box until he found a seven-inch piece of broomstick, glossy with frequent use. "The magic tortilla wand." He squashed the dough, dropped it into the flour, flipped it, sprinkled more flour on the top, and then began to roll it out. He worked on the dough like a painter on canvas, with pursed lips and intent gaze, as it rounded and thinned and assumed tortillahood. I was impressed.

"That's how Pancho says you pick a wife: wide hips and thin tortillas. Last year, he never let up until my tortillas were thin." He folded it deftly, lifted it, and then opened it onto the top of the stove. "No frying pan to wash."

"Right on the stove. Brilliant."

"Hah! You should see the Campos sisters make tortillas. They pat the dough out between their tender hands." He took a lump of dough and demonstrated, patting and flipping, but the tortilla fell apart. "That Aurelia Campos...prettiest girl I ever saw. She makes tortillas you could read the Bible through. And her mama watches her like a hawk."

On the stovetop, the first one steamed and bubbled and began to look like a real tortilla. He flipped it with fingertips, and it repeated the marvelous process.

"*Numero uno.*" He tore it in half and we shared it. It was a wonder of opposites: soft and crisp, thin and substantial, delicate and tough.

"Amazing," I said. It was something Li Po would have enjoyed.

"Now you try it." After a couple false starts, it worked. Then the cornmeal was ready, so he showed me how to mix a little flour into it and then roll it out. I elbowed him away from the dough in my rush to create. He decided to take a nap in the shade, under a big limber pine poised over the stunning drop to the creek. Another small magic in hand, I made tortillas, joyfully alternating corn and flour, until I had a stack of each.

Time for a ramble. I stoked the stove and damped it down, for the beans. Then I dug out my clandestine bag of ganja—two tablespoons to last the season—and twisted a smoke, which I intended to appreciate along with the verses of Tu Fu, naked and dead center in the most perfect of all possible flowery bowls.

I scrambled up a rockstrewn gully into the hanging valley, and threaded broken blocks and fir jungles to reach the border of remnant snow. The valley was a sink, and the melt percolated out of sight, emerging in the little stream where we got water for the camp. Patches of the snow were red with algae. Mitch had told me it was poisonous, which I doubted: he had a way of testing me with fibs. So I ate a small handful and it had no flavor, apart from ice and dust.

There wasn't much reason for any living thing to be here, other than the opening in space. But it wasn't an easy opening, or a secure one. There's something depressing about shattered limestone, a kind of despair in its naked, unstable, razor-edged disarray. The only law here was gravity: rocks fell until they stopped, usually on a gray stack of rocks that had fallen just before. When a pile grew too high, it collapsed. Eventually the shards would be soil, but that would take huge gulps of time. But it was good to be on ground the sheep would never cross: too hard and worthless, and in August, still partly under snow.

A strange little fugue played in my head: *Jesus wants me for a sunbeam, to shine for him each day*. I couldn't get rid of it, and I could hear, one by one, squeaky voices adding themselves, as the kids in my Sunday school class found their places in the songbook, or were nudged by their teachers. The image I had was of buttery sunbeams squishing down onto tidy flowerbeds and row crops, and over the shingled roofs of identical candy houses. In perfectly square pastures grazed herds of cartoon sheep, pink bows around their necks. *Ugh*.

There were definitely plenty of sunbeams up here, where nothing could graze except imagination. I didn't know if Jesus owned them, and I didn't care. But if I had to be one, I thought, I'd rather light up this rich and meaningless disorder.

Broken limestone, or dolomite—I didn't know how to tell them apart— clinked and grated under my feet as I hiked south under a cracked wall, through a confusion of sinks and moraines, and into jungles of stunted fir. I saw a faint trail and followed it, quickly realizing that it was made by feet much smaller and sharper than my own. My foot slipped and I went to all fours, but it wasn't solid enough to crawl. My boot soles, white crepe rubber, were too soft to edge, and if I fell it would mean an ugly slide that wouldn't kill me but would remove most of my skin, embarrassing as injuries go.

There's not really a word for how I got across. Above, the slope eased and I breathed more easily climbing to the dip in the ridge, and the canyon's south divide. The ridge was chalky, softer than the gray stuff of which the peaks were made, and Cedar Creek was a fanged hole with no descending trail. In my little daypack, the classics poked at my spine and ribs. I sat in the breeze and read a poem by Tu Fu, written to his friend Li Po:

> …You sing wild songs,
> Your days pass in emptiness.
> Your nature is a spreading fire,
> It is swift and strenuous.
> But what does all this bravery amount to?

I delivered a gentle shrug toward the east and traded the classics for my book of flowers: here liveth paintbrush, arnica, lousewort, gooseberry currant, buttercup, bearberry, and mats of wind-flattened juniper. Then I got stuck—short-style bluebells or alpine forget-me-nots? I stared at the drawings and couldn't decide. *Your days pass in emptiness.*

Why not? There was a tiny yellow flower that might have been lomatium and a small white anemone-type blossom with a yellow-green center and a delicate, hairy stem: *Pubescence*, the book said, enough to distract me into longing, for the warm slip of belly skin and the curly shock of unseen fur and the soft clutch centered on heat, and then the moist bloom. Cassandra.

Life is a spreading fire. What does it amount to, the body's loneliness? Flowers amount to seed, and black winter sleep, and then the damp seeds spring up and amount to flowers, and the sum is nothing. Days pass in flowers.

I stowed the book and looked around. To my right, at the center of the dip in the ridge, was a giant limber pine, a tree that flowed, rough and brown, like a river into the sky. The trunk had a heavy grace, like the forearms of working men. Opening my arms—just over six feet from fingertip to tip—I measured the ancient body of the pine, the bark scratching at my cheek, four times, and stopped with my left elbow touching the knot that was my starting point: twenty-one feet. *Endure*, it said.

Far below, I saw light flaring on the tails of the horses as they grazed. I could see Mitchell stretched out under a pine, hat over his face. The camp was clean, tortillas cool and wrapped.

Run, said the pine. So I flew across the slope, reckless in my bliss, and leapt narrow snow gullies to land running in the mud.

I came to a sloping meadow, centered on a huge gray block upon which a lordly marmot sunned. The marmot reared, examined me —*a foreigner, and a commoner*—and relaxed into a noble slouch. The meadow was a vale of impossible greens starred with pink, yellow, purple, white, and heartbreak blue.

Above, I saw a cow elk, sleek and gorgeous. She looked back at me. Her coat gleamed as she dashed away, and I could feel a stirring in my blood. Tracking her, I traversed, up, down, over, and through the arteries of snowmelt, across the swoops of drainage east to the snow. I clambered up onto the melting surface, kicking and gliding, punching white holes in the dusty mantle, swift and strenuous, my boots soaked through.

The elk was gone. I came on a rounded puzzle-mound of mud,

like a giant mallow chocolate, cracked at the top. I scratched its flank and found ice beneath. The world was inside out. I heard falling water on the breeze. A waterfall threaded over the rimrock and came down a steeply tilted trough of polished stone. Drunk with movement I scrambled and splashed up, and climbed the wall by the tiny falls, topping out, coming into another meadow, crowned with snow.

Go, it said. So I climbed the cornice, kicking steps, slicing my hands in for holds, up and up and over the melting lip. The snow leveled on the absolute top, and I stepped onto rocky soil, banding a line of krummholz fir. I burst through it and stopped. At my feet was a wild drop, cliff band to talus to meadow to forest around a tiny lake, and far, far down the long dark ridges was a river, Greys River, like a silver sword, sharp in its rocky cleft.

August 2

"Light the damn stove," Mitch said.

"Do nothing," I replied, "and all things will be done."

"Bullcrap. Says who?"

"Says Lao-Tzu."

"Son-of-a-bitch never herded sheep." He laughed.

I thought about that. "Maybe he just herded 'em really loose," I said.

But I lit the stove, started coffee, and set the beans near the pipe. Then I stepped out and stood until I heard a horse bell, not far off. Then Mitch told me that with the benefit of my ancient wisdom he could probably herd alone.

I was sated with exploration, so I cut up meat and started a cauldron of chili, red as a satyr's heart. And my cook's progress reached a milestone: a deep-dish pumpkin pie, baked in the Dutch oven. The pumpkin was canned, but I made the crust from scratch.

I could smell perfection. And when the lid came off, it was perfect. I sat and looked at the buckskin-colored crust, the glazed moon of pumpkin, the entire, steaming wonder of it. Mitch came back early and was properly awestruck. Then we ate hugely, gluttonously, sinfully, and absolved one another with groans.

Mitch took a canvas pack cover and a lash rope, and showed me how to make a boondocks hammock. "Cowboy heaven," he said. "There it is." We stretched it between big firs in the breeze and then contended savagely for it.

"It was my idea," he snapped.

True. He'd shown me how to pouch the canvas over a pebble and loop it with rope. "I did most of the work," I said, "and I'm heavier —test flight."

"You might rip it," he said, and straddled the canvas, daring me to throw him out. "Tie up another one." We had plenty of canvas and plenty of rope, but it wouldn't be the same. So I stomped off and sat in the dirt and let my book fall open to the *Analects* of Confucius, hoping for moral armament, which I found: "The inferior man loves only his property."

I considered yelling that, but Mitch was already asleep, hat over his eyes: he loved his naps. Feeling lonesome, I wandered down to the horses. Red came and nuzzled me as I scratched his withers, and sniffed me, as I sniffed him. I had the stronger smell. The flies that accompanied him showed a sudden interest in me. My jeans were caked with flour, the thighs dark with spills and soot. My T-shirt felt sticky.

Digging through my duffle, I couldn't find anything clean except a wool shirt, which it was too hot to wear, and a pair of poplin slacks, which I hated. So I filled the dishpan with water and set it on to heat. That wiped out the water supply. I caught Red, and got a pad and packsaddle, and draped two panniers to hold the canvas water bags.

It was an itchy trip. The sheep had crossed the creek, and there were pellets of dung floating in the pools, so I climbed to where the water rose from the slope and found that it didn't rise far enough. I had to dip it, a cup at a time. There wasn't a tree or even a bush to tie Red, and he kept dragging his lead rope. So I tied it around my ankle. He tugged, and I quickly reconsidered. I untied the loop in what I hoped was a soothing manner while he sniffed the part in my hair, and tethered him to the full water bag, which would at least slow him down.

When I got back Mitch was swaying and singing a minor-key hymn:

> All day over the prairies I ride,
> Not even a dog to run by my side,
> My fire I kindle from chips gathered 'round,
> And boil my coffee without being ground.
>
> My ceiling the sky, my carpet the grass,
> My music the lowing of herds as they pass.
> My books are the brooks, my sermons the stones,
> And my parson's a wolf on a pulpit of bones.
>
> My books teach me constancy ever to prize,
> My sermons that small things I must not despise,
> And my parson remarks from his pulpit of bone
> That the Lord favors them who look out for their own.

The tune was elusive, and then unforgettable. I let the song end before I led the horse into camp. He looked aslant as I unloaded the water, then covered his eyes again. The water on the stove was hot. We didn't have laundry soap, but dish detergent would do. Should I wash myself before the clothes? Or wash clothes and bathe while they dried? The latter. Humming the tune I'd heard, I poured half of the water into a cooking pot and heaped my dirty clothes into the dishpan.

"Goddammit! You better boil that when you get done!" Mitch glared from the hammock.

"Boil yourself, grandma."

"Hah! Maybe you could wash up a few things for me." He laughed and settled back.

"Dream on. I wouldn't touch your socks with a welding torch."

I hung my wet clothes on the tent ropes and branches. As I started to bathe, Mitch objected again: "You can't use the dishpan for that."

"What? Wait until I get back to the ranch?"

"Go down to the creek and jump in. That's what I do."

"Right in our drinking water."

"My germs are all the way to the Snake River by now."

"Too cold. Can't get clean."

"As long as the horses don't stampede when you lift your arms, it'll do."

He told me about Pancho's morning ritual, which was darkly medieval. Pancho had only a few pairs of socks and didn't trouble laundering them. "He'd wake up and pull them out of his boots and then break them."

"*Break?*"

"Roll them around between his hands, to soften them up," he said. I shuddered. "How did you stand the guy?"

"Got used to it. Horses don't smell good at first, or sheep."

"Sheep never do."

He shrugged and went back to his nap as I dried in the sun.

While my clean socks flittered in the breeze, I tried walking barefoot. I had the idea that toughening my feet was good practice, but up here the bedrock was cracked into shapes that were dangerous to bare feet: cubes, pyramids, and polygons. Besides, there were rock prongs sticking through the thin layer of soil. That I needed my boots to get around this place made me feel claustrophobic, but it was obvious I did.

Each place had its own laws. These mountains had hard layers and soft ones. Where it was hard, it was jagged, but there were handholds and footholds. Where it was soft, everything slid. Your boots shoved the slope downhill as you tried to go up. When you came down, the earth accompanied you.

That night, I heard coyotes. One howled, a questioning note. Another answered. Then another joined in and formed a wavering chord. As more coyotes sang, the night resounded as if darkness itself had found a voice. Mitch woke. "Damn critters," he said. The howls rose in crescendo and then fell into barks and yips. "Trouble," he said. "Bet they're in the herd."

He fumbled his way to the flaps. I heard a click and then the roar of a shot, stunning inside the tent. "Damn. *Sorry*," he said, and stepped outside, jacking another shell into the chamber. "But maybe I can scare 'em off."

He fired two quick shots, the flashes inking his outline. The howls diminished. After the fourth shot, the coyotes stopped.

August 3

The shots repeated themselves in my dreams, and I saw the bear, dead and flayed. I woke up and lay with open eyes until it was time to start the stove. We did our tasks and didn't say much, but the silence grew easier. The sheep were near camp, and we split up and walked around them as it grew light.

Back at camp, Mitch sat on a rock and charmed the sun up with his lonesome harmonica. I caught the horses and brushed each in turn, with crazy momentum, until they shone. When I turned them loose they bucked and stampeded, glowing like jewels against the green, sunlit slope.

That afternoon the sky was a drum that played itself. Thunder boomed peak-to-peak, and the canyons opened under the sound, hollow and hard. Blue softness filtered over the ridge, and a rainstorm broke, chill and silver, a pelting beauty that sent the horses snorting and ducking under pines, as leaves dipped and turned under the sky's weight, and made the tent belly and stream at the eave, the canvas soaked through in spots, passing circles and streaks of light.

I started a fire in the stove. Mitch came in, hefted his saddle into the tent, and tipped it up to dry. I draped a canvas over a low limb and edged it with rocks, a makeshift tent for the wet dogs, and shooed them under it. But Tikki-Lo snuck into the tent behind the stove, and shook. A dog-scented steam rose.

"Git outa here, you varmint!" Mitch sprawled on his bedroll, settling into the smell of the wet wool and pine smoke. The coffeepot ticked as the storm wall passed over, leaving everything soft, quiet, porcelain-clean. *Your days pass in emptiness.* Or in flowers. Cassandra.

"What?" Mitch asked. I'd spoken her name aloud.

"Nothing," I said. Around us, the forest paused between breaths.

In his saddlebag, Mitch had a roll of tortillas and a can filled with beans, closed with foil and a string. His steel canteen cup held a little bag of coffee and two sourdough biscuits, for breakfast. Rolled on the back of his saddle, his bedroll made a big hump, and I had his shelter half rolled over mine. Because the east ridge had good forage, he wanted to take the herd up to the rim where I'd gazed off. But it took long enough to get there from camp, and was risky enough in the dark, that he wanted to tepee out: his phrase. He'd camp on the ridge. If the herd strayed back toward the main camp, Pookie and I would catch them. If they tried to go east into the Greys River Canyon, he'd be there with a horse and two dogs.

He picked a spot in the lee of old pines, overlooking miles of air. He unrolled the shelter half, army surplus—two of them snap together to make an A-frame tent—as I sharpened deadfall sticks with my knife. Then we staked it out. He'd sewn a strip of light canvas along the ridge to shelter the open side, and he stretched it with parachute cord.

He poured out some grain on a flat rock for Tony. "He'll probably raise hell all night, but I won't get much sleep—have to night-herd. Come up early and spell me off." I envied his bivouac on top of the world: it had a lonesome nobility.

In camp I luxuriated, in sole possession of a tent that seemed suddenly huge. I built a roaring fire in the stove for heat and tied the flaps back for the view. A few tiny drops hung from the firs as the last light washed from the air. Pookie whined outside, so I called her into the tent. She nudged me with her head before lying down at the back of the stove and licking her paws.

"Don't tell," I said.

August 4

A bolt of lightning tore the lid off the dark. I could see maps in my eyelids. I looked out. A gust slapped the tent and the tops of pines boiled, but there were only a few spatters of rain as the storm moved across. Watching bolts hit the Star Peaks, I thought about Mitch up there. I didn't envy him. The sheep would be on the move all night, trying to dash over the top and shelter on the lee side in the thick timber, exactly where we didn't want them to go. He'd be up, I knew, and trying to hold them.

I should help, I thought, but crossing the head of the canyon was dangerous even by day. I couldn't make it at night on a lightning-spooked horse, and I was too exhausted to go on foot.

But I couldn't sleep. I imagined a white bolt groping down to finger the stovepipe, which would go incandescent as the tent erupted in flames. I tried counting sheep, but instead of leaping one by one, they thronged over the ridge and into impassable wooded breaks. Bursts of lightning woke me, and between them I fell into torpor, finally dragging out of my bag at 4:45. Mitch had left his little clock: the sheep will wake me up, he'd said.

I moved in a daze, head buzzing with contingencies. If Mitch got struck by lightning, then I'd ride out for help. How? Over Prater Pass? No. Load him on a horse and lead it down to the guard cabin at Deer Creek. How did a person struck by lightning look? What if the horse got struck? What if the dogs were eating the dead horse? My head spun with terrible sights.

I lurched out to pee and tripped over my bootlaces. I wanted to perform a courageous act, to equal Mitch's night out on the ridge, and in my disconnected state, I decided to ride Elhon. He'd been talking about making an honest horse of her. We'd saddled her a few times without too much trouble, and he'd circled her around a meadow. She was only a horse.

By first light, I got the saddle on. The trails were slick, and the big horse almost fell, so I got off and led her across the stream gully before I mounted again. The trail was barely visible in the rain-darkened soil. Ahead, it dipped under a brushy peninsula from which an old pine thrust roots into the air. The stream fell away faster than the trail climbed, and the next safe ground lay above a long drop. Elhon was reluctant, and I urged her gently, scared of her as much as the slope. Go, girl. Almost there. Then, from the forest edge, a weasel flicked out, quick as a lizard toward the stream.

I could feel her muscles bunch, and I grabbed for the horn as the weasel doubled and came back up the bank, right under her feet. She made two big jumps, straight back, and we landed on the narrow trail, but then she twisted and bucked out into space. The first buck took us twenty feet downslope. My feet popped out of the stirrups as I felt the dirt break loose under her hind feet. She bucked again. Thirty feet. Her front legs collapsed as her hindquarters whipped down the slope. I went flat out on her back, hands on the horn and boots in the air, as we surfed another thirty feet in a clatter of loose rock before coming to rest.

"*W-whoa*," I said.

I had the horn with both hands, and one rein. The cantle poked into my gut. My left boot touched the slope, and my right leg was stretched above the horse's tail. Her back feet were dug out of sight in a heap of debris. I could feel her shiver, so I cooed and quickly ran out of breath.

I rolled my weight up onto my left foot, careful not to push against the horse. She shivered again. If she lunged, I'd go under her hooves. I stroked her neck at the edge of the blanket. "Easy. Easy. Whoooooo." I managed a step up, keeping the rein lightly in my palm. Another step. Another. She heaved up and straightened her legs, and the slope shifted and gravel clattered into the creek, so I dropped the rein and clambered on all fours up to the first tree I could grab, showering her with dirt.

"Sorry, Elhon," I whispered. "C'mon. Up." The big horse stayed where she was, breathing hard, immobilized. I looked at the situation. Her two leaps had angled us away from the worst drop, to a set of ragged pinnacles where the creek plunged almost straight down. When her feet slipped, she'd swapped ends and was faced back the way we'd come, toward safety. That, at least, was good. She might slide or tip off the slope, but she'd roll into the stream just before it plummeted. If she didn't break a leg, I could lead her up the streambed to the trail crossing.

Pookie scrambled down and almost knocked me loose from my tree. I launched a slap and she cringed, anticipating the blow, but I stopped just short of her head. Then I stroked her. "Shhhhh. Good dog. Stay." I crept up into the brush, about where the weasel had emerged, and traversed the mats of juniper until I could step onto the trail.

"Elhon," I whispered. "C'mon. You can make it." She looked at me but wouldn't move. "Come on, big honey. Holy Christ. Please."

How could I lead her up? The reins were draped under her front quarters. I'd have to be almost on top of her to reach them. If she lunged, I'd go right underneath. But I couldn't leave her there. I took a tentative step, and Pookie shoved between my feet. "Damn dog. Get away. No stay. Sit. Stay." She retreated, whimpering. "Dogs. Horses. *Shit*."

There was a flurry behind me. The gold horse tensed, lunged, slid back, and then dug in, gaining her balance as dirt and rock rained into the creek. She got her front hooves on the trail and then her hind ones and then she ran blind, right for me. I scrambled straight up and grabbed a hank of stems as she thundered beneath. Then she stopped abruptly, and swung her head, disoriented. My hand stung. Shit! I'd grabbed a wild raspberry bush.

Pookie was fleeing toward camp. Elhon stood wild-eyed but on solid ground. I inched toward her, soothing her with my voice, and caught one rein, then the other. I stepped closer and rubbed her withers until the shaking stopped. "Poor baby girl. Okay."

I decided she wouldn't let me on her back, as if I wanted a second chance. So I led her back to camp, stripped my saddle, and turned her loose. I thought she'd tear off, but she stood stiff-legged, watching every move I made. I took the food sack and canteen out of my saddlebags and put them into my daypack. "Screw this rodeo crap," I told Pook. "I'll walk, and live."

As I left the camp, the big horse followed me. I tried to shoo her away, but she thought I'd saved her life, or something like that, and she wasn't about to let me leave. I had to lead her all the way back to the other horses before she'd let me go. By then, the sun was over the ridge. I felt half dead, and I still had to relieve Mitch.

"Pretty damn slow," he snapped. He had the shelter half rolled and his bedroll ready to go. "How come you didn't ride up?"

I lied. "The storm had 'em all riled up."

"I sure didn't sleep a wink. The lightning was close. I felt a couple jolts through the ground, so each time it started, I got in my bedroll for insulation. When it quit, I'd run out and chase the sheep off the ridge. The meadow's a damn mess." I looked at what had been a field of sunflowers and bluebells: brown muck. Not a plant was standing.

"Well, at least you got here. Walk this ridge with the dogs. The *borregas* are hungry after running all night. Should be a piece of cake." He tied the bedroll behind the cantle, and rolled the tent up tight and lashed it in front of the horn. "Guess that'll ride okay. I'll be back after I get some sleep." He swung his boot high to clear the bedroll, settled himself, and rode off.

I was barely able to stay on my feet, but the sheep fed calmly below and then bedded down. I dozed, my back against a rock with my coat folded for a pad as the sheepdogs flopped on their backs in the sun. Pookie was the only mobile soul among us, and the pikas— little rabbity things—had a fine time teasing her. Ma Pika would pop up with a *tzcherrrrrrrk*: half buzz, half squeak. Pook would pick her way over the boulders to chomp off her cute little round-eared head, and—*gone!* Then Sis would rear up 100 feet away and *tzcher-rrrrrk*. And the game would play out again: the dog laboring over the rocks, jaws agape, the pika diving, and then—*tzcherrrrrrrk*. Damnfool's tag with a permanent canine It.

At some point Mitch returned and told me he'd herd until sundown. I walked back to camp. I'd strained some muscles, unnoticed in the frenzy, but now I had to make an effort to keep my feet under me: to walk I had to stop thinking and to think I had to stop walking. I stopped at the spot where Elhon had almost killed us both. There were horse tracks and scuffed places, but you wouldn't notice unless they were pointed out. I climbed the loose slope back to camp and stood facing the tent, trying to summon the energy to get something to eat.

While I stood, a huge, brilliant cloud lifted from the rocky horizon until the sun was centered behind it, materializing soft and immense up toward the zenith, all glowing circulation, like a stirred bowl of pearls. It filled the sky with a tremendous presence, like God in a painting, but undeniably real.

Maybe it *was* God. I was too tired to judge, but I kept still under its gaze. At sunrise, the tall gold horse had almost killed us both. But I was alive to see this. It was beautiful. Sunlight through a cloud. Maybe that was enough. Maybe that was all. I looked up, hat in hand, my arms heavy, until it passed into the east and left the sky empty again.

April N. Rieveschl

Spirals

First publication

We were all waiting. I knew the routine. I had been dodging storms since I was a child. I could still remember the crabs and eels at my ankles, as the tide took to the streets, surging in great waves over the seawall. Waveland, Mississippi—it seemed a fitting name. There were many more: Carla, Betsy, Camille. I recalled them like distant relatives, all too familiar, and yet forgotten.

A restless wind blew, fluid and full of salt. The sea was airborne. Clouds rushed by like menhaden, on the run. I knew what it was doing out there, drawing energy from the warm waters off the Yucatan, swirling like a Mayan *bailarina*. "It" had become a "she," big enough to be named, big enough to have a mind of her own.

She stretched hundreds of miles from her center, the classic spiral, pulling the clouds to her. She was the shape of the galaxy, expanding. "Category 4," "a well-defined eye," "feeder bands," "reconnaissance aircraft"—words to convey control in the face of such evolving wildness. She was red on the radar, like a fire opal, mined from deep within the Mexican earth. Hurricane Opal's course could be followed but not predicted. She would defy the authorities and keep the residents of five states watching her every move.

When it was over, the papers described the scene as "catastrophic," "wide-scale devastation," and "destruction"; and so it was to many people who lost their homes. Whole houses had floated off their foundations, drifting into yards and colliding with other houses. Something immense had been here. I wondered what she had looked like—up close—wailing and howling in the darkness. Hurricanes, like dreams, seem to make landfall more often at night, that time when we encounter what we most fear—our own creative energy.

It was daylight now, but the water was dark and unfriendly; the energy was still in it, dissipating slowly. The beach was a mess of litter, rotting vegetation, and uprooted parchment tubeworms, a long whitish creature looking more like plant than animal. The birds—gulls, sandpipers, and pelicans—seemed not to notice. Maybe it was because they were of it, not separate. I, on the other hand, stood apart, on the periphery, trying to remember where I fit in. On approaching the water's edge, I then encountered an amazing sight. There were homes here too, shell homes scattered everywhere, hundreds of them, beautifully intact and mostly inhabited. This was a beach not known for its shells. A Scotch bonnet or shark's eye would be a rare prize. But now the sea wrack was a nest of twisted grasses and reeds hatching an array of shells: scores of bivalves—cockles, pen shells, angel wings, calico clams, and sunray Venus. Spider crabs with long hairy legs were caught hopelessly in seaweed nets. Another crab, this one the fiery carapace of a flame-streaked box crab, lay conspicuous among its shell prey. Armless now, it was no less a work of art.

It was the univalves, though, with their intricate designs that captured my heart—whelks, banded tulips, Florida horse conchs, queen's helmets, and more. Many were evacuated, others harbored dying gastropods and stunned hermit crabs, thrust out of their conventional reality. Tiny barnacles, chitons, and oysters that had set up house on the backs of these larger creatures found themselves trapped and destitute as well. I thought of the old myth of the Earth as a giant turtle. Maybe we too were building our homes on the back of another, unaware.

We saved many animals, returning them to the sea, red tongues hanging from their open valves, thirsty for water. The tide was low, for the moon had been full, and more shells dotted the sandbars, blending in with the lingering debris of boards, plants, and personal belongings; a large cockleshell, the halves so delicately connected, lay open, its gaping mouth a frozen scream, muffled beneath a sodden needlepoint pillow that had become lodged there. Farther down the beach, another pillow, its matching counterpart, drifted aimlessly. Whose hands had so lovingly crafted these? Were they of the same mind as those that shaped the cockle?

It was the shells that were the legacy of Opal. Their spiraled interiors seemed to mimic the structure of the storm, especially the lightning whelk, a lefty, its spiral rotating counterclockwise. Frank Lloyd Wright called shells "inspired form" and yet these shells had no signature, no authorship, no one needing recognition. To inspire means to animate with spirit. In the spires of the murex and the steeples of the conch flowed lines of a sacred space, calcified. Form followed function. I peeked inside, and the angel wings snapped shut, praying like hands, to be spared. The Mayans used shells as religious symbols. They too must have sensed the spiritual power of the shell. I picked up a conch and studied the orange and pink folds of shell, birthplace of Quetzalcoatl, "Lord of Life."

Gathering the empty containers, I felt a crazed delight, for such beauty could not be free for the taking. "Born to Shop"—Not. I was born to love shells. Others felt called too. By the third day, only Scotch bonnets and clams were left, cheap wampum, too common to deem valuable in this new economy.

I hoped that the ones we had returned to the sea had made it. There was one, in particular, that I prayed for—a grand queen's helmet, bigger than my head, that rested, half buried, atop a sandbar. We lifted her out, her rounded mass heavy like a bowling ball, and held her like a baby, her stomach—foot curling inward and full of life. I remembered the time when, cradled in my son's hands, a three-footed box turtle, all too familiar with adversity, responded to my soothing touch and voice, and emerged forthwith from her shell home, head and feet reaching out in a surprising show of trust. We had saved her life that day, as we now would her shell sister. She had to be old. I could imagine wearing this shell, helmetlike on my head, looking like some strange sentry, the sound of the surf piped to my ears—the original Walkman, but this one tuned you in, not out. And what was it I was tuning into? It was the season of storms. I recalled the words of Thomas Berry: "If you can't hear the voice of the wind, you better learn."

The shells were the wind chimes, the Tritons' trumpet, the song of the sea, the surf. As female symbols, they gave the wind a female voice. She had called the dunes back to her, indiscriminate—sea oats, asters, blazing stars, beach pea, pennyroyal, nettle, and Gulf Coast lupin. October was the month of yellow, the color of maize, the time we drank the goldenrod. The dunes in autumn rivaled the red maples of the Northeast. Gone. The tidal surge had consumed it all. A half mile inland, I found a seahorse, good luck, they say. This loss would be hard. Our secret swimming hole was out there, at sea...and what about the three-footed turtle? I looked up at the sky, something familiar. An old friend, the osprey, was back. He circled, in an ascending spiral. Animals and people do still talk to one another, I thought.

I was not prepared for this much change. We walked in silence, in a strange new land, a place that we had once known intimately, we knew not at all. As I worried for the loggerhead who would have no dunes to guide her selection of a next site, I spied a single monarch, "King Billy," his milkweed kingdom in disarray. The monarchs come every year, on their way to and from Mexico. The web of life was finely woven. It has been said that the fabric of interconnection is so complex that the flutter of a butterfly's wing could, by setting off a series of events, precipitate a hurricane. It flitted past. "Was it you?" I wondered.

About a third of a mile from the beach, the dunes become a woods of slash pines and scrub oaks. There was no clear line now. The trees, drenched in sand, had merged into dune, and dune into tree. White sand drifts were piled three to four feet high; branches protruded, heavy with white powder. For a moment, I was in Vermont in winter, barefoot. Dunes are moving, always, and in that one night, they had traveled years. Beyond that front line of buried forest, the trees could not hide their brown burns, nor the grasses and wildflowers, scorched as though by a summer drought, but more so, shocked by the winds of change.

This fragment of wild coast may not so readily recover. They are building bulwarks, bulldozing, fortifying—to protect the land from the next storm. Nearby, the homes, condos, and hotels are being rebuilt and repaired. I am not so afraid of the storms as of the walls we build. "Speak to the Earth and it shall teach thee" (Job 12:8). Listen to the shells and they shall sing.

The Mayans listened to the stars, and from them they learned to read the sky and measure Time. Elaborate calendars depicted cycles of Time, the "baktun," eras of creation and destruction, a continual cycle of repeating change. Time, curving around and moving forward, a spiral, nature's preeminent form, her logo, preserved in the petroglyphs of the American Southwest, remnants of visions of an ancient people long since vanished. The spiral speaks the wisdom of change, eternity, beginnings-and-endings.

There is another one out there, a spiral spawned in the opalescent waters off the Yucatan, its winds drawn from the Mayan jungle, bearing shell songs of long ago. Listen to the wind for, as it murmured King Midas's fate, it whispers untold secrets.

Contributors

Rick Bass has authored such celebrated works as *The Deer Pasture, Wild to the Heart*, and *Ninemile Wolves*. He resides in northwestern Montana with his wife Elizabeth and their two daughters. He is at work on a novel entitled *Where the Sea Used to Be*.

SueEllen Campbell teaches in the English Department at Colorado State University with her husband John Calderazzo. A graduate of the University of Virginia, she has written widely about twentieth-century literature and American environmental literature. *Bringing the Mountain Home* is her first book.

Lisa Couturier is a writer and essayist. Her work has appeared in *E: The Environmental Magazine, Wildlife Conservtion,* and *Sports Traveler*. She holds a masters degree in creative writing and environmental studies and is currently working on a collection of essays about women and urban nature. She lives in Manhattan with her husband and daughter.

John Daniel, a former student of Wallace Stegner at Stanford University, is the author of two books of poetry, a collection of essays (*The Trail Home*), and the memoir *Looking After*. He lives in the mountains near Eugene, Oregon, with his wife.

Jan Grover divides her time between northern Minnesota and Minneapolis. Her work has appeared in several anthologies and journals, including *Women's Review of Books* and *Utne Reader*. She is the author of *North Enough: AIDS and Other Clearcuts*.

Penny Harter lives in Santa Fe, New Mexico, where she teaches at the Santa Fe Preparatory School. Harter's work has been linked to the tradition associated with Robinson Jeffers, Gary Snyder, Wendell Berry, and Mary Oliver. *Turtle Blessing* is her first book.

Marybeth Holleman lives with her son in Anchorage, Alaska, where she teaches creative writing at the University of Alaska. She is working on a book of essays about her experiences in the Alaskan outback and has published widely in literary journals.

Adele Ne Jame has published widely in literary journals around the country. She lives in Honolulu, Hawaii, and teaches English at Hawaii Pacific University. The selections here are from her book *Field Work*. In 1995 she was nominated for a Whiting Award in poetry.

Homer Kizer lives in a small logging town in southeastern Idaho, where he supports himself through his writings and his wood carvings. Kizer is a graduate of the M.F.A. program in Creative Writing at the University of Alaska. His daring sonnet sequence has brought about renewed interest in the form.

Barry Lopez has authored such influential works as *Of Wolves and Men, Arctic Dreams* (winner of the National Book Award), and *Crossing Open Ground*. He lives with his wife, Sandra, an artist, in the Cascade Mountains of Oregon.

W. S. Merwin, recipient of a Pulitzer Prize in poetry, lives in Hawaii. In addition to being an accomplished poet, Merwin is also an essayist and an environmental activist. His books of poetry include *The Carrier of Ladders* and *The Moving Target*.

Dan O'Brien received the Iowa Short Fiction Award for his short story collection *Eminent Domain*. He has also authored such acclaimed works as *The Rites of Autumn* (nonfiction) and *In the Heart of the Nation* (a novel). He lives in Rapid City, South Dakota, with his wife Kris, a physician.

David Petersen lives in a cabin with his wife Carolyn in the San Juan Mountains of Colorado. His books include *Among the Aspen, Racks,* and *Ghost*

Grizzlies. He has edited the poetry and journals of Edward Abbey and will soon edit Abbey's letters.

Chip Rawlins lives in Boulder, Wyoming. A former seasonal worker for the U.S. Forest Service in the Wind River Mountains, he is now a full-time professional writer. His books include *Sky's Witness* and *Broken Country*.

April N. Rieveschl, a clinical psychologist, lives and works in New Orleans, Louisiana. Her work has been widely published in journals.

Alianor True graduated in 1997 from Cornell University with a bachelor's degree in science and technology. During the summers of 1996 and 1997 she worked as a firefighter for the National Park Service on the North Rim of the Grand Canyon. She is a native of Douglasville, Georgia.

Louise Wagenknecht has lived and worked in Idaho all her life. She divides her time between a sheep ranch and seasonal fire-fighting work with the U.S. Bureau of Land Management and the U.S. Forest Service. She is at work on a book about environmental issues in the Pacific Northwest.

David Rains Wallace has authored over a dozen works of natural history, including *The Dark Range, The Klamath Knot,* and *Bulow Hammock*. He and his wife Betsy, an artist, make their home in Berkeley, California.

Terry Tempest Williams has authored such classics as *Refuge* and *An Unspoken Hunger*. She led the fight for the Grand Staircase–Canyons of the Escalante National Monument in Utah and was present with President Clinton during the signing of the executive order creating it in September 1996.

Periodicals Consulted

Alaska Quarterly Review, Department of English, 3221 Providence Drive, Anchorage, Alaska 99508

American Poetry Review, 1721 Walnut Street, Philadelphia, Pennsylvania 19103

Antæus, Ecco Press, 26 West 17th Street, New York, New York 10011

The Antioch Review, P.O. Box 148, Yellow Springs, Ohio 45387

Arizona Quarterly, Department of English, University of Arizona, Tucson, Arizona 85721

The Atlantic Monthly, 745 Boylston Street, Boston, Massachusetts 62116

Audubon, 700 Broadway, New York, New York 10003

Backpacker, 33 East Minor Street, Emmaus, Pennsylvania 18098

Chicago Review, 5801 South Kenwood, Chicago, Illinois 60637

Cimarron Review, 205 Morril Hall, Oklahoma State University, Stillwater, Oklahoma 74078

Colorado Review, 360 Eddy Building, Colorado State University, Fort Collins, Colorado 80523

Denver Quarterly, Department of English, University of Denver, Denver, Colorado 80210

Esquire, 1790 Broadway, New York, New York 10019

Florida Review, Department of English, University of Central Florida, Orlando, Florida 32816

The Georgia Review, University of Georgia, Athens, Georgia 30602

The Gettysburg Review, Gettysburg College, Gettysburg, Pennsylvania 17325

Harper's Magazine, 2 Park Avenue, New York, New York 10016

Hawaii Pacific Review, 1060 Bishop Street, Honolulu, Hawaii 96813

Hawaii Review, Department of English, University of Hawaii, 1733 Donaghho Road, Honolulu, Hawaii 96822

High Country News, P.O. Box 1090, Paonia, Colorado 81428

Indiana Review, 316 North Jordan Avenue, Indiana University, Bloomington, Indiana 47405

Iris: A Journal About Women, Women's Center, P.O. Box 323 HSC, University of Virginia, Charlottesville, VA 22908

Kansas Quarterly, Department of English, Denison Hall, Kansas State University, Manhattan, Kansas 66506

The Kenyon Review, Kenyon College, Gambier, Ohio 43022

Left Bank, Blue Heron Publishing, 24450 N.W. Hansen Road, Hillsboro, Oregon 97124

Manoa: A Pacific Journal of International Writing, Department of English, University of Hawaii, 1733 Donaghho Road, Honolulu, Hawaii 96822

The Massachusetts Review, Memorial Hall, University of Massachusetts, Amherst, Massachusetts 01002

Michigan Quarterly Review, 3032 Rackham Building, University of Michigan, Ann Arbor, Michigan 48109

Minnesota Monthly, 15 South 9th Street, Suite 320, Minneapolis, Minnesota 55402

The Missouri Review, 1507 Hillcrest Hall, University of Missouri, Columbia, Missouri 65211

Montana Magazine, P.O. Box 5630, Helena, Montana 59604

Nebraska Review, Department of English, University of Nebraska, Omaha, Nebraska 68182

New England Review, Middlebury College, Middlebury, Vermont 05753

New Mexico Humanities Review, Department of English, New Mexico Tech, Socorro, New Mexico 57801

The New Yorker, 20 West 43rd Street, New York, New York 10036

Nimrod, Arts and Humanities Council of Tulsa, 2210 South Main, Tulsa, Oklahoma 74114

The North American Review, University of Northern Iowa, 1227 West 27th Street, Cedar Falls, Iowa 50613

North Atlantic Review, 15 Arbutus Lane, Stony Brook, New York 11790

North Dakota Quarterly, University of North Dakota, P.O. Box 8237, Grand Forks, North Dakota 58202

The Ohio Review, Department of English, Ohio University, Ellis Hall, Athens, Ohio 45701

Orion, 136 East 64th Street, New York, New York 10021

Outside, 1165 North Clark Street, Chicago, Illinois 60610

Pacific Discovery, Golden Gate Park, San Francisco, California 94118

The Paris Review, 541 East 72nd Street, New York, New York 10021

Prairie Schooner, University of Nebraska, Andrews Hall, Lincoln, Nebraska 68588

Puerto del Sol, Department of English, New Mexico State University, P.O. Box 3E, Las Cruces, New Mexico 88003

Santa Monica Review, Center for the Humanities at Santa Monica College, 1900 Pico Boulevard, Santa Monica, California 90405

The Sewanee Review, University of the South, Sewanee, Tennessee 37375

Sierra, 730 Polk Street, San Francisco, California 94109

Sonora Review, Department of English, University of Arizona, Tucson, Arizona 85721

South Carolina Review, Department of English, Clemson University, Clemson, South Carolina 29634

South Dakota Review, Box 111, University Exchange, Vermillion, South Dakota 57069

Southern Humanities Review, Department of English, Auburn University, Auburn, Alabama 36830

The Southern Review, Drawer D, University Station, Baton Rouge, Louisiana 70803

Southwest Review, Southern Methodist University, Dallas, Texas 75275

Tampa Review, P.O. Box 19F, University of Tampa, 401 West Kennedy Boulevard, Tampa, Florida 33606

The Threepenny Review, P.O. Box 9131, Berkeley, California 94709

The Village Voice Literary Supplement, 842 Broadway, New York, New York 10003

The Virginia Quarterly Review, Department of English, University of Virginia, Charlottesville, Virginia 22903

Wilderness, 900 17th Street N.W., Washington, D.C. 20006

Wildlife Conservation, Wildlife Conservation Society, Wildlife Conservation Park, Bronx, New York 10460

ZYZZYVA, 41 Sutter Street, Suite 1400, San Francisco, California 94104

Permissions